THE AKRON STORY CIRCLE PROJECT

RETHINKING RACE IN CLASSROOM AND COMMUNITY

THE AKRON STORY CIRCLE PROJECT

RETHINKING RACE IN CLASSROOM AND COMMUNITY

CAROLYN BEHRMAN

BILL LYONS

JAMES SLOWIAK

DONNA WEBB

PATRICIA HILL

AMY SHRIVER DREUSSI

WITHDRAWN

The University of Akron Press
Akron, Ohio

Copyright © 2017 by Carolyn Behrman, Bill Lyons, Patricia Hill, James Slowiak, Donna Webb, and Amy Shriver Dreussi

All rights reserved • First Edition 2017 • Manufactured in the United States of America •

All inquiries and permission requests should be addressed to the Publisher, The University of Akron Press, Akron, Ohio 44325-1703.

21 20 19 18 17   5 4 3 2 1

ISBN: 978-1-629220-52-9 (paper)
ISBN: 978-1-629220-53-6 (ePDF)
ISBN: 978-1-629220-54-3 (ePub)

LIBRARY OF CONGRESS CATALOGING-IN-PUBLICATION DATA
Names: Behrman, Carolyn, author. | Lyons, William, 1960– coauthor.
Title: The Akron Story Circle Project : rethinking race in classroom and community / Carolyn Behrman, Bill Lyons, Patricia Hill, James Slowiak, Donna Webb, Amy Shriver Dreussi.
Description: First edition. | Akron, Ohio : The University of Akron Press, 2017. | Includes bibliographical references.
Identifiers: LCCN 2017005526 (print) | LCCN 2017005607 (ebook) | ISBN 9781629220529 (paperback : alkaline paper) | ISBN 9781629220536 (PDF) | ISBN 9781629220543 (ePub) | ISBN 9781629220536 (ePDF)
Subjects: LCSH: United States—Race relations—Study and teaching (Higher) | Storytelling—Social aspects—United States. | Storytelling—Political aspects—United States. | Akron Story Circle Project. | Storytelling—Ohio—Akron.
Classification: LCC E184.A1 B347 2017 (print) | LCC E184.A1 (ebook) | DDC 305.800973—dc23
LC record available at https://lccn.loc.gov/2017005526

The paper used in this publication meets the minimum requirements of American National Standard for Information Sciences—Permanence of Paper for Printed Library Materials, ANSI Z39.48–1984. ∞

Cover design by Chris Hoot

The Akron Story Circle Project was designed and typeset by Amy Freels, with assistance from Tyler Krusinski. The typeface is Adobe Caslon with Futura display. It is printed on sixty-pound natural and bound by Bookmasters of Ashland, Ohio.

Contents

Foreword

The Pinnacle of the Color Line Project

Theresa Holden and John O'Neal

Over a ten-year period, from 1999 to 2009, we first created and, with our partners, helped to run Color Line Projects in six cities in the United States. Our partners were colleges, universities, and community or city arts organizations. The goals were lofty and challenging and we had many memorable moments that came close to achieving the mission and goals of the Color Line Project. The Color Line Project at the University of Akron not only met each of the goals, but also far surpassed our dreams for this important work.

The Color Line Project (CLP) was a multi-year, multi-community initiative of our organization Junebug Productions. CLP was a process designed to catalyze creative engagements among artists, educators, community activists, and their diverse constituencies. These engagements were intended to lead to the creation of high-quality art and to heighten our collective understanding of the dramatic impact of the Civil Rights Movement. Equally important, this process helps us work together to create activities, programs, and projects that challenge injustice today and improve the quality of life for all.

The Color Line Project was responsive to the fact that, despite its importance, the Civil Rights Movement is little known or understood and is devalued sometimes even by the people who participated in it. The project is also responsive to the need for archives of primary source material about the period. There is a certain urgency to the work because so many of those who were there are dying now. Most movement documentation was focused on leaders such as M. L. King Jr., while the grassroots salt-of-the-earth types, without whom there would have been no movement, have hardly been documented at all. These are the people whose stories the Color Line Project sought to prioritize.

Our Color Line Projects were carried out in the following six places: Rowan University, Glassboro, NJ; Palm Beach Community College, Lake Worth, FL; Cincinnati Arts Association, Cincinnati, OH; Flint Cultural Center Corporation, Flint, MI; Reston Community Center, Reston, VA; and The University of Akron, Akron, OH. The projects have been as unique as each of their locations. They each gave their Color Line Projects unique titles. The thousands of stories collected have created a rich treasure trove, which in itself proves the importance of such a project. However, the depth and width of the Akron Color Line Project, called the Akron Story Circle Project, was superlative.

The Akron Story Circle Project was and still is an incredible success because it discovered the power of stories. Our national CLP focused on stories because we believe people reveal more of their lives through their stories than through their arguments. Arguments can spawn defensiveness and may or may not reveal many telling insights. Stories on the other hand will always be insightful and authoritative and often will be entertaining as well.

We believe that by involving artists in the process of collecting stories from their communities and using them in their work, we strengthen the connections between the artists and their respective communities. When the communities see themselves reflected in the images created by their artists about them, the people will be made stronger, clearer and prouder of who they are and what they have done. Artists will emerge with stronger insights and appreciation of their roles in the life of their communities.

We believe that when educators see the stories of the people in their communities as vital to local and world issues and history, their students and the community will also grow stronger, and the educators will discover yet more ways to engage their students with their communities. And this is exactly what happened at the University of Akron.

As is evident in what follows, the Akron Project met each of our national CLP goals and strategies:

National Color Line Project Goals:

- to create public awareness of the impact of the Civil Rights Movement and the roles played by ordinary people in each locality;
  In Akron: The CLP project and story circles were used in the Rethinking Race week. Through invited speakers and the stories told, much was shared about the Civil Rights Movement; a reminder to both those who remembered the Movement and for those learning about it for the first time, of how far we have come, but how far we still have to go.
- to identify and engage local artists, educators, and activists in each community to collect the personal stories and oral histories of community residents and to help these artists, educators and activists find ways to use the stories and the process of collecting them in their own work;
  In Akron: Six incredible professors, Carolyn Behrman, Amy Shriver Dreussi, Pat Hill, Bill Lyons, Jim Slowiak, and Donna Webb, from six different departments, all took on the CLP with an energy and dedication unsurpassed. The professors welcomed us into their classrooms, where we offered our ideas and techniques to their students. Then with incredible creativity, each professor, using the story circle method, created projects for their students that met the educational goals of their subjects. Their students reached out into the wider community and used the vast resource of individual stories to carry out their inspired projects.
- to empower communities to hold their artists and educators accountable to the communities' collective interests;
  In Akron: The stories collected were "returned" to their storytellers in several ways, which are covered in this volume. For instance, a play derived from community stories is offered back to the people who told the stories; beautiful pieces of pottery, inspired by stories, are placed back in the that community for their appreciation. In each of the subject areas, the students whose projects reached into the community to gather stories "gave back" to that community, or will eventually, by what they have learned in their subject through the valuable insights they received from those very stories.

National Color Line Project Strategies:

- Local artists will use the collected stories and oral histories to make art;

- Educators will use them to study, to teach, and to employ the stories appropriately within their disciplines;
- Activists will be encouraged to use them in their efforts to mobilize and organize diverse constituencies;
- Junebug and the local partners will seek to network all these elements together so that they can learn from and assist each other.

This book shares the story of how these goals and strategies were accomplished with creativity and innovation by each of the professors.

The Akron Project captured the imagination of six remarkable professors, who in turn believed in the power of story with us and relayed this belief and indeed, passion to their students. These incredibly lucky students now have this simple, powerful tool in their hands to carry into their future, letting stories help build and heal their communities.

The Akron Story Circle Project was an incredibly rewarding project for us while we were working with each of the professors and all of the students. It was truly the pinnacle of the Color Line Projects. And now, what a reward for our ten years of work and dedication to an ideal to see the outcome of this enormous and brilliant project captured in this book. It holds important insights and hopefully will be used widely by educators and artists alike for years to come.

Introduction

James Slowiak

As I'm trying to remember how six University of Akron (UA) faculty members from diverse disciplines began to collaborate on what eventually came to be called the Akron Story Circle Project, the room begins to swirl, the pages of the calendar fly away like in an old Hollywood movie, and I'm taken back to November 2001 when I first met actor/director/playwright/activist John O'Neal (1940–). Here's my story...

John O'Neal's Junebug Productions, an African American theatre company from New Orleans, was in residence on the University of Akron campus, along with Roadside Theatre from Appalachia and Teatro Pregones, a Puerto Rican company from the Bronx. These three theatre ensembles collaborated on devising a performance, *Promise of a Love Song*, using the story circle process. I always had a strong interest in storytelling and wanted to introduce the UA community, especially UA theatre students, to this method as a way of creating performances. I put together a proposal and planned an initial fall semester residency, featuring *Promise of a Love Song* and all three companies, hoping to stimulate interest in the project among the students. A more intensive semester of work followed in spring 2002, involving only members of Roadside Theatre and a student-devised performance, *Circle Stories*.

When the three theatre ensembles arrived on campus, John O'Neal was scheduled to visit my Voice and Diction class. He entered the studio like a volcano, full of fire and force. His voice boomed, his body filled the space, and his eyes twinkled with mischief. When he discovered that I had worked with Polish theatre director and researcher Jerzy Grotowski (1933–1999), he teasingly asked me how many of my vocal resonators I had engaged that day. (Grotowski had identified more than thirty resonators in the human body.) I said: "Only one. My whole body!" He laughed uproariously and from that moment on, we were at ease with each other, knowing we could work together. Ours has become for me a cherished friendship and collaboration.

I often tell my students how the Japanese honor their senior artists with the Order of Culture, give them a lifetime annuity, and name them a national treasure. Well, in my eyes, John O'Neal is one of our national treasures. He cofounded the Free Southern Theater (FST) in 1963 as the cultural arm of the Civil Rights Movement. FST was influential in the Black Arts Movement (1965–1975) and helped establish the Black Theatre Movement in the United States. By bringing "theatre to those who have no theatre" FST gave voice to artists and communities who previously had no forum for their expression. The FST moved its base of operations from Jackson, Mississippi to New Orleans in 1965 and continued to seek ways that art could support the Civil Rights Movement through a professional touring company, a community involvement program, and training opportunities for local people interested in writing, performing, and producing theatre. After the group dissolved in 1980, John O'Neal continued to model FST's commitment to using art as a tool for community action and to promote social justice by forming Junebug Productions. In fact, the show John performed at the University of Akron in 2008, *Don't Start Me to Talking or I'll Tell You Everything I Know, Sayings from the Life and Writings of Junebug Jabbo Jones,* was the last production of FST and the first of Junebug Productions.

JOHN O'NEAL AND THE STORY CIRCLE PROCESS

Junebug "bases its approach on ideas and principles of democratic, grassroots, bottom-up development" advocated by Ella Baker (1903–1986). Ella Baker was a major figure of the Civil Rights Movement who often remained out of the spotlight and behind the scenes. She helped found the Student Nonviolent Coordinating Committee (SNCC), where, as mentor and advisor, her ideas of participatory democracy spread throughout the country and influenced all of the civil rights leaders of the time. The story circle process was developed as the primary tool to foster Ella Baker's brand of grassroots organization. Story circles were used during the Civil Rights Movement, not only to collect stories, but also to help plan and develop community work, evaluate projects, and create a more collective, less gendered hierarchy of leadership. According to Junebug Productions, the primary purpose of the story circle is "to share a simple and efficient structure that allows a space of equality in all gatherings where it is used and ensures that each person's story and voice is heard."[1]

Cultures around the world have long employed storytelling to transmit important values and beliefs and to build community. In nonprofit or social change contexts, the story circle model of storytelling can be used to bring people together on an equal playing field, allowing participants to operate as cocreators of a community's consciousness. The telling of personal stories invariably leads to a level of engagement in which participants transfer the story circle model to other aspects of their lives. Often, this new quality of participation shows them the way to realize their own potential as leaders.

STORY CIRCLE GUIDELINES

Before continuing the story of how story circles became an integral part of the teaching, research, artistic, and community practice of six University of Akron faculty members, I would like to look at the structure that has been transmitted to us by John O'Neal and other story circle practitioners, including Roadside Theatre. Here is the Akron Story Circle Project's version of Story Circle Guidelines:

1. We sit in circles of six to eight. A circle, not an oval or square, because being in a circle is important. In a circle everyone is in an equal physical space.
2. The facilitators introduce themselves and then moving clockwise around the circle each person simply tells the group their name and where they are from.
3. Be aware of how much time you have for the whole story circle process: the stories themselves, the cross-circle talking, and the report creation. Make sure you know what time your circle is to rejoin the larger group (if there is one) or what time the whole session needs to end. The facilitator should communicate these time factors to the circle.

4. Facilitators have a "Story Circle Log Sheet" on a clipboard in each circle to allow the research team to match up each story with a storyteller. This helps the transcribers if the stories are being taped. The circle decides on a way to keep time and on the number of minutes for each story. We suggest three minutes. Decide on a signal (hand sign, gently touching the storyteller on the shoulder, etc.) to be used when the time is up. The storyteller does not have to stop abruptly, just bring the story to a finish.

5. If there is to be a theme or prompt for the stories, the facilitator should explain the theme and answer any questions about the theme or the process itself.

6. Anyone in the circle may begin with a story.

7. As we move clockwise around the story circle, anyone can pass when his or her turn comes up. People who pass have a chance at the end of the circle to tell a story.

8. Do not take notes. Do not hold books or papers on your lap. Put your attention on listening. The essence of storytelling is listening. Listening is more important than talking. Don't worry about what your story will be, just actively listen to each of the stories being told and trust that the story circle process will bring you a story when the time is right. If several stories come to you as you are listening, reach for the "deepest" story that you are comfortable telling.

9. Each person just listens to the stories…no interruptions, no commentary, no body language other than active listening. We do not need to like or agree with anyone else's story, but just as we have the right to tell our own story, we need to respect the right of everyone else in the circle to tell his or her own story.

10. Tell stories…not political theories, arguments, opinions, or analysis. A story can be something that happened to you or it can be the story of a family member, friend, or acquaintance—a story you've heard.

11. Silence is always acceptable. Sometimes silence can be the most powerful story to tell. If there is silence after a story, that's good. It gives everyone a chance to reflect on the story and it allows the next storyteller time to begin or pass without feeling pressured.

12. After the circle is complete, the facilitator asks if anyone who has passed wishes to tell a story. They can pass again if they choose. Once all stories have been told, the facilitator invites "cross circle" questioning, commenting, and dialogue. Now is the time to ask for clarification on any story that you heard in the circle. Keep in mind how much time you decided to allow for this phase of the story circle process.

13. Then the facilitator asks each participant to think of an image for each story they heard in the circle and to share that image with the circle. This returns the earlier stories in the circle to mind and opens the way for a conversation in the circle that seeks to identify themes that emerged in the stories.

14. If the circle will be joining a larger group, then the circle needs to decide on how to "report back" on the essence or themes that emerged in your circle. This should be a collaborative undertaking and can be as creative as the group desires. Again, you need to keep to the allotted amount of time for this phase of the circle.

15. Finally, join the larger group, and report on your story circle.

If your group has time for more than one circle of stories, begin the process all over again. Remember: if the story circle process is being recorded (audio or video), make sure that you have secured appropriate release forms from all participants and assign someone to be in charge of the recorder(s) and the log sheet(s).

WHAT IS A STORY?

Surprisingly, one of the most difficult aspects of the story circle process in today's world is getting participants to understand what is a story. Perhaps it's because we've become so disconnected from our storytelling sources or that our senses seem to be already imprinted with Disneyfied images and X-Box excitement. Many participants feel ill at ease when asked to tell a story from their own experience and resort instead to giving their opinion about the prompt or theme. In these cases, it might be helpful to remind the circle what a story is:

• A story is a personal recollection of something that happened to you or someone you know.

- A story can have place, time, characters, narration, and/or dialogue.
- A story can be a simple event; it does not have to have a complete beginning, middle, and end.
- A story is not an argument, debate, or expression of one's personal opinion.
- A story can stand on its own legs; it does not need its message to be explained at the end.[2]

John O'Neal and Theresa Holden, in collaboration with many other groups and individuals, have worked for a number years to hone the story circle process into a workable tool for artists and community workers. Anyone interested in further exploration of story circles can find information on Junebug Productions website, http://junebugproductions.org.

JOHN O'NEAL AND THE AKRON COLOR LINE PROJECT

One way that John O'Neal refined his work with story circles was by establishing (with Theresa Holden) the Color Line Project, a national initiative to collect and archive stories of those involved in the US Civil Rights Movement and the reverberations of the movement in our lives today. John describes it on Junebug's website as

> a multi-year organizing project in which we use the Story Circle Process to collect stories from people who were involved with or who recognize that their lives have been significantly influenced by the Civil Rights Movement.[3]

Seven years after that first meeting with John O'Neal in a voice class, I joined a group of UA faculty and staff to plan a campus-wide event to celebrate the tenth anniversary of President Bill Clinton's first Town Hall meeting on race held at the University of Akron in 1997. In those planning sessions for Revisiting Race in America (which became an annual event later to be called Rethinking Race: Black, White, and Beyond), the six authors of this volume (who became the Akron Story Circle Project) came together and our stories began to interweave. I suggested we bring in John O'Neal as a keynote speaker to perform his solo piece "Junebug Jabbo Jones." I also suggested that we discuss starting a Color Line Project in Akron. I felt that this national initiative fit well with the University of Akron's goal of improving the understanding of race relations (including racial and ethnic conflicts) as well as further improving the racial climate on our campus. Professors Bill Lyons (Political Science), Carolyn Behrman (Anthropology), Patricia Hill (Communication), and Donna Webb (Art) immediately offered their enthusiastic support and the plans took off with funding from a variety of colleges, schools, departments, and on-campus and off-campus organizations, including the University of Akron's Center for Conflict Management (CCM) and Akron's Center for Applied Theatre and Active Culture (CATAC). Since what started as the Akron Color Line Project and is now called the Akron Story Circle Project has always been an important part of a larger campus cocurricular activity, Rethinking Race, Amy Shriver Dreussi (Associate Studies) joined us for the work creating this volume.

In February 2007, John O'Neal returned to the University of Akron campus to perform and, with his longtime associate Theresa Holden, to train faculty and students in the story circle process. During their time on campus, John and Theresa visited classes in Anthropology, Art, Communication, Education, Political Science, and Theatre. They dined with faculty and students, explained their projects, and conducted several days of workshops during which they initiated more than thirty of us to the story circle process and demonstrated some of its possibilities. We ended their residency that first year with a meeting to plan how Akron could join such places as Dayton, Ohio; Glassboro/Camden, New Jersey; Flint, Michigan; and others to establish a Color Line project of its own.

Junebug Productions lists the goals of the Color Line Project as:

1. Collect the many yet untold stories of "The Movement."
2. Help build a coalition of organizations that come together through this process.
3. Connect those coalitions around the country toward sharing, shaping, and implementing a vision and hope for a new Movement.

The CLP is designed to:

* Catalyze creative engagements among artists, educators, community organizers and their diverse constituencies;
* Heighten collective understanding of the impact of "The Movement;"
* Create high-quality art, innovative educational projects and productive community organizing/education;

- Facilitate a process that helps people in communities to work together to create activities, programs, and projects that challenge injustice and improve the quality of life for all.[4]

Junebug serves primarily as a resource and stimulus for each individual community's version of the Color Line Project. Armed with the story circle process and knowing that John and Theresa had our backs (so to speak), we began the incredible adventure toward finding Akron's answers to the questions posed by the Color Line Project. For many of us, it was taking a big step into the unknown. When we began this undertaking, little did we know how much it would change our teaching and research, our relationship with our community and with each other, and our personal attitudes and perceptions of race and privilege. Nothing would ever be the same.

THE BEGINNINGS OF THE AKRON STORY CIRCLE PROJECT

The University of Akron's Rethinking Race that first year was a big success, in part because of John and Theresa and the bonding they facilitated for the six core group members of the nascent Akron Story Circle Project. In Fall 2008, Barack Obama was elected President of the United States. In Spring 2009, five professors included story circle methodology in their course syllabi and either required or invited students to attend public story circles held during Rethinking Race 2009. John and Theresa returned to campus in February 2009 to visit classes and conduct story circles in the classroom environment and at several community settings.

That semester I taught a Special Topics class in the University of Akron Theatre Program called Color Line Project. Students in this class were trained in story circle methodology and conducted fieldwork at the Paul E. Belcher buildings, a senior-citizen apartment complex in downtown Akron near the UA campus managed by the Akron Metropolitan Housing Association (AMHA). Donna Webb had received a commission to design a mural for another AMHA building near Howard Street in Akron's North Hill neighborhood. She was talking to residents about the history of Howard Street and we decided that this topic would also provide a good prompt for story circles at the Belcher building.

Howard Street was the center of African American community culture in Akron during the first half of the twentieth century. Nightclubs, hotels, restaurants, and shopping all were a part of this bustling neighborhood. The sweet sounds of jazz and blues mingled with the smells of fresh fish and pomade on the crowded urban street lined with many African American owned businesses as well as shops representing a variety of other cultures and ethnic groups. Akron was the rubber capital of the world and that meant jobs to the thousands who streamed to Summit County's high point from all over the country, from all over the world. However, our story circles soon revealed that there was an ugly underbelly to the colorful stories of life on Howard Street. After several rounds of story circles, the color drained out of the stories and what remained was starkly black and white.

Racism ran rampant in Akron's factories, political chambers, and fashionable neighborhoods. An insidious form of segregation reigned in Akron for much of the twentieth century. In 1851, Sojourner Truth (c. 1799–1883) delivered her "Ain't I a Woman" speech in Akron. One hundred years later, the greatest African American entertainers of the day were still forbidden to stay in the exclusive downtown hotels and shopping at the city's chic department stores was relegated to certain floors for the black population. Even the Main Street Woolworth's lunch counter remained off-limits for citizens of color until well into the 1960s. From Howard Street one could hear clearly the trains as they rolled into the town's busy rail yards. And if one listened carefully, perhaps the whispers and heavy breathing of the African American workers who endlessly unloaded the blood-stained bales of raw rubber collected by their black or native brothers and sisters in Africa and the Amazon. In twentieth-century Akron, the stench of racism mixed with the suffocating fumes and filthy grit of vulcanized rubber eventually buried Howard Street, geographically and culturally, beneath the crush of urban renewal and rust-belt decay. In twenty-first century Akron, all that remains are the memories—and the stories.

My students were able to spark those memories and unearth some of the stories during story circles with the residents at the Belcher building. John O'Neal and Theresa Holden conducted one of these sessions when they returned to campus in February 2009. From this fieldwork and transcriptions of these stories and others provided by the University of Akron's Active Research Methods Lab, the students in the Color Line Project class selected a number of stories, scripted them, and staged them under my direction for presentation at the Belcher building and on campus in May 2009. This presentation served as a rough draft of the possibilities of the story circle method as a means of creating a community-based performance revolving around Akron, the Civil Rights Movement, and the city's history of race relations. Donna Webb's ceramics classes also participated in this initial presentation by providing sculptural set pieces and props that were inspired by the collected stories.

The reaction of the students and community members to this process was extremely positive. The meetings that took place (intergenerational and intercultural) left strong impressions on all involved. To perform the stories of actual people whom they had met and come to know by name provided lessons that stretched well beyond craft for the young actors in my class. They were faced with ethical and personal questions that will continue to influence their future work in theatre and in their communities. As a stage director and teacher, I began to understand that, in using the story circle process, the performance experience organically emerges from community and compassion rather than exploding forth from the exhibitionistic tendency common in contemporary theatre. This difference is critical and has the potential to create reverberations in the performer's work on herself, on her craft, her presence, her self-awareness, that can actually help to reshape our globalized and unjust world. I put this realization into practice in how I approached the continuing work collecting stories and the eventual rehearsals and scripting of *The Akron Color Line Project Performance*, presented at E. J. Thomas Performing Arts Hall in February 2011.

THE AKRON STORY CIRCLE PROJECT

All of this initial work with story circles and the Color Line Project inspired each of us to investigate the process in a variety of ways. Even now in 2016, story circles remain a central component of UA's Rethinking Race, especially as a tool for facilitating discussion and digesting material. We also continue to use them in our classrooms and communities, with our students and in various other situations. For example, in 2012 and 2013, the Akron Story Circle Project members conducted professional development workshops each August for Akron Public School teachers and staff working at Miller South Middle School for the Arts. Teaching the story circle process and seeking ways in which it can be utilized across the middle school curriculum has resulted in the school devising its own *Diversity Play*, featuring the children's own stories of confronting prejudice and intolerance.

This volume is an effort to share with you what we have learned in this process, to tell our story as members of the Akron Story Circle Project community. As John O'Neal might say, "That's my story and I'm stickin' to it!"

LOOKING AHEAD IN THIS VOLUME

We will conclude this introduction with a few clarifications on key concepts, an explanation of volume structure and a short summary of what a reader can expect from each subsequent chapter.

First, all indented and italicized quotes are from students in our classes or participants in story circles, taken from a story circle or a student analysis of story circle data. When an indented quote is also in quotation marks that indicates it is from a scholarly source.

Second, the Akron Story Circle Project started as a part of Rethinking Race and was initially called the Akron Color Line Project. We will use Akron Story Circle Project in this volume. Rethinking Race itself was initially called Revisiting Race and is still often referred to as Race Week; we will use Rethinking Race here.

Third, F2F refers to a type of Rethinking Race event called a Face-to-Face conversation. These are informal facilitated conversations. Each one is about a sensitive race-related topic designed to allow and encourage students to share their thoughts and become the central voices in a difficult dialogue.

Fourth, Rethinking Race is an annual cocurricular event that started at the University of Akron in 2007, growing out of similarly structured earlier events when the Center for Conflict Management (CCM) organized an Open Forum on Racial Conflict and a forum called Understanding US-Iraqi Conflict. The Dean of the College of Arts and Sciences then asked the CCM director (one of the authors of this volume) to work with an associate dean to create a similar week-long series of cocurricular events focusing on race to commemorate the tenth anniversary of President Bill Clinton's Town Hall on race held at the University of Akron. We assembled a team and created Rethinking Race.

The goal of the organizers of Rethinking Race has been to make this about *rethinking* (so we embedded these events into courses when possible) and bringing our campus community together around positive, serious, and sober (so therefore uncomfortable at times) conversations about race. We are all teachers, mentors, and volunteers. By year four, as the Akron Story

Circle Project grew, the leadership of Rethinking Race was institutionalized under the director of our Institute for Teaching and Learning and the
director of our Office of Multicultural Development. These two colleagues
and friends, Helen Qammar and Fedearia Nicolson (who was in the original organizing group as well), brought energy, ideas, and resources to the
table and Rethinking Race grew under their leadership to an event attract-
ing ten thousand participants in 2014.

This volume is organized to move the reader from examples of undergraduate classroom-based, pedagogical use of story circles (Lyons, Hill),
through a graduate/undergraduate course-based collaboration examining
story circles as a research method for the social sciences (Behrman and Spickard Prettyman), to a case of community-based research and service-learning
engagement with a community partner (Webb). Continuing with the theme
of a widening circle of engagement but returning to the roots of the Akron
Story Circle Project, in chapter 6, Dreussi, who has served Rethinking Race
for several years by gathering assessment information, shares community and
student reported experiences with Akron Story Circle Project activities at
Rethinking Race events. This is followed by the full script of the play, *The
Akron Color Line Project Performance*, described briefly above. The volume
closes with some final thoughts about storytelling, democracy, and our goals
as teachers and citizens in contemporary America.

You may be surprised by the appearance of the chapters for two reasons.
We have encouraged each other as authors to embrace the notion of storytelling by including our stories and experiences in our texts. This means that
chapters contain many narrative-style statements from the authors as well
as quotes from students and participants in story circles. The other unusual
content which separates this volume from most academic collections are the
comments in each chapter. These additions to each authors' chapter are in
effect a drawn-out conversation among the authors of the volume intended
to reveal more about the concerns we have explored together and to engage
the reader in our exchange.

This addition has roots in our long collaboration which has been charac-
terized by a wonderful collegial ethos. There is no particular hierarchy in our
group. Each member has brought distinctive perspective and expertise to the
collective. We have supported each other's research activities, classroom exercises, community events, presentations, and performances, acting as sounding

boards, facilitators, data collectors, copresenters, witnesses, audiences, and "talk-back" leaders. As a result we have spent much time seeing each other work but we have also taken the time to sit, eat, and converse about our shared interests. We find that our conversations often help us strengthen our teaching and research practices. The "bubbling" is intended to invite the reader into some of those conversations to the extent that printed text can do so.

NOTES

1. From a handout provided by Junebug Productions.

2. From a handout written by Theresa Holden, Junebug Productions, Inc.

3. For more information on John O'Neal and his thoughts on storytelling, story circles, social justice, Junebug Jabbo Jones and the Free Southern Theatre, see: *A Conversation with John O'Neal:* http://vimeo.com/80959243.

4. From a handout provided by Junebug Productions.

Teaching about Racial Conflict with Story Circles

Bill Lyons

The story... is one of the basic tools invented by the human mind, for the purpose of gaining understanding. There have been great societies that did not use the wheel, but there have been no societies that did not tell stories.
—Ursula K. LeGuin

I. INTRODUCTION

We are all curious and struggling—with our students, with each other, within ourselves, our disciplines and our communities—to connect and empower through interactive and collaborative community building.

This chapter examines story circles in the context of two courses, both of which were constructed to integrate the annual, campus-wide, cocurricular event Rethinking Race into class assignments. The courses occurred sequentially in the spring and summer of 2008. In both, story circles were used in class. Students were taught to use the story circle technique to gather stories about race and analyze these as primary source data. In addition, students were required to participate in Rethinking Race events that included public lectures, F2F conversations, films, and more... all focusing on race and racial conflict.

F2F here refers to a type of Rethinking Race event called a Face-to-Face Conversation. These are informal, facilitated conversations about sensitive race-related topics designed to allow and encourage students to share their thoughts and become the central voices in the event. Rethinking Race material and story circle data combined with a selection of scholarly readings on race, crime, and politics to constitute the texts for each course. This chapter describes these experiences and lessons learned.

Figure 1. Talk back after a cocurricular event sponsored by the Akron Story Circle Project. Three Akron Story Circle Project faculty are included here: (from left to right) Jim, Carolyn, two students, Bill

Here is how the chapter will proceed. First, some backstory. Second, the chapter describes the structure of the two cocurricular courses. The third section provides an illustrative sampling of the stories collected by my students and their analysis of these stories. Then the chapter concludes by more deeply examining the relationship between three aspects of the class structure and the skills required for active democratic citizenship: creating productive 'difficult dialogues' that reject dualistic thinking, starting with the best available data, and getting in our students' way with deliberative storytelling.

A. Some Back Story

In the fall of 2003, James Bowier, a student from the Black United Student Association at the University of Akron, dropped into my office. We had never met. He wanted to work together on a project for Black History Month. We decided to cocreate and coteach a special topics class called Understanding Racial Conflict. Forty-eight students enrolled in that class and were divided into permanent groups of four (half black, half white, half male, half female) for the entire term.* Each group prepared and produced a segment for an end-of-term service-learning project, which was a

Figure 2. Story Circle with Donna

campus-wide Open Forum on Racial Conflict attended by over two hundred students, faculty, and community members. James' idea struck a nerve that brought people together.[1]

*Carolyn: Remarkable that you managed to get such a perfect distribution. Did you recruit for this class or was this good fortune?

Bill: Yes, a student of mine (James) took the lead in our recruiting efforts through the Black United Students Association. This does raise an interesting and important question about using story circles. In the two classes described here we had a great mixture of students. Since then, however, there was at least one occasion when some of the in-class circles were populated entirely with white suburban students. How intentional should we be in constructing story circles to structure in a meaningful exchange on the conflicts highlighted by whatever prompt we use? What do others think?

Carolyn: In my Human Diversity course I actually abandoned a plan to use story circles in a unit focused on race because only four of thirty students were not white Americans. I used them a little later in a unit on intersectionality (race, class, and gender) instead.

Donna: Having spent a year working in a largely African American community, I find that I am more and more impatient with the racial mix of the University of Akron. Creating working groups that are more like the racial balance of the city of Akron is now one of my goals. I try to include people of color in what I do. Whether it is a stated goal or not, I see similar practices carried out by other members of the Akron Story Circle Project.

Another thought: things are better in more racially balanced groups. We in the Akron Story Circle Group don't just think that conversations and insights *should* be better in a racially diverse group; we *have experienced* the improved quality of learning in these groups.

Less than five hours after writing the above, I arrived at a conference in Milwaukee. Theaster Gates, Director of Arts and Public Life at the University of Chicago, was the keynote speaker for the more than four thousand potters who gathered at the National Council for Education in the Ceramic Arts in March of 2014. When asked how we might create an NCECA that is more diverse, he advised us to each invite a person different from us to the conference next year. He said that the personal invitation is the most potent form of inclusion. An invitation to join a story circle or to tell a story is just this kind of powerful call.

Jim: In a recent discussion about diversity with a colleague on the West Coast, she marveled that I was still so concerned about inclusion and making sure that all groups were represented in our theatre season and by the kinds of plays presented. She made it seem that the Midwest was behind in getting beyond these kinds of issues. But the lack of African American representation in the arts community in Akron is very disturbing and the university has to take a leadership role instigating this change.

Amy: I routinely have this problem of under-representation of minorities in my general education diversity classes. No one, and particularly no student, should bear the burden of speaking for the entirety of their race…and yet, it happens. Nice work recruiting a diverse mix! I would love that!

This chapter examines the experiences of students in two subsequent courses that built on these 2003 experiences as a part of Rethinking Race in 2008. It was my experience with the students who took the 2003 Understanding Racial Conflict class that sparked my interest and gave me the courage to begin to take race more seriously in the classroom.• The two classes I discuss in this chapter, and Rethinking Race, which these courses are linked with, grew out of the success of this student-initiated, student-driven, and student-produced Open Forum on Racial Conflict. For me, all of this traces back to when James walked into my office. When we listen to our students with open minds and open hearts, great things happen.[2]

•Pat: Great self-reflection. I am glad you recognize that it genuinely took courage to engage in classroom conversations about race and racism with your students. Teachers must prepare for conversations about race and racism, and our success depends on our willingness to persist in the process.

Bill: How did others come to focus on working with students to analyze stories about race?

Pat: I have always tried to make a connection between my teaching ethos and my everyday experiences as an African American woman. A pedagogical goal is to get my students to realize that in order to live peacefully together on this planet, we need to open our

Figure 3. Story Circle Project faculty and author of this chapter, in Dear World Photo kiosk at Rethinking Race

hearts and minds to truly listen and engage topics like race that make us downright uncomfortable.

Jim: I think that for a long time I just assumed that issues of race and inclusion would take care of themselves. I always applied "color-blind" casting to choosing actors for the productions I directed. And the professional company, New World Performance Laboratory, that I codirect has always been culturally diverse in its makeup. But I never went out of my way to make race or racism an issue in my teaching or performances. I think the fact that I had to be "discreet" about my own identity as a gay man influenced this avoidance of other hot topic issues. But as I became more confident in my own craft and personal life, I found that I needed more and more to push certain buttons in my work as an artist concerning society's persistent prejudices. I re-connected with John O'Neal at a Network of Ensemble Theatres (NET) conference and encountered folks affiliated with Alternate Roots in the summer of 2006, and soon after Bill asked me to join the Rethinking Race committee. I jumped at the chance and realized that as a theatre director and teacher, I can do what it is I do (create the space for others to create) while developing a civic practice that involves constructing a forum for these "difficult conversations" to take place. It's been a grand adventure and one that only seems to lead deeper and deeper into authentic action and more profound and meaningful contact.

Carolyn: The Human Diversity course I mentioned is a 200-level, general education course. The class was developed to explore questions of how human beings vary physically, where that physical variation comes from, and the ways it matters. The class covers dimensions of differences from skin color to body size, physical abilities to incidence of diabetes. One of the first things we do is face up to the paradox of race—that, as a categorical construct, it is biologically invalid but that it is simultaneously extremely important socioculturally. The origin of our "racialized world view" figures significantly in the first few weeks as the students and I are getting to know each other. After we look at the historical development of this perspective and the consequences we all live with, I found (thanks to all of you) that dealing with the dimensions of racial difference in the room is vital. Direct language and a straightforward attitude toward my own standpoint (being a white, upper-middle class, middle-aged woman) sets a tone in the classroom. And then the story circles generally help students own their own standpoints and appreciate others.

II. STORY CIRCLES IN CLASS

I was initially afraid to use story circles in my regular classes; I was afraid of losing control of the conversation.✦ In this chapter you can hear my students' voices—from in-class writing, discussion board threads, and formal paper assignments—and see that they came to my rescue.✦ For many of us, perhaps most particularly those who are white like me, participating in story circles brings both sides of Mark Twain's observation.

> It ain't what you don't know that gets you into trouble.
> It's what you know for sure that just ain't so.

✦**Donna:** For me, asking students to do something so unexpected in an art class has prevented me from using story circles very often in my studio classes. Students have established ideas about where ideas for their art should come from and examining their own stories is not among them for the most part. This fear is somewhat irrational for several reasons: Art created through personal narrative forms an important thread throughout history and particularly so in the twentieth century, when religious and mythic themes became less important. This would then invite the question of where these narratives come from. Secondly, the few times when I have ventured to include story circles, students were engaged and surprised at their own stories. It is more an issue of leadership. Working with the Akron Story Circle Project is very helpful in creating the feeling that telling stories is a natural and inevitable process.

✦**Bill:** In what ways did taking such a risk as a teacher help anyone else learn more, and in particular, learn to trust our students more? My students regularly challenged me to think more deeply, including rethinking about my own standpoint. Anyone else have similar experiences?

Jim: This aspect of trusting our students is something which has now permeated all aspects of my teaching and directing. Every class discussion is now structured in some way like a story circle for me. And each student is a potential storyteller with something to offer. I'm much less of a tyrant in the classroom and more apt to find the unexpected and unfamiliar as I teach, making it as much a journey for me as for the students.

Story circles helped me see and hear about an entire universe of experiences I did not know, and more importantly, tore back the curtain on other stories I thought I knew for sure that "just ain't so." While we can all dismiss data that does not reinforce the familiar, it is much more difficult to dismiss stories told by peers sitting next to us about our own city, as this student noted.•

> *Hearing the stories of racial profiling that occurred right here in Akron to an amazing degree really surprised me. While reading about this practice occurring in a white suburban area did not surprise me, the stories of local students did.[3]* •

•**Amy:** Absolutely! It's the personalization of the issue that makes it resonate. Otherwise it's just another abstraction for most students, many of whom seem to be up to their ears in abstractions. Putting a face on the issue allows them to connect and even emphasize.

•**Donna:** I thought that problems caused by race largely disappeared for well-educated African Americans. My understanding changed as I listened to the well-educated, talented, and beautiful students in Jim's theatre class. Every story told by the young African American students included a comparison of lighter and darker skin colors. Stories like, "My sister married a man who was darker than she and one of their children has very light skin or I have skin that is darker than my sisters and therefore I have been considered the less pretty sister." The stories that did not include these kinds of comments were the exception.

A. Story Circles, Round One: Law & Society Course

The first of the two classes described here was Law & Society. The goals of this course focus on how the law comes to have meaning in society and the ways that various agents—from lawyers to clerks, talking heads to interest group activists, public and private leaders—participate in this process. This course analyzed the law by focusing on the relationship between race, crime, and politics as a 300-level political science course and a core course for our Conflict Management program.

As a part of our second annual Rethinking Race, my Law & Society class invited John O'Neal and Theresa Holden from the Color Line Project (discussed in the Introduction to this book) to our class to conduct story circles on race and train students in the story circle technique.[4] • We conducted story circles three additional times during the class and several of the students also participated in story circles that were part of Rethinking Race. The course included three writing assignments based on the data gathered in these story circles. Students had to write a short paper, participate in online discussions, and write a longer paper analyzing the stories collected, the relationship between the stories and the scholarly articles assigned, and reflecting on their own experiences with the story circle data collection and analysis process.

Bill: These were amazing experiences. My students were blown away by John and it gave me a chance to model—by manifestly listening and engaging and learning from John—being a good citizen-student with my own students. I might not have felt confident enough to integrate story circles into my syllabus had it not been for John's assistance. Anyone else experience this team-teaching boost?

Pat: The story circle training taught me the importance of listening to each other as we share what disturbs and troubles us—about our fears, and about what gives us hope. John and Theresa's visit reinforced both my understanding of this and provided a valuable tool for how to talk about race.

Carolyn: Listening to others talk about race issues in terms of personal experience and then finding the stories within myself was both wonderful and hard in these first story circles and the discussions that followed them. Something that was hard and that surprised me was how comfortable I have become with not fully acknowledging race issues in my personal life. Even with my two closest black friends, sisters who are basically part of my extended family, as our mothers were best friends, race was always with us and never really acknowledged as an issue. I think my relationship with them has changed in ways that are at times not comfortable, easy, or entirely welcomed the past few years as I have brought my experience in these dialogues home to my relationship with them. I have grown up a bit, I think, through our bumpy exchanges that happen to coincide with racialized events like the deaths of Trayvon Martin, Tamir Rice, and John Crawford, among others.

Jim: Bill talks about team teaching. I guess I would tend to use the word collaboration. I wish that our institution allowed for more collaboration among disciplines for teaching. I think that we could really enhance each other's classrooms in a variety of ways. The Story Circle Project has allowed me to rethink and reinvent many ways that our fields of inquiry intersect and how the arts and social sciences in particular can work together to create a civic practice that includes art action and social action.

B. *Story Circles, Round Two: Summer Conflict Management Course*

Many of the students in the Law & Society course expressed a desire to continue working with story circles and, in particular, suggested that story circles ought to include not only their peers, but African Americans from multiple generations. As a result, in a summer course the next term, we partnered with the Akron Urban League to conduct eight story circles, each facilitated by two UA students from the Law, Mediation & Violence class, collecting nearly one hundred stories.●

●**Bill:** This raises another interesting point that I suspect is shared by others working on this volume. We were only able to make this connection with the Urban League because a former student of mine works there. Our own embeddedness in the communities surrounding UA facilitated bringing story circles to them and their stories to us.

Carolyn: This is true, Bill. Sometimes that embeddedness involves many threads of connection, too. Many threads connect me to the wonderful experience my undergraduates had at a local public middle school working with fourth- through eighth-graders, gathering stories for their production, *The Diversity Play.* This original play has drawn much praise and been invited to be performed at area universities. One of my students chose to write his final exam essay on this experience, and I have suggested he submit this excellent essay to a student writing competition. My own children attended that magnet arts middle school in Akron where, through them, I met the theatre teacher Wendy Duke, who now, many years later, directs *The Diversity Play.* She is a former student of Jim's. In a separate undertaking, we, the Akron Story Circle Project, have twice been engaged by the Akron Public Schools to work with middle school teachers, including Wendy, in the use of story circles as part of middle school curriculum development. I had a student, India Burton, in a Human Diversity class in 2008, who stood out for her academic skill but also for her community engagement. She went on to work with Jim on the *Color Line Project Performance* and has commented on the script (see chapter 7). India became Wendy's codirector for *The Diversity Play.* All these connections are, I suppose, to be expected in a small city, but I am impressed with the strong quality of the work that stems from these endeavors. I think the level of quality must rise from the strength and flexibility of the method and from planners' deliberate efforts to connect the lived experience on one end—through a filter that is shaped by a sense of social justice—to intelligent analysis of social reality on the other end.

Jim: I think story circles have naturally gotten all of us out of the ivory tower of the academy to become much more involved in our community. Even if we already were operating within our various communities in a number of roles (parent, church member, artist, researcher, etc.), story circles have created a different web of contacts and connections or allowed us to see our contacts and connections differently. Because I think that's one of the real reverberations of this process: how it changes our ways of seeing. Suddenly our world becomes something very different than what we had imagined. Our image of ourselves and our world is measured against the reality of the stories we hear and so many delusions and illusions fall away. It's a real *via negativa*—a stripping away of what is false or blocking our own authenticity—and at the same time, a *via positiva*—a meeting full of wonder and mystery. At the intersection of these two paths lies a transformation in the way of seeing ourselves and the world around us.

More than ninety percent of the stories had been transcribed and stored in an archive in UA's Active Research Methods Lab (ARM Lab)[5] by the end of the day following our story circles at the Urban League, a testament to student enthusiasm and engagement. In addition to our scholarly readings, once the stories were transcribed our focus turned to analyzing these as primary source texts. We did this in a structured way, as outlined by the assignments below.

1. Response Papers

These are short (two single-spaced pages) papers written in response to each assigned text and due before we begin working with that text in class. In the first half of each paper, students summarized the central argument and the best data presented in support of that argument, and then constructed their most thoughtful scholarly response *to that argument* in the second half. These papers provided ample opportunity for faculty-student and student-student interaction to clarify the art of summary, making sense of data and scholarly arguments, and integrating these into one's own thoughtful presentation of an argument in response.♦

> ♦**Bill:** It likely varies by field and instructor preference, but these assignments are critically important, interactive opportunities for me to reinforce in text-specific and individualized ways what we mean by *engaging seriously and thoughtfully with a scholarly argument*; particularly when we are engaging in difficult dialogues about controversial conflicts, starting with concrete illustrations allows me a chance to model intellectual engagement with the data—wrestling with complexity, choosing language carefully and more were all important to the later success of this class experience.
> **Carolyn:** You have modeled this so well, Bill, that I have adapted your approach to fit my introductory course in Human Diversity!

2. Initial Reactions Paper

Only moments after conducting the story circles the students recorded their own initial reactions to the stories and the story circles, providing a chronology of how the story circles unfolded on one side of the page, with their reactions, impressions, and observations on the other side of the page. This paper sets a tone of ongoing and open exchange about the stories for the class,✦ as another student pointed out, noting that the instructor:

> *engaged the whole class. He let us feel as if our opinions and knowledge matter beyond just getting a good grade. The feedback that was given was a lot more helpful than I have received in other classes.*●

> ✦**Bill:** This paper is also an excellent illustration of the benefits of interdisciplinary work, since the idea and structure for these assignments grew out of conversations with Carolyn about how anthropologists construct their field notes. Are there other illustrations of how our cross-disciplinary conversations in this project improved our work?
> **Donna:** My sabbatical (Faculty Improvement Leave) and the resulting research would not have been possible without the interdisciplinary experiences I have had first with Jim's

theatre class and with the Akron Story Circle Group and with Synapse Center for Arts and Science. I believe that the arts have much to contribute to both social change and the integration of scientific information into our daily lives. As important as data is both in the hard and social sciences, the meaning of that data in our lives must be created through story telling. Sometimes that story is told by visual means.

Pat: I admit that working within my discipline is familiar and comforting, and the thought of venturing out was a bit daunting at first. However, I have come to understand that disciplinary specialization constrains faculty from broadening their intellectual horizons. To contribute to the fund of knowledge that helps us all solve the problems of the world, we need to consider interdisciplinary work. I revel in our opportunity to work in an interdisciplinary fashion. It has been invigorating, and I believe it has provided each of us more opportunities for creativity and intellectual breakthroughs.

Jim: This project has allowed me to investigate the interdisciplinary nature of theatre and to bring your various disciplines and points of view into the process to inform and question my own work in the rehearsal studio. I have been happy to include members of the team in early rehearsals for a variety of performances, not just story circle-related productions. The ways in which the team's feedback challenged and informed work on *The Dionysus Project* (a three-play investigation of the Dionysus myth and its manifestation in today's world), for example, helped to guide the project through its research into ecstasy, addiction, possession, obsession, repression, and passion. I think the theatre is a natural laboratory for discovering how to collaborate.

Amy: I am blessed to serve in a multidisciplinary department, Associate Studies, where I can simply walk down the hall for a different perspective from, say, an economist, mathematician, or someone who teaches composition. We are all enriched by the experience.

•Bill: We all know that formative assessment is important for many reasons. Here we see that one of those reasons, particularly when it is structured to play out over many (somewhat shorter) assignments, is that the individualized feedback demonstrates to often cynical students that we are interested in what they think, in the questions they bring to the table. Our in-class discussions often started with 'student x, you said this in your abc assignment, and I have a couple of questions about that because I would like to hear more about what you are thinking here.' The very personal and intimate nature of story circles amplified the power of ongoing instructor feedback. Did anyone else experience it this way?

Carolyn: You are an excellent teacher, Bill, and a part of your skill lies in your ability to give ongoing, cumulative feedback that seems to me to work like signposts leading students toward both academic understanding and greater self-awareness. That said, I agree that the impact of the story circle experience on a class can be an increased sense that we all "know" each other and also that we care to know each other. This allows the feedback to fit into a framework of relationship and I think we all hear and receive comments on our work more effectively in that context.

Figure 4: Amy at Rethinking Race event

3. Central Themes Paper

In class, student cofacilitators first worked through a list of ten questions, presenting their conclusions to the class, and critically responding to the presentations of their peers. During this week we were reading a Cornel West essay titled "Nihilism in Black America" (1993) to focus our analysis of the relationship between structure and agency.♦ We were also reading two chapters from *Punishing Schools* (Lyons and Drew 2006), providing an illustration of how to write about narrative data. During this week-long process, the instructor started each of the five days with a one-page handout and mini-lecture. Additional scholarly articles (selected on the basis of themes that were emerging from class discussions) on race and crime were used, in short bursts of five to eight minutes followed by discussion, to demonstrate how one might apply concepts from this literature to make sense out of narrative texts such as the stories we had collected.

♦**Amy:** Since you shared this with me, Bill, I've used it many times. It works so well to frame the discussion for my students.

Jim: This brings up another common thread for us in the arts and social sciences that I had not previously thought about. In theatre, Grotowski talks about the *conjunctio oppositorum* (conjunction of opposites) between structure and spontaneity. It is one of the paradoxes of creativity that spontaneity cannot exist without structure. First one must

> build the banks and then the river of life can flow. If there are no banks, there is only a
> swamp. So often we think that spontaneity, improvisation, or inspiration comes from
> nowhere, but if it's authentic and lasting, it actually comes from a great deal of prepara-
> tion and structure.

At the same time, we focused on how to use the stories to thicken our understanding of the specific concepts in the literature and, more generally, the nature of racial conflict, power and subordination, and intellectual inquiry. Identifying themes was challenging and time consuming work, but turned out to be an essential part of doing justice to the storytellers.*

> *Bill: This is another instance where my work was improved through collaboration around
> story circles. The story circle process, which we explained in our introduction, high-
> lights the importance of identifying themes. Since my students had done this in circles,
> and my exposure to circles pushed me to expand my description of 'summarizing argu-
> ments and data' to include identifying themes in stories (from scholarly sources or our
> own circles), the conversations that resulted and the thought behind the themes that
> emerged were significantly more powerful here. Such a small adjustment, just tweaking
> how I talked about scholarly engagement, resulted in such a huge gain. Anyone else
> experience this?
> Donna: During my year-long project at Cascade Village I did many kinds of art projects
> in an effort to determine what kind of public art would be welcomed at Cascade Village.
> During that time I lived with a group of stories from story circles told by residents early
> in the year. Since we had recorded and transcribed them they were available to me. I
> reread them numerous times. Slowly the themes emerged and I realized that the stories
> were important not only because they represented an important art form already present
> in the community—that of storytelling—but also because they revealed themes impor-
> tant to the community and seemed to contain hope for the solution of problems there.
> Pat: Carolyn's chapter speaks somewhat to the arduous nature of story circle method,
> which illuminates injustice by engaging themes about people in a social context—how
> they view the world and how they negotiate everyday experiences with race.
> Carolyn: In my field we tend to read qualitative and quantitative scholarship in relatively
> equal amounts. I find that getting students to analyze trends in quantitative examples
> is easier sometimes than getting them to see and talk about themes in more qualitative
> sources so I often use a wonderful article on identifying themes by Ryan and Bernard
> (2003).

4. Individually Written Themes Paper

In this paper, students were asked to build on our central themes discussion by identifying at least five specific concepts, relationships, or ideas from the literatures we had read. They were asked to select those that (1) they thought would help them do justice to the storytellers and their stories, (2) *they could use* to help readers better understand the stories, and (3) they thought would deepen our understanding of the concepts.

5. *Mature Draft of Final Paper*

Students were required to share four copies of their mature drafts, organized with common subheadings agreed upon in class discussion, at the start of our final week. After in-class peer critiques and individualized feedback from the instructor, students were instructed to re-think and revise these drafts to produce final papers of twelve to fifteen pages.•

> •**Carolyn:** This is a wonderful sequence of assignments drawing students into three important exchanges that hone their writing skills in different ways. The first is a dialogue with content (scholarly literature and primary sources) that emphasizes coherent description and identification of themes and patterns that link and build arguments. The second is a dialogue with the instructor in both oral and written form that builds rapport, models appropriate ways to critique and support and this helps students trust their written voice, enhancing authorial confidence. Finally, the sequence engages students in an exchange about their work with other students. This dialogue—well bolstered by the first two—clearly brought about the great strides in development that the students quoted here identify.

A white male student commented at the end of the five-week session that he "could not have written the final paper if we had not had the earlier paper assignments to build on and show us, like a road map, how to take on such a complex challenge one step at a time." Another exemplary student commented, "Here we read articles that were applicable to racial conflict and participated in deep discussions that helped the students grasp the material." As another student observed, in other courses she would "simply drift by, meet the requirements and be done. But in this course, it actually forced me to learn more. I actually feel like I learned something and did something important."•

> •**Amy:** Wow! Really, isn't that why we teach—in the hope of making impacts like these?

III. SAMPLING THE STORIES WE GATHERED

With this basic structure of Law, Mediation & Violence in mind, this section provides an illustrative sampling of the nearly one hundred stories

Figure 5: Akron Color Line Project/Story Circle Project Team

my students collected and analyzed. We heard stories about explicit racism, exclusion, and hangings in the south during the 1950s. We also heard stories about cross burnings outside of Akron,* about a black student currently at UA being asked in confidence by a white, elderly friend if she could see his tail, and countless descriptions of unwarranted and humiliating traffic stops in and around Akron.

> *I got a call early like nine from one of my buddies. He wanted me to ride to Akron and to pick up his mom. So he come; he get me. We comin' down State Road. We see the police cars. We in [nearby city]. We see police cars everywhere. . . . If you ever been on State Road, it veers off Howard or Main Street. So we took the Howard way. . . . We goin' down Howard, we see Akron police out too. Apparently somebody shot somebody with a shot gun and uh it's like a three-hundred-pound black guy maybe four-hundred-pound . . . so, we get down by like Howard going down the hill (inaudible) all the cop cars all the way up the hill they was following us the whole way. . . . I didn't know somebody got shot till afterwards. So they pull us over in the middle of the hill. . . . They said the guy was in a rusty Chevy Capri; mind you, a blue one. Uh my friend has a Chevy Capri four-door but uh he got a very clean Chevy, mind you, so uh you can't, there's no way you can get primer mixed up with this clean car. . . . So they pulled us over. . . .*
>
> *So [the lieutenant] he hopped out, they all hopped out, surround us like six cars (inaudible) with their guns. . . . I was scared like "What's going on" [the cops said] "Get your hands up, get your hands up!" My hands already up . . . he*

yanked me outta the passenger side you know, "Get down on the ground!"... The dude just, I dunno if he just didn't like black people (inaudible).

[The] sergeant, you can tell he wanna shoot me. He had the taser in my face and he had the regular gun in my face. And I was really scared. And he yanked us out the car he throw my arm behind my back like, like all in one motion. I was already on my knees and he like just he kind like throw me to the dirt. And I remember his partner just comin' over and just stomped me in the face, like my tooth gone till this day right here (pointed to his tooth) just stomp me in the face kicked at least three times... the suspects they was lookin' was in a rusty car, a 300 pound guy so. So this is a big dude. You know I'm a little dude. My other dude is no bigger than you maybe (pointing to another participant).

You know, I just think it's sad how they just... cause one black person did something we all suspects... I guess I heard the saying you know I guess we all look alike but, uh, you know you can't get me mixed up with some three hundred pound guy. It was horrible. (Al-Obaid 2010, 6).•

*Donna: According to the master's thesis by J. L. Maples, "The Ohio Ku Klux Klan, 1921–1928," Akron had the largest Klan membership in the country during the late 1920s. John did his research by interviewing surviving members of the Klan as well as their contemporaries who were still alive in the early 1970s. John has agreed to participate in a story circle with us. I suggested the prompt: *stories I have been told about racism in Akron.* This is an activity that can only happen because I work with the Akron Story Circle Group.
Amy: The Ohio Historical Society has a collection of jaw-dropping photos of Klan parades down Main Street in Akron in the 1920s, complete with separate (of course!) floats for the KKK Auxiliary.

•Amy: It is hard to imagine a different context in which a student would have been willing to reveal so much.

And stories about being targeted by authority figures for extra scrutiny were not only about police profiling. A storyteller discussed what one student-author called "an instance of being racially classified as a threat to society and the disenfranchisement she felt while grocery shopping with her family" (Bailey 2010, 4). Here is how the story appeared (in italics and indented), including the analysis of this story offered by the student cofacilitator (also indented but not italicized).

So, I really have had few bad experiences, and the one that that really brings in my mind now... was um, my experience in the grocery store with my family: my daughter and my husband. He had just come back from Vietnam. We are in the grocery store and we were standing in the aisle…making a decision about something that we were going to buy, and the cart…was in the aisle and enough room was there for a cart to come by in the opposite direction. There was a little white lady, who wanted to us to move out of the aisle so she could come by because she did not want us in the aisle with her.

Well, my husband having been in Vietnam is not the best person to be saying "boy, move out the aisle. Let me by." He said, "You can come by." She left her cart, went up to the grocery store manager, had him to come back, and let him know that we were harassing her.

Here we see a predicament in America's racial conflict, where the member of the powerful, dominant group claims to be so weak and helpless as to be "harassed" by the simple presence of an African American unwilling to step off the sidewalk or otherwise disappear to ensure her comfort.…She expected the manager or someone in authority to simply enforce her vision of a racially pure society in that grocery aisle.

And the manager approached us with an attitude that we were automatically in the wrong and that we were bothering her.…I just don't know when I've ever felt so degraded and so disrespected and it just had to be the grace of god that he looked and saw my husband in the uniform and the lady was just…going on about how colored people should not be, uh well she used the term why Negros should not be allowed to shop in the same places and how we just did not appreciate things (Gray 2010, 6).♦

> ♦**Pat:** This story of racial profiling is powerful and demonstrates its devastating effects on a personal as well as a group level in a democratic society. Racial profiling is often paired with potentially negative action, as we saw in circumstances surrounding the killing of Trayvon Martin. The sharing of experiences like this helps to bring awareness of not only what racial profiling is, but also how it affects lives. In the struggle to end racial profiling, the first step is developing awareness of the issue so that policies to ensure equal treatment of all might be implemented. This is yet another example of the profound value of story circles.
>
> **Donna:** Pat, I so agree with you. My experience in story circles led me to question the killing of Trayvon Martin in a way I might not have thought to do before hearing the stories of people with values much like my own describing experiences that made me say "how can that be?"

IV. CLASS STRUCTURE: PRODUCTIVE APPROACHES TO DIFFICULT DIALOGUES

Those are the types of stories our students collected and analyzed. In this section, we will hear from these same students as they describe the importance of carefully structuring in-class and cocurricular experiences (like those in Rethinking Race used as a text in the first course here), to avoid reinforcing racial divisions and encourage, instead, more productive conversations, what we call here *difficult dialogues.*

When students engage seriously in college life, this inevitably means encountering situations in which they are uncomfortable and these are opportunities to reflect, learn, and come together. "To learn from one another, students from different backgrounds, and from different racial and ethnic groups, must interact" (Light 2001, 190). Combining scholarly articles with story circles and Rethinking Race events as non-traditional texts, and then going through the structured and iterated engagement process described above created a learning experience designed to challenge rather than reinforce negative stereotypes masquerading as conventional wisdom as this student noted.

> *Each keynote speaker and face-to-face conversation helped to educate me on issues of racism and gave me tools in order to try to resolve them in my life. Donna Brazile... helped me to realize that I can make progress by holding honest conversations with people of different race and religion. It was a truly great experience to see people of different race and gender coming together.*✦

✦**Carolyn:** This student and Brazile make me think about when higher education is at its best. Indoctrination is learning "what to think," higher education is "learning how to think" and we do that when we challenge our preconceived notions through direct experience with people and ideas that are unfamiliar.

Jim: Not just "how to think," but how to learn, how to understand (stand under, as I said previously), and how to take action. For me, as a theatre teacher, this is the most satisfying part of my work. In theatre, the main tool is action. When a student truly understands this crucial aspect of theatre training, he or she is prepared to take action in his or her own life as well, not just as a character onstage. Using the stories from story circles as material for creating performance adds a more personal, more urgent dimension to that part of the process. It really brings it home, so to speak, and we are no longer dealing with distant creations from the minds of revered poets or playwrights, but we are dealing the material of our own lives and our own community. In this way, we are taking action to make our community more livable.

According to Lee Warren of the Bok Center, as educators we are all challenged by difficult dialogues in the classroom, and the core of transforming these "hot moments" into learning moments is to find ways to "*manage ourselves* so as to make them useful" as opportunities to "learn in

Figure 6: Jim at rehearsal

and from the moment" (2000, 1). But the course structure described above operated as a set of agreed-upon (if always open to renegotiation) ground rules to frame our difficult dialogues around both scholarly data about race in society and stories about race in the room. This encouraged the myth-busting and re-thinking central to transforming uncertainty into adventure.

The unanticipated challenge, the hot-moment suggestion or comment or reaction, became a learning moment because we were present and the course structure prepared us to engage with our own emotional and cognitive confusion. Without attention to how difficult dialogues make salient the relationship between structure and agency, we might miss learning opportunities, or worse, allow difficult dialogues to reinforce existing power imbalances and prejudices.[6] Instead, in these classes story circles helped us be prepared to *use* conflict and confusion to teach democratic citizenship skills.

Difficult dialogues, done well, provide us with opportunities to "wrestle with messy problems that have no clearly defined answer, a skill that will help [us all] as voters when [we] evaluate policy trade-offs. It is also a skill that many employers say they value" (Berrett 2014, 2). Most important political, social, cultural, even economic questions that make it onto our public policy agenda are complex and lack a single, clear-cut, data-driven solution. They require us to balance competing demands and values, weigh policy and constituency trade-offs, in contexts where resources are limited and unequally controlled.•

This type of problem solving—the heart and soul of democratic politics—requires nuance and subtlety, data and experience, listening and a shared goal of finding common ground even while we likely still disagree. Lacking the one uncontroversial solution imagined in familiar platitudes, these are the types of questions that a zero-tolerance culture will almost certainly answer badly, but with great confidence.♦

♦**Donna:** I like too the way the story circle asks us to respect each person's story. This encourages the finding of common ground.

These are questions where the solutions depend on *achieving* agreement, agreements that are usually tentative, partial, and provisional. Achieving agreements in these areas nearly always requires us to be uncomfortable, to accept uncertainty, to be willing to collaborate with others who bring complimentary skills and perspectives to the conversation, whose stories are unlike our own—sometimes dramatically so.

This type of learning is one reason we value discussion-based teaching. Doing it well requires us to be comfortable being uncomfortable, because we will not always know the right answer ahead of time.♦ Doing it well requires us to be ready to be honest in these dialogues when we are confused or when a question or comment has caused us to rethink or reconsider. If we are so unschooled in difficult dialogues that we cannot help a room puzzle through the difference, for instance, between politics and partisanship, it is time to be honest: simply choosing to avoid charged conversations, because they are charged, is like refusing to do our homework.

♦**Pat:** While we may work to engender in our students feelings of safety and comfort in the classroom, dialogues about race or racism tend to take us out of our comfort zones.

Polite conversations may not get to the heart of important issues. Our pedagogy should help students get comfortable with the incendiary.

Instead, be present. Help students puzzle through the questions by doing it with them with a shared goal of enhancing everyone's understanding of the controversies—and the value of serious inquiry. Ask questions when we do not know, instead of changing the topic to something we are comfortable being the expert on, to demonstrate that we are interested in the questions and concerns expressed by the people in the room and that we hope they might be similarly interested in the questions and concerns that animate us.

Expect intellectual inquiry to challenge participants to reconsider the familiar, rethink 'common sense,' and replace identities forged in a hyper-racialized context with one recognizing our place in a diverse global community. Well-structured, difficult dialogues are one way to do this. My students loved it, and for all the right reasons.

Tim Wise really opened my eyes to problems induced by racism here in the United States. I learned that one reason I do not see racism as a problem in today's society is because I am not forced to experience it on a daily basis. I came to further realization about Tim Wise's "white privilege" during one of the story circles. One of the black students told a story of when he and a few of his friends stopped to eat at a restaurant located in a predominately white area.

He explained how the people who were eating and working stopped in their tracks and stared at him and his friends. They did not stick around to eat. To add insult to injury, a police cruiser followed them in their car until they had left the area. In my opinion, this story was more influential than any article or statistic because of the similarities that we share. Even though he is a black man, we are both students at the University of Akron, we both grew up in a culturally diverse atmosphere, and we both have a multitude of friends who are black and white.•

•**Carolyn:** It is important to keep these conversations balanced on that delicate edge between what is too painful, too personal, sometimes narcissistic, sometimes revealing of our failure to recognize other participants' social realities, and what is too removed or too academic. The stories and the literature at their best work together to guide students to see connections and then contextualize them.

"Even though he is black, we are both students. . . ." We can be both different and in the same community. Our stories express both universal

Figure 7: Story Circle with Jim

themes and local identities as both Pat and Jim emphasize in other parts of this volume. The more I have worked with students in story circles, the more persuaded I have become that we likely fail as teachers if our lesson plans do not generate hot moments, difficult dialogues, of both the foreseeable and the unanticipated variety.♦ Certainly, if our goal is to advance our understanding of race and racial conflict, being present, ready and willing to, as Tupac Shakur demands, learn the "skills it takes to be real," requires us to both bring our students into difficult dialogues and to engage with them as colearners wrestling with these real world conflicts.[7]♦

> ♦**Amy:** Agreed! It can be so difficult to break through that curtain of passivity in the classroom, that "I'm here but not really here" gaze.

> ♦**Bill:** And this just happens to also be an important reason that we believe democracy can link individual initiative to innovation and collective prosperity, because this process is also the process of solving problems, driving innovation, and achieving agreements.
> **Jim:** This makes me think of John O'Neal's admonition to trust the circle. By that he meant that you don't need to come into the circle with a set story in mind. The group will often generate ideas that are important to and come out of that particular story circle. It may be that finding the way in difficult dialogues could have that same provisional nature.

Warren (2000) notes that we ought to listen for "the song beneath the words" for the sub-text in any story, because it is here we are more likely to discover potentially shared interests, to see the spin, and to *experience* the value of *engaging* thoughtfully—with others—in difficult dialogues. Gradually, or sometimes more suddenly, curtains are pulled back and we begin to see ourselves and our circumstances in ways that challenge unexamined or even untold stories.

> *After going to F2F conversations and just seeing the closed-mindedness of other students who I don't share a class with, I'm starting to think that the Law & Society class should become a general education requirement.*

This student found, in the structure of the course, a safe place enabling a skill set valued by a community that made more productive engagement in difficult dialogues possible.✦

> ✦**Bill:** Here I am trying to describe 'the relationship between structure and agency' with different language. It is possible, however, this just makes it more confusing. Thoughts?
> **Carolyn:** The structure/agency debate gets an appealing twist here because your student wants you to change university structure (creating a new general education requirement) to bring other students the sense of agency he has found by seeing the difference between his awareness of structurally-based inequalities gained through your class and other students' lack of that awareness during a Rethinking Race event!
> **Pat:** I do think it is possible to create a space where all students feel comfortable all the time. However, we need to help students feel trusting and trusted. Bill, I believe you are doing this in this course.

Tom Angelo (1993) provides several powerful and research-based insights on the relationship between class structure (like response papers or minute papers)● and productive dialogues—structure and agency. Response papers, minute papers, discussion threads, story circles and Rethinking Race events structured these classrooms around interactively engaging each student's imagination and curiosity.

> ●**Bill:** Minute papers ask students to spend one minute at the end of class identifying something they learned that day and something about the material that remains unclear. In addition to these and the usual office hours, weekly written feedback on assignments, and interactive feedback during class time, the course also included weekly discussion threads. I was amazed at the response. Difficult dialogues that silenced about half the class in weeks one and two gradually became more comfortable in this space for even

the quietest of students, as these students posted vigorously into threads and to me personally in response to my posts. As a result, these students then began participating regularly in conversations during class as well, until nearly every student was speaking multiple times in every class meeting.

The face-to-face conversations reinforced the idea that actions speak louder than words when it comes to my relations with people and racism. I never understood how my parents could not have a problem with people of other races yet at the same time deny me the choice of dating someone who was not white....

The thing is, people can talk as much as they want to about how bad things are but if they do not do anything or if they do the opposite of what they say is right, there will be no progress or change for the better. These events were a great experience. I hope to spread the information, ideas and concepts I have learned to my family, friends, and those who I will be working with in the future.

Our classrooms were structured, as Lev Vgotsky famously directed,[8] to *meet our students where they are.* Students were regularly invited to reflect on course material (and, in particular, on why we should care about this material) and bring their questions to class as a part of their assignments. When I used the photo booth at Rethinking Race to create a picture of "Hispanic Bill," I was trying to model a more open-minded approach to these questions and the photo did spark interesting conversation.♦ All of this ongoing and frequent faculty interaction with students around student questions demonstrates the value of honest engagement by connecting new data (scholarly articles, our own experiences, Rethinking Race texts, and story circle data) to student questions and concerns to reinforce the personal value of this scholarly material and of scholarly inquiry itself.[9] Just as Angelo focuses on the importance, and difficulty, of unlearning...this course was designed to highlight for participants the importance of rethinking, reconsidering, and reframing throughout.

♦**Amy:** Very cool! I have to admit that I thought this photo booth for Rethinking Race was just a gimmick. However, my students responded very strongly to the experience of seeing themselves in different skins. It was very meaningful to them.

Jim: In my Contemporary Theatre Styles course I show a video of a performance installation called "Cornered" by Adrian Piper. *The New York Times* describes it as follows: "In the riveting video 'Cornered' (1988), the artist herself sits demurely at a desk backed into a corner. Calmly she declares, 'I'm black,' (which is not obvious as she has light skin and

> straight hair) and proceeds to quietly harangue us about why we (presumably white) viewers might be bothered by this announcement. Do we think she is causing unnecessary trouble? Would it be better for her to pass for white? Then she argues that because of widespread miscegenation, most supposedly white people are actually black according to the laws of certain Southern states. So, at the end, when she demands to know what we are going to do with this new information, we are cornered ourselves, pushed to decide whether to continue accepting the racist status quo or begin to live differently."
>
> I think it's a brilliant and disturbing piece that always makes my students, both black and white, question many of their prejudices and preconceptions about race and where they stand on these difficult issues.

V. CLASS STRUCTURE: STARTING WITH THE BEST AVAILABLE DATA

In the Law & Society class, we started with twenty recent articles from scholarly journals in political science, sociology, communications, and law to critically examine the relationship between race and crime, punishment and politics.[10] There are many misconceptions and deeply held, but inaccurate, myths about race and crime that need to be carefully reconsidered in order for any serious conversation about racial conflict to move forward productively. This type of work, of course, is always a tough sell at the start of each semester.

> *I was extremely skeptical of the research articles that we covered in class. It seemed as if every article was skewed and loaded or had a certain margin for error. There was a particular article about police legitimacy that confused me because I had never experienced the possible injustices of the criminal justice system. My thoughts on policing were positive and I found it difficult to believe that racial profiling by police officers was a form of racism. It was not till later that I realized this was partially because of my race.*
>
> *Some of the stories from the circles helped me to better understand the data provided by Meehan and Ponder's "Race and Place" argument. We heard one story about a person that got pulled over in a neighborhood that apparently did not match the person's profile. The officer asked why she was so far away from home and what she was doing. This is very similar to the inquiries of the officers on the in-car computers used in Meehan and Ponder's study. It was apparent that officers stop people based on race and whether they're out of their stereotypical areas.*

If I were constructing that same syllabus today, I would almost certainly assign Michelle Alexander's book, *The New Jim Crow.*[*] In *The New Jim Crow,* Alexander[•] argues that as *an entirely foreseeable consequence* of our now decades long War on Drugs (WOD), "mass incarceration [has] emerged as a stunningly comprehensive and well-disguised system of racialized social control that functions in a manner strikingly similar to Jim Crow" (Alexander 2012, 4).

> ✦**Donna:** I chose *The New Jim Crow* for a reading group I formed at Cascade Village. It was the only time that I had a group of politically active young adults join one of my projects. On the last day of the reading group we went to the university to participate in story circles led by the Akron Story Circle Group and to hear Michelle Alexander speak. The members of the group went on to create a local group of Stand Up Ohio, to lead a rally in support of public schools in Akron and to lead the successful move for a fair hiring practice for returning citizens in Akron. One of the group ran an unsuccessful campaign for a city council seat against the president of city council. I continue to learn a great deal about leadership from this group.
>
> **Amy:** I was watching the reactions from your reading group on the evening of Michelle Alexander's speech. They were totally engaged and in total agreement with what she was saying. It was, for me, the best part of the evening.

> •**Amy:** She was amazing!

Alexander argues that the WOD is structured to incentivize mass arrests of young black men for minor and non-violent drug offenses *more often committed by white youth*, followed by an unconstrained prosecutorial enthusiasm for the conviction and imprisonment of an unprecedented number of—largely black—Americans (Alexander 2012, 61). She describes a 'racial caste system' centering on the WOD (Alexander 2012, 190), but starting in the public impoverishment of inner city schools, connecting disadvantages *concentrated in poor, inner city, black communities*—that is, about place and not race—to a broad menu of policy choices we make without examining the disparate impact on our power-poor neighbors of color.

The fact that most of us do not even see this creates an intellectual and emotional obstacle to productive difficult dialogues about race. Structures, like the WOD and punishing schools, encourage and enable police officer, prosecutor, and young black male behaviors that result in this racialized incarceration explosion. Structure interacts with agency here to reproduce and reinforce the Jim Crow ideology as a new conventional wisdom confirmed by the prison population: black are criminals. And this makes an already difficult dialogue all the more difficult to unpack.

Rather than rely on race, we use our criminal justice system to label people of color "criminals" and then engage in all the practices we supposedly left behind. Today it is perfectly legal to discriminate against criminals in nearly all the ways that it was once legal to discriminate against African Americans.

Once you are labeled a felon, the old forms of discrimination—employment discrimination, housing discrimination, denial of the right to vote, denial of educational opportunity, denial of food stamps and other public benefits, and exclusion from jury service—are suddenly legal.

As a criminal, you have scarcely more rights, and arguably less respect, than a black man living in Alabama at the height of Jim Crow. We have not ended racial caste in America; we have merely redesigned it (Alexander 2012, 2).

It turns out, upon closer examination, that there are reasons African American men are failing as fathers and partners and these reasons center on the disadvantages concentrated in their neighborhoods and schools, the particular ways structure and agency interact in our poorest neighborhoods.[11] As Alexander details, however, the pain associated with this ongoing punishment includes discrimination in employment, housing, and educational opportunity. This paints a picture of two Americas,♦ where some are raised in families and communities treated as virtuous citizens and others as disorderly subjects.[12] Our students picked up on this theme in the story circles.

I learned that your up-bringing and whom you are around affects the way you view race. Those in minority families have been brought up preparing to be discriminated against and knowing that no matter what they do, they will be affected by these things. I definitely think that you should keep these story circles in your class for the future. They not only give another aspect to the subject, but it also gives the class a chance to better understand each other and where they come from.

♦**Amy:** Daniel Patrick Moynihan said it in 1965. It was disturbing then and revisiting it today is even more so.

I find it difficult to imagine what it would be like to grow up "preparing to be discriminated against" and living in what Cornel West called the "Nihilism of Black America."[13] According to Alexander, our choice to police in this way is "unraveling community and family relationships, decimating networks of mutual support, and intensifying the shame and self-hate experienced by the current pariah caste" (Alexander 2012, 17) and it is all perfectly legal and therefore beyond invisible in society, let alone in our classrooms.

Disguised by our taken-for-granted and conventional framing of crime and punishment as 'just common sense,' apolitical, and about them rather than us, this incarceration explosion has political utility. It benefits some and it depends on a very specific, and widely misunderstood, set of stories we tell about race and crime. Here the data is helpful, but the conversation remains uncomfortable and challenging. We work our way through the data showing that most drug dealers and users are white, whites are also more likely to engage in drug-related criminal activity, and racial profiling is a waste of taxpayer dollars (because it does not work), while blacks make up the huge majority of minor drug arrests and an even larger portion of drug convictions (Alexander 2012, 7). The War on Drugs is a web of misconceptions that make difficult dialogues harder. The data is, however, helpful.

> *The data upon reading are just that—data. When you participate in activities such as story circles [it] allows you to put a face to the numbers given. It also gives you an understanding of the underlying issues that go into behaviors highlighted in a person's story.... [P]articipating in these story circles and race week I've seen how productive they are and how they connect people together who otherwise wouldn't have a connection.... I feel it's a good way to allow people to see the type of person you are and the experiences you have had that make you the person they see in front of you.... I know people are different and they come from different walks of life with different experiences but story circles allow people to connect.*
>
> *I learned we all have more in common with each other than we think. There are aspects of each of our lives that we can relate to and understand without bias and I found that interesting. While we may look different on the outside, come from different cities or towns, grow up in different kinds of family we all are participating in the same world and we all are trying to find what's right, do what's right or simply survive this crazy thing we call life.*

"People come from different walks of life and story circles allow people to connect." Story circles allow us to see and appreciate our different life experiences without erasing our shared values; in storytelling, difference and unity coexist. Making sense of the relationship between race, crime, and punishment requires examining the best available data and seriously scrutinizing our political spectacle. Doing this we see that the power of a widely shared faith in white supremacy is a concrete legacy of slavery that re-emerges in techniques used to control freed slaves during the Jim Crow era, to reframe civil rights activists as criminals, and today to sustain these trends in a racialized criminal justice system.* Information like this is not the end of the story, but quite literally the first in a series of stories to examine together as we struggle with our history and present. One goal here is to invite students to think and rethink together. Richard Light argues that faculty "should make a thoughtful, evidence-based, purposeful effort to get in each student's way" (2001, 209). The data help us get in our students' way. Story circles help us contextualize the data, amplifying its disruptive influence.

> *Bill: This short summary suggests that the data all point in one direction, which is not
> the case. But the data do profoundly challenge conventional wisdom, the WOD, and
> other myths about race. How do you address this with students?
>
> Donna: At Cascade Village I heard the stories of people who shared values so close to my
> own that I could see no significant difference. Most of them also had relatives in jail or
> prison. One amazing young man who is a leader in our community has a father and
> four uncles in prison. Another young woman who ran for city council this past year
> has a cousin who has been arrested more than sixty times for drug-related offenses. At
> the very least these stories set up doubts about the workings of our criminal justice
> system. At the very least, we must ask, "how can this be?" Once those doubts take hold,
> we must become more observant and critical.
>
> Carolyn: In Human Diversity we focus on the Eugenics Movement and examine a series
> of articles and new reports across the seventy-year period since World War II. The
> students are asked to examine events and analysis of events for evidence of the racial-
> ized world view that shaped the foundation for this movement and of the biological
> determinism that drove (drives) it. We scrutinize their stories of race conflict for evi-
> dence and well, I am not sure that directly answers your question, Bill, but there is a
> parallel between our two approaches, I think.
>
> Jim: This comes back, for me, to the problem of reverberation that I discussed elsewhere.
> Yes, we can have these incredible experiences, see the light, so to speak, but how do we
> get it to "stick" for our students? How do we keep them from going back immediately
> to their habitual behaviors? Or shouldn't we worry about that? I guess I want to create
> lasting change, but is there such a thing? Change by definition is a process. So I try to
> content myself with what social critic and cultural historian Morris Berman, in his
> book *The Twilight of American Culture*, calls the monastic option: people who are quietly
> working in their own ways, in their own communities, to critique society and preserve/
> transmit the positive aspects of humanity. "This may not, of course, actually transform
> American life, but it might leave a memory trace, a fragment of cultural preservation

Figure 9: Donna and Carolyn telling stories

to be picked up in more propitious times." Such traces are, perhaps, the best we can hope for. And this Story Circle Project has left a big trace for all involved. The motto of my theatre company, New World Performance Laboratory, is a haiku by the Japanese master Basho:

Journeying through the world
To and fro, to and fro,
Cultivating a small field.

VI. CONCLUSION: STORYTELLING TO GET IN OUR STUDENTS' WAY

In *Making the Most of College* (2001), Richard Light provides compelling data to support the claim that our most successful students understand that they learn more when faculty have high expectations and facilitate student efforts to integrate scholarly insights into open conversations focused on real world problem solving.[14] Students, according to Light, are highly critical of *platitudes* about diversity and, instead, focus on the necessary preconditions campus leaders must create to ensure that diversity-talk supports interactions where we learn from those with different backgrounds rather than reinforce the stereotypes diversity talk is meant to combat.•

•**Carolyn:** Yes. It can be far too easy to slide into these platitudes especially in the last class of the day. Structuring classes to create these dialogues, keeping them informed by literature and designed to make space for respectful voices, and working across disciplines and outside the single classroom to relevant, structurally-supported, interdis-

> ciplinary, cocurricular activity makes good teaching easier. This way we build safe-
> guards against our own weaknesses as *human* teachers.

The class structure described above was one critically important element of establishing preconditions to move our conversations from the empty recitation of platitudes and posturing to serious engagement with multiple competing perspectives on an already sensitive topic.

> *These story circles allowed me to see the scope of racism's effects. I heard white students that were troubled by racist views in their communities, African American students who spoke of the equal treatment of whites at a nearly all-black school, and several people that, like me, had not been exposed to diversity before coming to college.*
>
> *These circles allowed me to connect with classmates of all races and realize that although we came from different backgrounds we had a lot of the same difficulties but also incredible differences. I think this is a great teaching method. In addition to the learning opportunity, it takes away awkwardness within a class. For me, when I feel comfortable with my class-mates, I feel more confident in participating in discussions and voicing my opinion.*

Students pointed out that ethnic and racial diversity *actually enhances learning* when we set a tone of openness and enact a culture of inquiry. "And campus leaders at all levels must reinforce it. The perspective is not liberal or conservative. It is just an open-mindedness. It is an eagerness to meet and engage with people who look different from oneself and come from different backgrounds" (Light 2001, 135).

> *Although I have been close with some African Americans before coming to Akron, I have never been comfortable with discussing issues related to race with these individuals. As many other sensitive whites could relate, discussing issues of racism that African Americans face on a daily basis can be challenging.*
>
> *Personally, hearing second-hand stories of racism and reading through journal articles leaves me with a sense of guilt and shame for my race, but the stories of the racism that my fellow classmates face made the issue strike close to home. Listening to these first-hand accounts made me realize that feeling guilty and ashamed for my race wasn't the way to respond to the racism inflicted to others, but being proactive and "talking about race to become uncomfortable" was the approach I needed to take.*

Figure 10: Pat in a Story Circle with Carolyn and Jairo

Consistent with the literature on the preconditions for deliberative democracy,[15] platitudes about diversity cannot overcome, and will often reinforce, stereotypes and prejudice unless structures are in place to support and encourage open-mindedness, active listening, and being fully present.◆

> *Just as the story helped me understand their data, the "Race and Place" article helped prepare me for the story about profiling. Before reading the article and knowing how widespread the issue of racial profiling is today, I would have been shocked to hear of these kinds of things happening. Since I was aware of the problem, the story just served as proof of the damage it does on a personal, rather than statistical basis. I would definitely be interested in participating more in a Story Circle project. I would actually like to take this kind of research and examine racism in my hometown and within the school system.*

◆**Pat:** Your chapter reveals that telling stories and reflecting on racial positions goes a long way in opening doors to critical conversations.

We value diversity because it protects our species, drives innovation, and keeps life interesting. As an observation and shared aspiration for survival and prosperity, a commitment to diversity should translate into an appreciation of the *value* of conflict and disagreement. This class was an effort to teach our students not to fear conflict or conversation about controversial topics like race, but instead to see these as opportunities to learn the skills of democratic citizenship: listening, scrutinizing, storytelling, negotiating, achieving agreements. And it is important to learn to do this with others, *with those who disagree* or have very different lived experiences and sometimes competing perspectives. In the end, we will always, at least, *share the struggle* (Walsh 2007, 252) to balance civility and contestation, listening and speaking, diversity and unity in the stories we tell—from classrooms to larger public spheres.

NOTES

1. It turned out that James was not able to coteach the course, because he had to drop out of school that term unexpectedly. But he did graduate. In fact he just got married and is doing well.

2. As a result of these students' effort the class was recognized by the campus Office of Multicultural Development for innovative diversity programming, by the office of then Representative (now US Senator) Sherrod Brown, and by students campus-wide when they selected me as Faculty of the Year for 2003.

3. All indented and italicized quotes are from students in the Law & Society class, from story circles or their analysis of story circle data. When an indented quote is also in quotation marks that indicates it is from a scholarly source. The student statements included here are from a variety of assignments: in-class writing, discussion board threads on our campus LMS, and formal papers.

4. For more on the Color Line Project, see Yuen.

5. The ARM Lab is part of an NSF-funded project. The facility offers support to faculty and researchers focusing on human behavior from any discipline, facilitates undergraduate research, and encourages interdisciplinary and community-based collaborations.

6. See David Foster Wallace, pages 110–18 in particular.

7. "In particular, students mention professors who encourage students to disagree—constructively—with what they are presenting. There is a delicate line between ceding all responsibility to a student and encouraging that student to take a reasonable amount of responsibility for shaping his own ideas and arguments. Faculty who are able to walk that line are remembered with honor by their students (Light, 119–20)."

8. Richard Light (84) reinforces the importance of meeting students where they are so we can discuss what matters to them about the scholarly inquiry playing out in any particular class, department, or campus community.

9. One of the metacognitive points, for instance, that this course repeatedly emphasized in the importance of focusing on asking better questions (and multiple ways to do this, together), rather than simply focusing on finding the one right answer.

10. See note 11 for many of the articles that were included.

11. See Sampson and Bartusch 1998; Lyons and Miller 2012; Barker 2006; Payne and Gottfredson 2003; Sunshine and Tom Tyler 2003; Wacquant 2001; Meehan and Ponder 2002; Fluery-Steiner 2002; Mendelberg 1997; Chiricos and Welch 2004; Behrens, Uggen, and Manza 2003; Western 2002; Pager,2003; Clear, Rose, Waring, and Scully 2003; Tonry 1999.

12. See Yngvesson 1993.

13. West was one of the twenty articles assigned in the course. "We must acknowledge that structures and behavior are inseparable, that institutions and values go hand in hand. How people act and live are shaped—though in no way dictated or determined—by the larger circumstances in which they find themselves. These circumstances can be changed....Second, culture is as much a structure as the economy or politics; it is rooted in institutions such as family, schools, churches....[So,] how people act and live are shaped by the larger [political and economic, and cultural] circumstances in which they find themselves...[and] these circumstances can be changed. Third, we must delve into the depths where neither liberals nor conservatives dare to tread, namely into the murky waters of despair and dread that now flood the streets of black America. To talk about depressing statistics of unemployment, infant mortality, incarceration, teenage pregnancy, and violent crime is one thing. But to face up to the monumental eclipse of hope, the unprecedented collapse of meaning, the incredible disregard for human (especially black) life and property in much of black America is something else." (1993, 11–13).

14. Light reports that "students often give the most rigorous and demanding classes their highest ratings" because these faculty "helped students make connections between serious curriculum, on the one hand, and the students' personal lives, values, and experiences, on the other...[they] build such connections into their teaching" (2001, 110).

15. See Barabus 2004. Barabus argues that the literature on deliberative polling, among other work, demonstrates that there are four critical preconditions for effective deliberation (that is, designed to achieve informed agreements about shared interests and concerns, versus discussions that are designed to reinforce divisive positions and thwart agreements needed to make democracy work). These conditions are open-mindedness, disagreement, a shared goal of achieving agreements, and clear/balanced information. Disagreement refers to ensuring that the people who disagree speak to and hear from each other. "Deliberation," as Barabus puts it, "is structured so that people with diverse views commingle." Thus, democracy (and both classroom as well as social learning, see earlier Schattschneider quote) requires us to learn the skills it takes to actively listen to those with views unlike our own, to learn to be patient and thoughtful so we might respond respectfully, adopting a curiosity stance—seeing deliberation as a opportunity to learn and more productively address the conflicts we face—together.

REFERENCES

Al-Obaid, Rafah. 2010. "Racial Conflicts in America." *Transdiscinplinary Journal of Conflict Management* 1: 1–9. http://www.uakron.edu/conflict/research/transdisciplinary-journal-of-conflict-management.dot.

Alexander, Michelle. 2012. *The New Jim Crow: Mass Incarceration in the Age of Colorblindness.* New York: The New Press.

Angelo, Tom. 1993. "A Teacher's Dozen: Fourteen General, Research-Based Principles for Improving Higher Learning in Our Classrooms." *AAHE Bulletin* 45, no. 8: 3–8.

Bailey, Alyssa. 2010. "Law, Mediation, and Violence." *Transdiscinplinary Journal of Conflict Management* 1: 20–31. http://www.uakron.edu/conflict/research /transdisciplinary-journal-of-conflict-management.dot.

Barabus, Jason. 2004. "How Deliberation Affects Public Opinions." *American Political Science Review* 98, no. 4: 687–701.

Barker, Vanessa. 2006. "The Politics of Punishing: How Institutionalized Power, Activist Governance and Citizen Participation Matters to the Rise and Fall of Incarceration." *Punishment & Society* 8, no. 1: 5–32.

Behrens, Angela, Christopher Uggen, and Jeff Manza. 2003. "Ballot Manipulation and the 'Menace of Negro Domination': Racial Threat and Felon Disenfranchisement in the United States, 1850–2002." *American Journal of Sociology* 109, no. 3: 559–606.

Berrett, Dan. 2014. "Thorny Exchanges on Campus Can Hold Educational Value." *The Chronicle of Higher Education* (January 20): 1–11.

Braithwaite, John. 1989. *Crime, Shame and Reintegration.* New York: Cambridge University Press.

Brunson, Rod, and Jody Miller. 2006. "Gender, Race, and Urban Policing: The Experience of African American Youths." Book review in *Gender and Society* 20, no. 4: 531–52.

Chiricos, Ted, and Kelly Welch. 2004. "Racial Typification of Crime and Support for Punitive Measures." *Criminology* 42, no. 2: 359–90.

Clear, Todd, Dina Rose, Elin Waring, and Kristen Scully. 2003. "Coercive Mobility and Crime: A Preliminary Examination of Concentrated Incarceration and Social Disorganization." *Justice Quarterly* 20, no. 1: 33–64.

Coleman, James. 1988. "Social Capital in the Creation of Human Capital." *American Journal of Sociology* 94: S95–S120.

Cross, Patricia, and Mimi Steadman. 1996. *Classroom Research: Implementing the Scholarship of Teaching.* San Francisco: Jossey-Bass.

Drew, Julie, William Lyons, and Lance Svehla. 2010. *Sound-Bite Saboteurs: Public Discourse, Education, and the State of Democratic Deliberation.* New York: SUNY Press.

Dyson, Michael Eric. 2001. *Holler If You Hear Me: In Search of Tupac Shakur.* New York: Basic.

Fisher, Roger, William Ury, and Bruce Patton. 1991. *Getting to Yes: Negotiating Without Giving In.* New York: Penguin.

Fluery-Steiner, Benjamin. 2002. "Narratives of the Death Sentence: Toward a Theory of Legal Narrativity." *Law & Society Review* 36, no. 3: 549–76.

Frankfurt, Harry. 2005. *On Bullshit.* Princeton: Princeton University Press.

Gray, Douglas. 2010. "A Black Perspective on Racial Conflict in Akron." *Transdiscinplinary Journal of Conflict Management* 1: 39–67. http://www.uakron.edu /conflict/research/transdisciplinary-journal-of-conflict-management.dot.

Hacker, Andrew. 2003. *Two Nations: Black and White, Separate, Hostile, Unequal.* New York: Scribner Press.

Harris-Lacewell, Melissa 2003. "The Heart of the Politics of Race: Centering Black People in the Study of White Racial Attitudes." *Journal of Black Studies* 34, no. 2: 222–49.

Huchings, Pat, ed. 2000. *Opening Lines: Approaches to the Scholarship of Teaching and Learning*, Menlo Park: The Carnegie Foundation for the Advancement of Teaching.

Juergensmeyer, Mark. 2005. *Gandhi's Way: A Handbook of Conflict Resolution.* Oakland: University of California Press.

King, Martin Luther. 1977. *Strength to Love.* Minneapolis: Fortress Press.

———. 2010. *Where Do We Go From Here: Chaos or Community?* Boston: Beacon Press.

Kuh, George D., Jillian Kinzie, John H. Schuh, Elizabeth J. Whitt and Associates. 2005. *Student Success in College: Creating Conditions that Matter.* San Francisco: Jossey-Bass.

Light, Richard. 2001. *Making the Most of College: Students Speak Their Minds.* Cambridge: Harvard University Press.

Lyons, William, and Julie Drew. 2006. *Punishing Schools: Fear and Citizenship in American Public Education.* Ann Arbor: University of Michigan Press.

Lyons, William, and Lisa Miller. 2012. *Putting Politics in Its Place: Reflections on Political Criminology, Immigration, and Crime. Studies in Law, Politics and Society. Special Issue: The Legacy of Stuart Scheingold,* edited by Austin Sarat, vol. 59. Bingley, United Kingdom: Emerald Publishing.

Manning, Kathleen, Jillian Kinzie, and John Schuh. 2006. *One Size Does Not Fit All: Traditional and Innovative Models of Student Affairs Practice.* New York: Routledge.

Meehan, Albert, and Michael Ponder. 2002. "Race and Place: The Ecology of Racial Profiling African American Motorists." *Justice Quarterly* 19, no. 3: 399–430.

Mendelberg, Tali. 1997. "Executing Hortons: Racial Crime in the 1988 Presidential Campaign." *Public Opinion Quarterly* 61: 134–57.

Mill, John Stuart. 1975. "On Liberty." in *Three Essays: On Liberty, Representative Government, and the Subjection of Women.* Oxford: Oxford University Press.

Novkov, Julie. 2008. "Rethinking Race in American Politics." *Political Research Quarterly* 61, no. 4: 649–59.

Olson, Joel. 2008. "Whiteness and the Polarization of American Politics." *Political Research Quarterly* 61, no. 4: 704–18.

Pager, Devah. 2003. "The Mark of a Criminal Record." *American Journal of Sociology* 108, no. 5 : 937–76.

Payne, Allison, Denise Gottfredson, and Gary Gottfredson. 2003. "Schools as Communities: The Relationships Among Communal School Organization, Student Bonding, and School Disorder." *Criminology* 41, no. 3: 749–78.

Patterson, Kelly, Joseph Grenny, Ron McMillan, and Al Switzler. 2011. *Crucial Conversations: Tools for Talking When Stakes are High.* New York: McGraw-Hill.

Piper, Adrian. 2000. "Art in Review." *New York Times,* November 17. http://www.nytimes.com/2000/11/17/arts/art-in-review-adrian-piper.html.

Ryan, Gery W., and H. Russell Bernard. 2003. "Techniques to Identify Themes." *Field Methods* 15, no. 1: 85–109.

Sampson, Robert, and Dawn Bartusch. 1998. "Legal Cynicism and (Subcultural?) Tolerance of Deviance: The Neighborhood Context of Racial Differences." *Law & Society Review* 32, no. 4: 777–804.

Schattschneider, Elmer E. 1975. *The Semisovereign People: A Realist's View of Democracy in America.* New York: Holt, Rinehart, and Winston.

———. 1969. *Two Hundred Million Americans in Search of a Government.* New York: Holt, Rinehart, and Winston.

Shakur, Tupac. 1992. "Changes." *YouTube.* http://www.youtube.com/watch?v=vL5sdu3pNrU.

Sunshine, Jason, and Tom Tyler. 2003. "The Role of Procedural Justice and Legitimacy in Shaping Public Support for Policing." *Law & Society Review* 37, no. 3: 513–47.

Tinto, Vincent. 1993. *Leaving College: Rethinking the Causes and Cures of Student Attrition,* Chicago: University of Chicago Press.

Tonry, Michael. 1999. "Why Are Incarceration Rates So High?" *Crime & Delinquency,* 45, no. 4: 419–37.

Valentino, Nicholas, and David Sears. 2005. "Old Time There Are Not Forgotten: Race and Partisan Realignment in the Contemporary South." *American Journal of Political Science* 49, no. 3: 672–88.

Wacquant, Loïc. 2001. "Deadly Symbiosis: When Ghetto and Prison Meet and Mesh." *Punishment & Society* 3, no. 1: 95–134.

Wallace, David Foster. 2006. *Consider the Lobster And Other Essays.* Boston: Back Bay Books.

Walsh, Katherine Cramer. 2007. *Talking About Race: Community Dialogues and the Politics of Difference,* Chicago: University of Chicago Press.

Warren, Lee. 2000. "Managing Hot Moments in the Classroom," *Derek Bok Center for Teaching and Learning.* Last modified March 17, 2016. http://isites.harvard.edu/fs/html/icb.topic58474/hotmoments.html.

West, Cornel. 1993. *Race Matters.* Boston: Beacon Press.

Western, Bruce. 2002. "The Impact of Incarceration on Wage Mobility and Inequality." *American Sociological Review* 67: 526–46.

Yngvesson, Barbara. 1993. *Virtuous Citizens, Disruptive Subjects: Order and Complaint in a New England Court.* New York: Routledge.

Yuen, Cheryl, with John O'Neal and Theresa Holden. n.d. "Animating Democracy: Junebug Productions Color Line Project." 1–16. http://animatingdemocracy.org/sites/default/files/documents/labs/color_line_project_case_study.pdf.

Let My Story Speak for Me

Story Circles as a Critical Pedagogical Tool

Patricia S. Hill

"To hear each other (the sound of different voices), to listen to one another, is an exercise in recognition."
—bell hooks, "Transformative Pedagogy and Multiculturalism"

I. INTRODUCTION

This passage by cultural critic bell hooks reminds us that as the world becomes smaller through changing demographics, technological imperatives, and a globally interconnected economy, it is vital that students develop both a sense of global citizenship and a critical comprehension of complex issues that challenge the human race. This chapter draws on the tenets of critical pedagogy and standpoint scholarship to identify and discuss both the value and application of that literature to the utilization of story circles as a trans-formative learning technique in my Intercultural Communication class.⁺

⁺**Donna:** I have never heard of standpoint theory. I see now that the stories we collected from the community are a wonderful tool for challenging the status quo.

In this course, students start with simple acts—listening, seeing, recognizing—•structured in and through stories that lead us all into engaged conversations about the world we share. Unfortunately, as black feminist researcher Patricia Hill Collins (1998) suggests, in the face of tremendous change, injustice still contextualizes our contemporary society. As such, she maintains that teaching should equip our students so that they might learn to "talk back" to the world (71). Our university-level curriculum and instruction should help our students pose critical questions about social justice as well as examine popular culture, social structures, and government actions. However, most classrooms in the United States operate with teaching practices that "stifles dialogue and interactions between pupils and their ideas" (Lyle 2008, 225). In such an environment, students are disconnected from the opportunity for "fruitful conversations that support the ability to conceive of themselves in many different ways" (Dillion 2011, 217). Our pedagogy must pave the way for students to achieve a transformed view of our world where we all work collectively to achieve a goal of justice and harmony.

•**Jim:** This sounds exactly like what my colleague Jairo Cuesta and I do in our performance ecology research and workshops. Performance ecology is an attempt to rediscover the urge to act. Through a series of structured physical and vocal exercises, songs, and dances, both inside and outside, we work on the simple actions: to see, to listen, and to meet. The work usually culminates in what we call a rendering—a structured, harmonic improvisation that works on the participant's perception, precision, and ability to adapt.

"Pedagogy is the craft of teaching—the use of various approaches and strategies to stimulate learning" (Schniedewind 1987, 30). Critical theorists define education as a way to empower and transform students in an effort to bring about social justice (McLaren 2003, Wink 1997). In line with critical educators (e.g. Apple 1998, Ellsworth 1993, Giroux 1988 and 1990, Giroux and McLaren 1996, Giroux and Simon 1988, Gore 1993, Lather 1991, Solórzano and Yosso, 2002), critical pedagogies explore the "influences of educational knowledge... that perpetuate or legitimate an unjust status quo" and are concerned with "social injustice and how to transform inequitable, undemocratic, or oppressive institutions and social relations" (Burbules and Berk 1999, 46–47). bell hooks (1994) argues that students today want a meaningful education, one in which their professors will not offer them information without addressing the connection between what they are learning and their overall life experiences.✦ hooks calls for pedagogy that encourages students to value their own and each other's voices, including working toward a "shared and a common good that binds us" (1994, 40).✦ Moreover, she questions the rationalistic foundations of traditional pedagogical perspectives by offering examples of the ways she has constructed her own critical pedagogical stance (hooks 1981, 1984, 1994). Informed by the works of Brazilian educator Paulo Freire (1970) and theoretical standpoints of other African American women scholars, hooks (1994) advances assumptions of critical pedagogy as a "practice of freedom" and a way to enhance learning.•

> •**Bill:** Really like what you are doing here. Richard Light similarly documents this student thirst for meaningful educational experiences. Dyson in *Holler If You Hear Me* provides evidence that Tupac also observed and articulated this desire. This is one of the inherent values of story circles for me. It makes it nearly impossible to avoid seriously and thoughtfully engaging with all the "so what?" questions surrounding the scholarly material we ask our students to engage with every semester.

> ✦**Bill:** In our conclusion, we see that political scientist Katherine Cramer Walsh's analysis of public dialogues (very much like story circles) finds that "Storytelling is important here as it served to expose people to the possibility that people of different racial backgrounds could have very different experiences in everyday life—from shopping to interactions with the police—in the very same geographic community. And it was also important for its ability to alert people to the reasons that people of different racial backgrounds might have different perspectives" (236). Walsh concludes that this storytelling is two-way communication through which we expand our spectrum of legitimate perspectives, rejecting *either/or* framings in favor of *both/and* listening and scrutinizing, balancing civility and contestation, dialogue and debate, building social capital, and demonstrating in practice that attention to difference is necessary if we want to achieve agreements, find unity, and build communities.

> •**Bill:** I like this framing as a *Way*, a practice, an approach to life, a path. This frame guides us to think about ideas as actions (like Merton's contemplative prayer), and about interactions that are ongoing marking out a life's journey. "A path," as Cardinal Zen put it, "will appear when enough people walk on it." See also *Gandhi's Way*, and Gandhi pointing out that we all need to "be the change we want to see in the world." Wittgenstein as well, who said: "live in a way that makes what is problematic disappear." And, of course, early Christianity was called the *Way* and Buddhism refers to the *Twelvefold Path* and the *Middle Way*. Story circles bring classroom conversations down to the road level, where we can feel the gravel beneath our feet and appreciate the long and winding nature of the road itself.
>
> **Carolyn:** I also paused at the word *way* here and find your discussion of it, Bill, very enlightening. For me, at first the word called up thoughts of how each class (the thing we as teachers set up) and each storytelling (the thing each story-teller in the circle chooses to share) is a small journey that we embark on consciously. There is a lot of freedom in the process, but it also a *compelled* process, especially when we do it in our classes. A little free association here: that image of small journeys and the notion of choices we make

in what we choose to tell reminded me of a story told to me by a mentor in graduate school. He told of a young man in India who had been raised in a loving family and strong community in a mountain village, but the young man dreamed of an education in the city. His family assisted him in making arrangements but could not really imagine, as indeed he could not, what the path ahead would bring. The day arrived when the young man was to depart and his father took him to the train station. As they passed below a lintel onto the platform, the young man noticed an inscription scratched onto the lintel that was weathered with time. It was faded so he asked his father what it said. It is advice to any traveler, the father informed him. It says: "Must this journey be taken?" This admonition to stop and reflect before acting is not intended to prevent the journey, but suggests that we each pause to consider what will change in the relationships around us depending on when, how, and where we choose to go. I am not saying all this to suggest that we discourage storytellers from sharing experiences that are close to the heart, but I am suggesting that the process is an invitation to be vulnerable and that that is a different kind of risk for each depending on their standpoint.

Jim: A "way" is a process, not a product or a pre-determined result. This is a constant battle for those of us in education and especially in the arts: to keep our attention on the "way." Even when everything around us is pushing us to come up with results. In theatre, we are faced with the question of reflecting life as it is or as it could be. How do we get beyond the repetition of the same stories of injustice and ignorance and begin to reflect the stories of freedom and hope? Why is change so slow? Carolyn's story reminds me of a story from Stephen Nachmanovitch's *Free Play: Improvisation in Life and Art*. He begins the book with this story from Japanese folklore: A new flute was invented in China. A Japanese master musician discovered the subtle beauties of its tone and brought it back home, where he gave concerts all around the country. One evening, he played with a community of musicians and music lovers who lived in a certain town. At the end of the concert, his name was called. He took out the new flute and played one piece. When he was finished, there was silence in the room for a long moment. Then the voice of the oldest man was heard from the back of the room: "Like a god!"

The next day, as this master was packing to leave, the musicians approached him and asked how long it would take a skilled player to learn the new flute. "Years," he said. They asked if he would take a pupil, and he agreed. After he left, they decided among themselves to send a young man, a brilliantly talented flautist, sensitive to beauty, diligent, and trustworthy. They gave him money for his living expenses and for the master's tuition, and they sent him on his way to the capital, where the master lived.

The student arrived and was accepted by his teacher, who assigned him a single, simple tune. At first he received systematic instruction, but he easily mastered all the technical problems. Now he arrived for his daily lesson, sat down, and played his tune—and all the master could say was, "Something lacking." The student exerted himself in every possible way; he practiced for endless hours; yet day after day, week after week, all the master said was, "Something lacking." He begged the master to change the tune, but the master said no. The daily playing, the daily "something lacking" continued for months on end. The student's hope of success and fear of failure became ever magnified, and he swung from agitation to despondency.

> Finally the frustration became too much for him. One night he packed his bag and slinked out. He continued to live in the capital city for some time longer, until his money ran dry. He began drinking. Finally, impoverished, he drifted back to his own part of the country. Ashamed to show his face to former colleagues, he found a hut far out in the countryside. He still possessed his flutes, still played but found no new inspiration in music. Passing farmers heard him play and sent their children to him for beginner's lessons. He lived this way for years.
>
> One morning there was a knock at his door. It was the oldest past-master from his town, along with the youngest student. They told him that tonight they were going to have a concert, and they had all decided it would not take place without him. With some effort, they overcame his feelings of fear and shame, and almost in a trance he picked up a flute and went with them. The concert began. As he waited behind the stage, no one intruded on his inner silence. Finally, at the end of the concert, his name was called. He stepped out onto the stage in his rags. He looked down at his hands, and he realized that he had chosen the new flute.
>
> Now he realized that he had nothing to gain and nothing to lose. He sat down and played the same tune he had played so many times for his teacher in the past. When he finished, there was silence for a long moment. Then the voice of the oldest man was heard, speaking softly from the back of the room: "Like a god!"

This pedagogical approach reflects certain beliefs about the teaching/learning process that guides selection of educational strategies and techniques. These assumptions are in line with Freire's (1970) notion of "conscientization," in which students are liberated from domination by their own critical awareness. Educator Joan Wink (1997) has built her teaching practices around critical pedagogy and contends that

> Most of us went into education "to make a difference." For many, this phrase soon became just another reason to be cynical. Critical pedagogy has not only taken this cynicism away from me, it has given me hope. It has led me to believe that I really can make a difference. Conscientization, self and social transformation, empowerment, problem posing, praxis, action. They are no longer words to learn, they are no longer things I do now, they are ideas I strive to live everyday (153).◆

◆**Pat:** Participating in story circles and the sharing of experiences has also given me hope.
Carolyn: This is very important. We all are participating in the educational process because we recognize that when classes work it is because we achieve a level of engagement in which the participants feed each other. We feed our curiosities, our intellects, and our need for human exchange of ideas that bring us understanding and a sense of genuine meaning. I think there are many paths to successful educational exchange but this combination of critical perspective and hooks' humanism that you highlight here, Pat, seems foundational in our time.

A guiding principle of this pedagogical stance is to view the classroom as an environment in which all participants are actively engaged with the material being studied, with self, other, and with the external world in ways that facilitate mutual growth and construction of knowledge.✦ Emphasis is placed on empowering the student, allowing them to find their voices and connect their lived experiences to knowledge acquisition.

> ✦Bill: Yes. Very Important. Story circles help us help our students engage with texts, with each other, and with our larger communities. The ideas noted above from Wittgenstein and Gandhi and Cardinal Zen remind us of the importance of *engaging* with texts and peers and mentors and communities as an approach to living and this approach is highlighted (in contrast to the often disengaged ways we too often go through the day) when we tell and hear each other's stories, when we blend words and things we do and aspirations we strive to become each day. David Foster Wallace's Kenyon commencement address comes to mind here as well.
> Jim: Yes. Knowledge is doing and must be embodied. But how do we do this in an "information" culture as opposed to a "knowledge" culture?

Much like critical pedagogy, standpoint theory gives educators a framework to understand how to motivate students and strive to cultivate a classroom environment that respects and promotes the centrality of everyday experiences in the construction of knowledge.● Standpoint theory implies that we perceive and construct the world differently depending on the societal positions we occupy as members of social and cultural groups (Collins 1990, Harding 1986, Hartsock 1983, Wood 1992). Everyday experiences include constructions of previous education in school or at home and self identification with an ethnic group, gender group, age group, socioeconomic class, ability, sexual preference, etc.✦ Collins (1986) maintains that a teaching approach informed by standpoint theory emphasizes experiential learning strategies, which link theory more meaningfully to direct experiences and empower students to think critically. Further, students are encouraged to openly draw on their own experiences (and be open to the experiences of others) to interrogate how "what they know" reveals something about their social location. This allows students to be empowered through the recognition and validation of their own everyday experiences, encouraging them to both draw on and share these experiences while engaging course material. Thus, informed by these frameworks, teaching practices would guide students to:

- examine their experiences to position themselves relative to each other and to institutions, and
- dig for and narrate occasions when they have found themselves in tension with social and cultural norms.

Amy: I have so many nontraditional students who enter my classes with tremendous real-world experience but feel very intimidated about the academic world. This perspective would be so empowering for them!

Carolyn: It seems to me that this is a practical level of awareness that, as teachers, we have to re-awaken to regularly. I have a colleague with a physical disability who was stunned and saddened when he was confronted by a student who spoke up about her sense of exclusion when an assignment was predicated on what the professor thought would be a shared childhood experience for the class but which is something extremely low-income families like hers could not offer their children. He reported that at first he denied to himself that this was a problem, but then on reflection felt he should have been especially sensitive to difference. I think it is the exceptional person who can remain sensitive to all standpoints at all times, but what Pat is saying here is that we can weave "awakening practices" or "recognition activities" (just making terms up here!) into the fabric of our courses that keep us alert as teachers and enrich the classroom experience for all. Story circles offer a method for doing this.

Jim: I like your invented terms, Carolyn, and I am totally in agreement about weaving these kind of practices into our teaching. It's essential.

In addition, using these frameworks, the educator would have tools to expose students to counternarratives and encourage them to cultivate their own sense of group identity relative to their history and political-economic hierarchies. These tools allow a teacher to be taught as well as teach and to apply their knowledge to real world issues of social justice.

I follow hooks and other critical/standpoint theorists to inform the pedagogical practices designed to promote deep learning in my classes. I believe that we have an obligation to embrace pedagogical practices that assist our students in breaking down provincial ways of looking at the rest of the world and questioning our own assumptions. Our curriculum and instruction should move outside the classroom to connect with real-world problems. As such, our aim must be to facilitate students' questioning of their own assumptions and to engage them in issues that many would rather avoid.* Similarly, Bill Lyons has observed that educators should "move beyond the now commonplace focus on 'respecting others,' to re-imaging the community we share with each other" (personal communication).

> **⁺Bill:** This is what I love about Rethinking Race, and why Rethinking Race is such a salient theme in my classroom, use of story circles as a part of integrating this larger cocurricular series of events into course assignments designed to bring scholarly insights and real world problem solving into the same room.
>
> **Jim:** Sometimes this is very difficult. The pull backwards is very strong. I am always astonished how students can have "life-changing" experiences during a theatre production process or study abroad program or even in a particular class and then resort to habitual behaviors and perceptions almost immediately. The "stick-time" seems to get shorter and shorter. The real work is how to increase this "stick-time," how to integrate it into their lives so that the change in behaviors and perceptions "sticks" with them longer.
>
> **Carolyn:** Jim, I agree that this is a key part of the challenge and one I would like to continue to explore. Take a look at Tadmor et al.'s work on implicit bias and "epistemic unfreezing." They find significant short-term value in multicultural experiences and open the door for examining how and how long people "unfreeze" from implicit bias. Maybe we can explore creative ways to apply this knowledge.

This chapter addresses these queries and draws on the tenets of critical pedagogy and standpoint scholarship to identify and discuss the application of that literature to the utilization of story circles as an experiential learning technique in the classroom. For purposes of clarity, I first provide the background and development of my particular use of story circles in the classroom. Second, I discuss story circles as a critical instructional strategy to help students learn to value subjective knowledge as legitimate, and to risk expressing their intuitive understandings in in-depth ways most have not done before in a classroom setting. Next, I offer a practical application of story circle pedagogy from my own teaching practices to reveal the powerful ways the story circle strategy can facilitate students' consideration of theirs and others' concrete experiences. I conclude with a discussion of how educators might embrace pedagogical stances that embody teaching with a "vision of a better life" (Giroux and McLaren 1989, xii), where the accepted canons of knowledge can be challenged and attention can be given to creating classroom space that best fulfills all student needs.

A. My Introduction to Story Circles

In February 2009, I participated in a Rethinking Race: Black, White and Beyond event at The University of Akron. Amy Dreussi's chapter in this volume provides an extended background of the Rethinking Race series of events, but to help contextualize the value of the series to my Intercultural Communication class, I will reiterate some history of Rethinking Race Black, White and Beyond. The celebration first began as an annual campus-wide series of cocurricular activities in February 2008. Commemorating President Clinton's choice of The University of Akron as the location for his first Town Hall Meeting focused on race issues in America, the events were dedicated to engendering greater understanding of racial and ethnic relations, power, privilege, and the prejudicial "-isms" that punctuate everyday experiences. Through dynamic speakers, creative and theatrical productions, story circles, films, a unity celebration, and thought-provoking "Face-2Face" conversations, Rethinking Race created a safe space for faculty of all disciplines, staff, students, and community members to critically reflect on and dialogue about race, ethnicity, and beyond. The vast array of these events presented multiple opportunities for participants' critical self-reflection and dialogue on diverse perspectives. The events of Rethinking Race also allowed participants to explore their views and biases, openly and honestly. Over the past several years, the Rethinking Race events have facilitated and inspired instructors in various disciplines to accomplish a number of pedagogical goals and enhance the classroom learning experience. Instructors incorporated students' attendance at events into classroom assignments ranging from reaction papers to making connections with theoretical concepts. Moreover, the events have provided a shared experience for what bell hooks (1986) calls a "common starting point" from which diverse audiences could dialogue about important issues.● This is increasingly important on college campuses because in today's world there are fewer opportunities for public engagement to take place.◆

●**Amy:** I recall a comment made by a student after a story circle about how nervous she was initially because race is such a sensitive topic and because she was not accustomed to speaking in front of others. She was grateful for the opportunity to get beyond those concerns and have a meaningful dialogue with persons who, minutes before, had been total strangers.

◆**Carolyn:** Especially on campuses like ours with our significant numbers of working and commuting students.
Jim: The theatre, of course, is the ideal forum for such public engagement.

Bill: Events—from theatrical performance to classroom story circles and more—providing public spaces for diverse audiences to dialogue about important issues; as Amy points out, this is often scary for a young student unaccustomed to engaging with those who see and experience the world differently. Thinking about these as Pat does here, as intentional efforts to create or catalyze "common starting points" is another way to see how these events contribute to building community and making democracy both more possible and more desirable.

One of the first events I participated in during Rethinking Race was called story circles. This particular event was a training opportunity for the story circle method facilitated by John O'Neal and Theresa Holden from the New Orleans community-based Junebug Productions' Color Line Project. It was at this event that I became aware of other like-minded social justice educators from various disciplines seeking enlightenment. Story circles are exactly that—a gathering of individuals together in a circle with the objective of sharing their own real life experiences—listening to and learning from the experiences of others. As you learned in the introduction to this volume, each story circle is made up of a small group of participants from a larger group with varied characteristics. The conversation begins with a prompt—in our case, the prompt dealt with the telling of a story about an aspect of one's racial experiences. After everyone has had an opportunity to tell their story, common elements/themes of the stories are identified. These were then reported back to a larger collective in various forms, including dance and/or acting performance, song, poems, as well as the creation of artifacts. Uniquely, the story circle process leads participants to share in-depth and typically emotionally laden truths. According to Donna Webb, storytelling done in story circles allows the tellers to "highlight their creative abilities both as storytellers and as those who make creative decision in difficult situations" (personal communication).

The story circle training enabled us all to share ideas and experiences through what Lindlof and Taylor (2002) describe as a "chaining" or "cascading" effect (182). Talk links to, or tumbles out of, the topics and expressions preceding it. As we progressed in the training, we quickly experienced a profound depth of one another's everyday experiences. Carolyn Behrman's chapter in this volume discusses a number of ways that story circles can be a powerful tool for "group bonding" (77).

II. STORY CIRCLES AS A CRITICAL INSTRUCTIONAL STRATEGY

Story circles are understood as a tool of instruction because they make use of the act of telling a story to facilitate a greater understanding of both self and other. Story circles are in line with critical pedagogy in that they are a way to promote talk in a classroom that "create space for multiple voices and discourses" (Lyle 2008, 225). Moreover, story circles not only facilitate the sharing and building of meaning collaboratively; they also encourage "communication through authentic exchanges" (Lyle 2008, 225). Bochner (2007) writes that in the telling of stories, we are gathering "knowledge *from* the past and not necessarily knowledge *about* the past" (203; Bochner's italics). Each of us has only to remember stories we have told about our lives—and how the recounting of experience differs in relation to the person(s) to whom we are talking. Personal narratives develop as lives do, and personal accounts of experience differ from telling to telling.✦ Thus, personal accounts are never only personal and individual. The telling of experience is constructed in relation to how we have come to understand the world. This follows Wallace's (2002) claim that the process of structuring experiences into stories is rooted in oral traditions and provide a means of establishing a common experience between the teller and listener, of "creating a connection between them" (411).● Gates (1989) maintains that storytelling in the oral tradition is first and foremost about healing and nurturing through communion with one another.

✦**Donna:** When I asked three storytellers from a story circle to retell their stories first to children and later to an adult audience, I heard the stories develop from three-minute "gems" packed with meaning in a small package to longer, more introspective stories with new details and insights.

Jim: This also speaks to my thoughts on the effect that embodying someone else's story has on the storyteller. When one enters whole-bodily into the experience of another, something in the storyteller, the doer, changes and does not change back. We tell stories to understand—to stand under—the experience.

Bill: Great point Pat, Donna, and Jim. As contexts change, as time passes by, between tellings…there is a lot more going on than I ever saw before we starting working with stories.

●**Donna:** Three storytellers from Cascade Village presented their work at the Akron Art Museum in a SlideJam. All of the other presenters, including me, relied heavily on notes to speak. Val, Val, and Eddie told their stories extemporaneously and in that way distinguished themselves from the other speakers. The audience could be heard responding to their stories.

There is renewed attention across disciplines to the human impulse to narrate. This interest arises from foundational work in psychology by Bruner (1990), who refers to the study of stories as the "biology of meaning" and points to the fact that people naturally organize experience in narrative form. Labov (1972) in linguistics advances storytelling as a method of "recapitulating" past experience because "stories have a specific past event and an evaluative function in that they reflect the point of view of the narrator" (359–60). In the field of communication, Fisher (1987) argues that people are essentially storytellers, and that the study of narrative brings us closer to understanding human communication and action because it allows us to understand the reasons humans use for selecting certain narratives over others in explaining their world. This body of research teaches us that through stories, we come to define and sometimes redefine our experiences to know the salient and distinctive experiences in a person's life.◆

> ◆**Carolyn:** This is wonderful material. It speaks to the part of my chapter where I talk about how students read the circle and their peers and allow/choose a story. I see this as another valuable aspect of the story circle process—opportunity for students' socio-emotional development.
> **Pat:** They lead to the possibility of finding something new, remembering something forgotten.
> **Donna:** I have been struggling to find a way to suggest the role of art and art making into our discussion and this material makes that possible. Poetry, art, music, etc., lead to the possibility of "finding something new, remembering something forgotten." Stories create a portal between life and art. When we say stories are an expression of lived experiences, we might say as well that stories make us aware of lived experiences and highlight their importance.
> **Bill:** Stories create a portal. Awesome.
> **Jim:** I love this idea of "the biology of meaning." It makes me imagine that each story becomes imprinted on us genetically—or that all the stories are already in each of us in some kind of state of potentiality and to live is to bring those stories to life.

Echoing assumptions of standpoint theorists, stories also can be viewed as a vehicle for people to access their everyday experiences, since they have features such as places, time, problems, solutions, and other connectives that locate individuals within a particular frame of reference. Story circles not only facilitate the telling of stories of both self and other, but they also have the potential to "rework classroom space" (Collins 1998, xi) and encourage a student's critical thinking. This is particularly useful in situating students within a historical context and applying their knowledge to real-world problems. Further, this pedagogical stance is of particular value in teaching for social justice because it seeks to broaden the classroom content to more adequately represent diverse traditions. These guiding principles allow students to be empowered through the recognition and validation of their own personal experiences, encouraging them to draw on their personal experiences while engaging theory.*

*Bill: This is an important value added from using story circles, and it is infused into the class organically.

Pat: The sharing of stories enables students to see conjunctions and disjunctions among their lived experiences and explore connections with larger social and cultural constructs.

Donna: When viewing or otherwise experiencing art we often find that artists who use the most personal material in their art making find the largest and most universal audience. In other words, personal experience *is* universal. This is one of the reasons that stories are so powerful.

B. *Let My Story Speak for Me: A Practical Application for Transforming Our Classrooms*

I teach a course entitled Intercultural Communication. As a class that fulfills a general education "diversity requirement," it is typically well populated. The stated goals of the course are:

1. To introduce background, principles, and theoretical frameworks of intercultural communication and their significance in contemporary American society;

2. To foster a safe place in the classroom for open and honest discussion about the relationship between culture and communication; and

3. To facilitate a process whereby students can develop knowledge, critical thinking, and communicative skills that they can apply to their everyday life experiences.

I. BACKGROUND

One of the challenges that I encounter in this Intercultural Communication course is creating a space to allow dialogue to happen on topics that are considered "difficult" and/or "sensitive" by many students. Discussion of topics such as culture can be affectively loaded for both educators and students because they are linked to strongly held beliefs, values, and feelings. These diverse feelings can present an even greater challenge. In teaching this course, I have become aware that many students may find it especially difficult to rethink socially endorsed beliefs and stereotypes on complex issues of oppression, racism, sexism, homophobia, etc. Also, many may fear, when the end point is unclear, that the intellectual and emotional journey will be fraught with uncertainty.● Strewsbury (1993) argues that pedagogy should provide students with opportunities to develop their intellectual independence and interdependence. She maintains that students should collaborate with each other on assignments and in discussions, and in applying their knowledge to real world problems. I have noted from course evaluations that students often report on the value of participating in a *personalized, non-judgmental environment* where they feel free to ask "taboo" questions, make mistakes, share experiences, feelings and opinions, and expose their limited understanding of a particular issue.◆ Students also relate how they value the opportunity to verbalize disagreements, name conflicts, and ask difficult questions.

●**Bill:** Learning to engage productively in what we call (elsewhere in this volume) "difficult dialogues" is an essential skill for effective democratic citizenship and conflict management, in the classroom and beyond (15).

Pat: These difficult realities must be negotiated in some fashion—story circles facilitate the move from difficult dialogues to critical conversations.

Donna: I would add that story circles allow us to discover what the "story" is. That is, what is the experience, what is the language that describes that experience and why does it matter? Once all that surfaces in the story circle, difficult dialogues and critical conversations can be focused on the shared experience of the story.

Jim: I recall a graduate class in Contemporary Theatre Styles when I showed a video on the work of choreographer Bill T. Jones. His life partner, Arnie Zane, died of AIDS several years before the video and Jones spoke eloquently and sincerely of their relationship, love for each other, and life and work together. At the end of the class, a student, whose fundamentalist beliefs had been a stumbling block throughout the class, came up to me and said that he had no idea that two men could love each other so deeply. He had been moved by Jones's stories of his love and said that he saw and heard something that he didn't know existed in same-sex relationships. His views changed then and there.

◆**Amy:** This seems to be a recurring theme in Face2Face Conversations About Race as well—a sense of relief to be able to discuss these volatile issues in an open manner.

Bill: My students have expressed this relief many times after story circles, Face2Face Conversations, or other Rethinking Race events. There appears to be a hunger out there to learn to engage on controversial issues in a loving and safe and illuminating way.

2. STORY CIRCLES AS INSTRUCTIONAL STRATEGY—WHY?

Utilizing the theoretical lens of critical pedagogy and standpoint theory, I asked myself how I could best connect with these students in the discussion of topics that are deemed "sensitive." After my experiences with the story circle training, it was clear the answer existed in "story"—that my students and I could *let our stories speak for us*.* As stated earlier, story circles encourage questions and conversations. They provide a catalyst for communication by starting with what one knows best—one's own story. This honors diverse experiences by including each person's story. Because many students are starved for an opportunity to talk about issues of oppression and race in a safe environment, this experiential activity has the potential to fulfill that need for them. When students share and listen to their peers, I often see increased understanding of the complexity of our diverse experiences. Thus, a long-term reward from students' experience with the story circle process is that as students share their concerns, desires fears, accomplishments, and dreams trough their stories, they become members of what Bruner calls a "culture creating community" (1986, 34).•

*Donna: This is very important. As an art form, stories both express the viewpoint of the artist and exist separately in the world. Everyone knows for example that a painting is not the artist even though it may have been created by him or her. After the initial telling, the story can exist and function as a vehicle for change as it is passed on by others.

•Donna: Yes, this is how the stories are passed on.
Jim: Psychoanalyst Julia Kristeva calls this creating "soul space." To speak of the soul may not be academically popular, but storytelling, art, theatre creates "soul space." They are human activities that are absolutely necessary for our health and survival in a post-human world.

3. ASSIGNMENT

Experiential learning is privileged in the Intercultural Communication class through the use of story circles in conjunction with discussions of identities, stereotypes, and biases as an opportunity to identify generalizations. The story circle strategy exemplifies my belief that topics deemed "sensitive" in intercultural communication can best be addressed through the sharing of experiences—through stories. As a class, we all participate in the story circle process with a beginning prompt: "Tell a story of a time when you encountered a racialized experience." The class is then divided into small groups of no more than six for the actual story circles. I first utilized this pedagogical tool in a class discussion of how our identities are complex intersections located in shifting and structured power relations. I wanted to empower my students to become active participants in the story circle process, and so I engaged them by sharing the following experience as my story speaking for me:

> *I have known myself (in terms of my ethnic identity) as many different labels. While I now consider myself an African American, I have also over the years categorized my identity according to what I believed society considered me at the time—"Black," "Negro," and once-upon-a-time, as "Colored." I first came to know myself as Colored during the height of the civil rights movement of the 1960s. I was in elementary school and was the only little "Colored" girl in the class. I was frequently made fun of and had frequent battles with other children because I was perceived of as "inferior." But, the notion of being inferior as "Colored" really hit home when my family and I visited my Aunt, Uncle, and three cousins in Mississippi over summer break.*
>
> *I recall that the older of my cousins once told me that he hated when we visited because it caused "trouble" for them. I remember him saying that we (my siblings and I) "got to leave, but they had to stay there." I recall a trip to town with my older cousin and my siblings to pick up some items from a local store. This was my first opportunity to actually go to the store. Prior to our departure, my cousin sat my siblings and me down to "school us" on how we HAD to behave on the trip to town and especially in the store. He told us that in the town, we would walk on the road and not the sidewalk where the Whites walked. He also told us that we needed to at all times, keep our eyes focus on the ground and "NEVER," and he emphasized "NEVER" look at the Whites directly in their eyes. He said when we got to the store, we were not to speak, and he would do all of the talking to be sure that we didn't "sass" anyone.*
>
> *I recalled feeling very fearful that I might unintentionally engage in some type of behavior that might be deemed problematic by any one of the Whites we encountered. For me, the most memorable part of the trip to town was when I asked my cousin if we could stop to get something to drink before we went into the store because I was feeling uncomfortable from the anxiety I was experiencing. He pointed to a water fountain with the word "COLORED" posted above it and told me that this is where I would have to drink.*◆

♦**Carolyn:** I'd really like to hear you comment briefly here about how this story was received by the class, or how it and other stories shaped or informed the subsequent discussion of identities.

Donna: While it would be helpful to know a statistic such as, "in 1962 X number of towns in the US has separate facilities such as drinking fountains for African Americans," it is also important to know that a young Pat Hill was told that if she wanted a drink it must be taken from the "colored" drinking fountain.

Pat: Student comments to my story included words like "shock," "disbelief," "disgust," and "guilt." A comment that I found most memorable was from a student who revealed that they had "never spoken about racism" in their lifetime. In the telling of this story, there was a re-emphasis that a central principle of a free, democratic society is that all human beings should be allowed to live equally satisfying lives in their own unique and diverse ways. This, I believe, helped the students to accommodate the stories espoused by others as a way of producing and consuming some new knowledge.

Amy: I find myself alarmed at the suggestions by white students that diversity programming and coursework is aimed at making them feel guilty about the racism of the past. I quickly tell them none of them were in the state legislatures that passed Jim Crow laws, none of them beat up civil rights marchers, none of them kept black people from exercising the franchise, etc. They can't control the past and should not be made to feel guilty. However, if after learning about racism, past and present, they do nothing to rectify it moving forward—well, there's an occasion for guilt.

Jim: I think one of the most stunning aspects of The Color Line Project Performance for students watching was the nearness of the racism. When things were brought home to Akron, it really made an impression. Uncovering the racism among us, in the small ways that it rears its ugly head, makes it more real. And Amy is right, not to make anyone feel guilty, but to take action now.

Following our discussions that day, several students indicated how the story circles were enlightening, in that they facilitated access to knowledge. This was exemplified by a student who commented in the "cross talk" session that she had never been involved in a dialogue with a professor sharing personal experiences from an African American woman's perspective. Moreover, the discussion revealed that story circles provided encouragement for students to create an inclusive climate as we shared individual and cultural experiences and thus developed a more refined understanding of the connections between being in a comfortable space, where others listened to how we were experiencing the affirmation of our identities, and awareness of our situations.

When using story circles in my Intercultural Communication classes, the experiential learning continues when the students write reaction paper essays reflecting on impacts of and insights gleaned from the story circle process. These essays included students' observations as well as emergent themes that were revealed to them through the story circle process. To help contextualize the experiences, students reflected on specific questions including: (a) What was the main point of the story? (b) What were key words and/or phrases used to tell the story? (c) Did the story resonate with your own everyday experiences? Lindlof and Taylor are instructive in describing how "storytelling in groups enable people to make their experiences intelligible to each other" (2002, 180). As described below, student reaction papers explicitly revealed that story circles could be understood through two overarching themes. First, perspectives on the story circle process were discussed in terms of *positionality of reality*—meaning the stance through which the students ultimately process the activity (actively or passively). Second, the students' perspectives revealed a clear discussion of *context*—referring to the focus on personal vs. social issues in which their comments were directed. With students' permission, the following are brief exemplars of their comments.

4. POSITIONALITY OF REALITY

Many of the essays show that as the students were actively engaged, they were "stunned" and "shocked" by what they experienced. In one essay, a student commented, "not only did I find the story circle to be an uplifting experience; it was completely foreign for me." One student revealed a detached reaction regarding a discussion of whiteness that was uncovered in his story circle. He indicated,

> *I was personally unfamiliar with some of these experiences in the discussion of being white. I grew up in a neighborhood that was not very culturally diverse and am finding it hard to believe that these things happen to people on a daily basis.*✦

✦**Carolyn:** Our students come to the university from such a range of places and levels of experience. Judging from this comment, the process you lay out here gives perspective and then encourages reflection and revelation in a way that is safe.

Pat: My teaching experiences have revealed that students can sometimes be cynical about issues of racism and white privilege. My story (above) was told to draw out participants to reflect on their positions that we might better speak "with" each other about "dark" and often "hidden" sites of injustice. Patricia Hill Collins argues that African American women and other historically oppressed groups have experiences [and thus stories] that are different from those of mainstream American society (1998). As such, the sharing of these stories have the potential to generate new angles of vision on injustice.

In class discussions, I have found that some students have unconsciously coded "culture" as something unique that only "people of color" have. Such thinking speaks to the value of interrogating constructions of whiteness as a way of learning to see the world in new ways.• Recent research has acknowledged the growing importance of incorporating whiteness studies scholarship into Intercultural Communication curriculum (Martin and Davis 2001, Martin and Nakayama 1999). In fact, Martin and Davis argue that an intercultural communication classroom that does not focus on the race/ethnicity of white Americans is akin to "leaving a picture unfinished" (2001, 299).◆ Jackson and Heckman (2002) note that making important concepts such as whiteness and white privilege visible and salient to students helps foster greater intercultural understanding and awareness of oppression and privilege.

•**Carolyn:** Coming at this as an anthropologist, it seems to me that we are most ethnocentric when dealing with variation of ethnicity and experience *within* our shared wider culture.
Jim: There is something I need to say here about the theatre as a laboratory for working out some of these issues of privilege and perception and reflecting back to the culture the new possibilities. Unfortunately, the theatre often resorts to reflecting what society wants or expects to see and not a picture that tells a more inclusive story.

◆**Donna:** My colleague, Kevin Concannon and I hosted a Face2Face to talk about White Art and Black Art. There are many Afro American artists but no White Artists. If artists are to remain leaders in cultural change, this is where we should expect to see some provocation. Look at the results you get when you Google "White Art" and compare them with the results of "Black Art."

5. CONTEXT OF THE INTERACTION
Because many of the students located themselves in very personal stories of their racialized experiences, many discussed how the stories highlighted stereotypes, injustices, and misunderstandings as social problems. Murji and Solomos define racialization as "the process by which ideas about race are constructed, come to be regarded as meaningful, and are acted upon" (2005, 1). It was typical for them to say that the stories had inspired them to reflect on their own lives, as a student explained:

After the explanation of the rules, the group divided into smaller groups. I noticed that the comfort level in the group seemed to rise. My group opened up and was more receptive to the idea of applying critical thought to personal events. This experience was instrumental in understanding the reasons behind why John O'Neal and Theresa Holden are attacking the issue of race with the story circle method. By sharing, we can provide a guide for others who are dealing with the same problems.

Another student shared an understanding of racism as a larger-than-life issue:

There was a definite group effect in our circle. I felt the group become more intimate as we exchanged personal stories and accounts of our experiences with race. Most of the stories had a feeling of restlessness with our experiences in problems of race. There is a sense of shock to the huge events that had, or still are taking place.

One student indicated that she thought "racism is everywhere and there is not much that can be done about this to change people." Other contemplations revealed how the space that was created for the telling of stories enabled revelations and enlightenment to emerge, as another student shared:

My group was comprised of six members who all had a unique story to tell about race. As a group, we felt awareness was a key issue because each of us was conscious and concerned about the issues of race. I was one of the first people to tell a story, and by the end of the circle, I had other stories that I wanted to tell. This really opened my eyes.

Still another student shared that racism was something that "we" needed to work on:

I didn't know how telling stories could be so powerful or how profoundly they could affect me in so many different ways. I am still trying to make sense of this experience and be more aware of how I treat other people. We have a lot of work to do.

Put simply, these elaborations reveal the powerful ways story circle methodology can facilitate a student's greater understanding of complex issues. In line with qualitative research methods, story circles have the ability to both preserve an individual's interpretation or recollection of events and offers the benefit of showing in its full complexity, the world of another.

6. REFLECTIVE PRACTICES

Processing, debriefing, and feedback are central to teaching with an eye on social justice. Upon completion of experiential exercise, processing and feedback take place to help participants understand their impact on each other, contextualize interpersonal and intergroup communication, and bring undercurrents of conflict and criticism out to the open where they can be constructively addressed. Facilitating learning through this reflective process is essential in addressing issues and inequity and injustice. I utilize the following questions for facilitating processing of the story circle activity:

1. What happened in this exercise?
2. What feelings did you have as you completed this activity?
3. What is one thing you learned from this activity?
4. What surprised you about this activity?
5. What do you want to find out more about as a result of this activity?
6. What can you do with this information in the future?*

> *Donna: This is such an important question. Creative use of this new information is a key to real social change.

In responding to these questions, students are encouraged to say more about what they understand the issues to be, so that they are pressed to go beyond a surface analysis to think of the issues underlying their positions. It is my experience that students often base their positions on traditional societal norms and beliefs, which they take for granted without deeper reflection. Feeling comfortable with these challenges to "common sense" understanding of issues of power, privilege, and social inequality is frequently difficult for students who have never considered these issues before. In this process, students from the dominant social group often struggle with the idea that their social group membership grants unearned privileges not available to members of subordinated social groups.• On the other hand, although students from subordinate groups are generally more aware of the impact of social group membership on their identities and status in society, they become more aware of the complexities of social identity and group relationships as they engage in dialogue with peers similar to and different from themselves.

> •Amy: Students can readily grasp the racism side of the equation but I find that they really struggle with the notion of the privileges of being in the dominant group. Story circles are really useful to facilitate this understanding.
> Bill: I find this in my classes too, and this resistance has almost always turned out to become an entrance into one of our most powerful discussions of the term.

III. CONCLUDING REFLECTIONS

Informed by the tenets of critical pedagogy and standpoint scholarship as a teaching practice, this chapter has elaborated on the value and utility of story circles as a transformative learning technique in the classroom. I believe the constitutive nature of stories makes them not simply a critical pedagogical tool; they also create a critical space for engagement, learning, reflection, and transformation of thinking on "sensitive" issues (Giroux 2002).

In sum, the essence of student reactions revealed that story circles enabled a beginning point for the articulation of everyday experiences from diverse standpoints. This is in line with standpoint theorists' claims that our knowledge is emergent from our context and our situated experiences (Collins 1990, Harding 1986). By listening to others tell their stories, we not only gain insight and understanding of the human experience; we also gain a recognition of diverse everyday experiences. On a micro level, these student reflections revealed the compelling ways that story circles were acknowledged as rare and valuable opportunities for the students' own critical self-reflection and greater comprehension of issues of race and social justice. On a macro level, these reflections speak to the complexity and continued significance of race, racialized experiences, and oppression in our contemporary society.

These reasons speak to the value of creating an inviting space in our classrooms for the telling of everyday experiences through stories. But the stories do not stand on their own. We must acknowledge that teaching is a process whereby educators are constantly making meaning from texts and providing students with opportunities and assistance for examining their social realities critically. My hope is that my teaching philosophy, goals, and practices keep pace with the realities of the world as it shifts technologically, demographically, and economically. As a nexus for greater comprehension, story circles are embraced in my classes as fundamental for engagement of questions about life and living in speculative and dramatic ways of students who will be called upon to work with and for others from varying backgrounds. By creating a positive and engaging learning environment and employing alternative modes for dialogue across diverse communities, educators can play a crucial role in the conversations of the future.♦

♦**Donna:** This chapter is very stimulating to me. It seems that Intercultural Communication is by definition a creative act since you are bringing things together that have not been together before.

REFERENCES

Apple, Michael W. 1996. *Cultural Politics and Education*. New York: Teachers College Press.

Bochner, Arthur P. 2007. "Notes Toward an Ethics of Memory in Autoethnographic Inquiry." In *Ethical Futures in Qualitative Research*, edited by Norman K. Denzin and Michael D. Giardina. Walnut Creek, CA: Left Coast Press, 197–208.

Bruner, Jerome. 1990. *Acts of Meaning*. Cambridge, MA: Harvard University Press.

———. 1986. *Actual Minds, Possible Worlds*. Cambridge, MA: Harvard University Press.

Burbules, Nicolas, and Rupert Berk. 1999. "Critical Thinking and Critical Pedagogy: Relations, Differences, and Limits." In *Critical Theories in Education: Changing Terrains of Knowledge and Politics*, edited by Thomas Popkewitz and Lynn Fendler. New York: Routledge, 45–65.

"Cardinal Zen." n.d. Wikipedia. Last modified March 7, 2016. http://en.wikipedia.org/wiki/Joseph_Zen.

Collins, Patricia Hill. 1986. "Learning From the Outsider Within: The Sociological Significance of Black Feminist Thought." *Social Problems* 33: 14–32.

———. 1998. *Fighting Words: Black Women and the Search for Justice*. Minneapolis, MN: University of Minnesota Press.

———. 1990. *Black Feminist Thought: Knowledge, Consciousness and the Politics of Empowerment*. New York: Routledge, Capman and Hall.

Dillion, Lisette. 2011. "Writing the self: The emergence of a dialogic space." *Narrative Inquiry* 21, no. 2: 213–37.

Dyson, Michael Eric. 2001. *Holler If You Hear Me: In Search of Tupac Shakur*. New York: Basic.

Ellsworth, Elizabeth. 1993. "Why Doesn't This Feel Empowering? Working through the Repressive Myths of Critical Pedagogy." In *Teaching for Change: Addressing Issues of Difference in the College Classroom*, edited by Kathryn Geismar and Guitele Nicoleau. Cambridge, MA: Harvard Educational Review, 43–70.

Fisher, Walter. 1987. *Human Communication as Narration: Toward a Philosophy of Reason, Value, and Action*. Columbia, SC: University of South Carolina Press.

Freire, Paulo. 1970. *Pedagogy of the Oppressed*. New York: Continuum.

Gates, Henry Louis. 1989. "Introduction: Narration and Cultural Memory in the African American Tradition." In *Talk that Talk: An Anthology of African American Storytelling*, edited by Linda Gross and Marian Barnes. New York: Simon & Schuster, 15–21.

Giroux, Henry. 1988. *Schooling and the Struggle for Everyday Life*. Minneapolis: University of Minnesota Press.

———. 1990. *Border Crossings: Cultural Workers and the Politics of Education*. New York: Routledge, Chapman & Hall.

———. 2002. *Breaking in to the Movies: Film and the Cultural Politics*. Malden, MA: Blackwell.

Giroux, Henry, and Peter McLaren. 1996. "*Teacher Education and the Politics of Engagement: The Case for Democratic Schooling.*" In *Breaking Free: The Transformative Power of Critical Pedagogy*, edited by Pepi Leistyna, Arlie Woodrum, and Stephen Sherblom. Cambridge, MA: Harvard Educational Review Press, 301–31.

Giroux, Henry, and Roger Simon, eds. 1989. *Popular Culture: Schooling and Everyday Life.* Granby, MA: Bergin & Garvey.

Gore, Jennifer. 1993. *The Struggle for Pedagogies: Critical and Feminist Discourses as Regimes of Truth.* New York: Routledge.

Harding, Sandra. 1986. *The Science Question in Feminism.* Ithaca New York: Cornell University Press.

Hartstock, Nancy. 1983. "The Feminist Standpoint: Developing the Ground for a Specifically Feminist Historical Materialism." In *Discovering Reality*, edited by Sandra G. Harding and Merrill B. Hintikka. Amsterdam: Dordreicht Reidel Publishing, 283–310.

———. 1997. "Comment on Hekman's 'Truth and Method: Feminist Standpoint Theory Revisited': Truth or Justice?" *Signs* 22, no. 2: 367–74.

hooks, bell. 1989. *Talking Back: Thinking Feminist, Thinking Black.* New York: South End Press.

———. 1993. "Transformative pedagogy and multiculturalism." In *Freedom's Plow,* edited by Theresa Perry and James Fraser. New York: Routledge, 91–97.

———. 1994. *Teaching to Transgress: Education as the Practice of Freedom.* New York: Routledge.

Jackson, Ronald, and Susan M. Heckman. 2002. "Perceptions of White Identity and White Liability: An Analysis of White Student Responses to a College Campus Racial Hate Crime." *Journal of Communication* 52, no. 2: 434–50.

Kristeva, Julia. 1995. Address to the participants at the conference "Why Theatre?" University of Toronto.

Labov, William. 1972. *Language in the Inner City.* Philadelphia, PA: University of Pennsylvania.

Lather, Patti. 1991. *Getting Smart: Feminist Research and Pedagogy With/in the Postmodern.* New York: Routledge.

Light, Richard. 2001. *Making the Most of College: Students Speak Their Minds.* Cambridge: Harvard University Press.

Lindlof, Thomas, and Bryan Taylor. 2002. *Qualitative Communication Research Methods.* 2nd ed. Thousand Oaks, CA: Sage.

Lyle, Sue. 2008. "Dialogic Teaching: Discussing Theoretical Contexts and Reviewing Evidence from Classroom Practice." *Language and Education: An International Journal* 22 no. 3: 222–40.

Martin, Judith, and Olga Davis. 2001. "Conceptual Foundations for Teaching about Whiteness in Intercultural Communication Courses." *Communication Education* 50: 298–313.

Martin, Judith, and Thomas Nakayama. 1999. "Thinking Dialectically about Culture and Communication." *Communication Theory* 9: 1–25.

Murji, Karim, and John Solomos. 2005. "Introduction: Racialization in Theory and Practice." In *Racialization: Studies in Theory and Practice,* edited by Karim Murji and John Solomos, Oxford: Oxford University Press, 1–27.

McLaren, Peter. 2003. "Critical Pedagogy: A Look at the Major Concepts." In *The Critical Pedagogy Reader*, edited by Antonia Darder, Marta P. Baltodano, and Rodolfo D. Torrez. New York: Routledge, 69–96.

Nachmanovitch, Stephen. 1990. *Free Play: Improvisation in Life and Art*. Los Angeles: Jeremy P. Tarcher, Inc.

Schniedewind, Nancy. 1987. "Teaching Feminist Process." *Women's Studies Quarterly* 15, no. 3/4: 15–31.

Solórzano, Daniel G., and Tara J. Yosso. 2002. "Critical Race Methodology: Counter-Storytelling as an Analytical Framework for Education Research." *Qualitative Inquiry* 81: 23–44.

Strewsbury, Carolyn M. 1993. "What is Feminist Pedagogy?" *Women's Studies Quarterly* 15: 6–14.

Tadmor, Carmit, Ying-yi Hong, Melody Chao, Fon Wirunchnipawan, and Wei Wang. 2012. "Multicultural Experiences Reduce Intergroup Bias through Epistemic Freezing." *Journal of Personality and Social Psychology* 103 no. 5: 750–72.

Wallace, Catherine. 2003. *Critical Reading in Language Education*. New York: Palgrave MacMillan.

Wallace, David Foster. 2005. "This is Water." Commencement at Kenyon College, May 21. YouTube. https://www.youtube.com/watch?v=8CrOL-ydFMI.

Walsh, Katherine Cramer. 2007. *Talking About Race: Community Dialogues and the Politics of Difference*. Chicago: University of Chicago Press.

Wink, Joan. 1997. *Critical Pedagogy: Notes from the Real World*. New York: Longman.

Wittgenstein, Ludwig. 1980. *Culture and Value*, translated by Peter Finch. Chicago: University of Chicago Press.

Wood, Julia. 1992. "Gender and Moral Voice: Moving From Women's Nature to Standpoint Epistemology." *Women's Studies in Communication* 15: 1.

The Story Circle Method and the Social Science Toolkit

Carolyn Behrman and Sandra Spickard Prettyman

> *Maybe stories are just data with a soul.*
> —Brene Brown, social worker and researcher, TEDx Houston, June 2010

I. BEHRMAN'S INTRODUCTION

Beginning with a story...

In late January of 2009, my thirteen-year-old daughter and I returned from a festive weekend in Washington, DC. She and I had canvassed for Obama in Ohio, going door to door in sometimes hostile and sometimes welcoming urban neighborhoods. To celebrate her first successful political efforts, we accepted an invitation from two sisters, old family friends, who had been very active in the campaign in DC. One sister held an elegant afternoon tea for volunteers, the other a sort of mini-inaugural ball at her home the following evening. Between these events, we walked the city from exuberant exhibits of campaign-related art in Georgetown to raucous music and street performances in Dupont Circle and on the Mall; DC was bubbling with enthusiasm. It seemed that everywhere we went people were full of hope for a future America a little less racially divided. On the day of the inauguration itself, we got up very early and drove six hours home to arrive at the University of Akron's Student Union just in time to watch the ceremony on a huge screen surrounded by a buzzing, excited crowd of students. At a hushed moment when Obama stepped forward on the screen a voice at the back of the auditorium cut the air: "Fucking Socialist A-Rab." The room went from hushed to utterly silent. I froze. What would follow and how would I help my daughter understand it? Often profanity causes people to giggle and an outburst such as that generally emboldens those who agree or provokes those who are offended. But this time there was a breath-long stillness and then, as one, the people in the room returned their attention to the screen; en masse they refused to give the provocateur his response. The previous low murmur resumed. My throat tightened with the sense of dignity, maturity, and hopefulness that infused that moment.✦

✦**Donna:** When I am privileged to hear a story like this told by a colleague or a student, I feel that the knowledge that I gain has a human face. The colleague or student has a child and their family activities reveal how education and values "live" outside the university and inform our private lives.
Bill: Story circles do bring human faces, with families and complicated lives, into the classroom in life-affirming ways, helping us better understand and learn to navigate the world we live in. This particular story really grabs my attention and would provide a fantastic starting point for a meaningful in-class discussion.

This is the sort of story that I might tell in a story circle with a prompt to "tell a story of race or race conflict." In a story circle, the other participants would listen to such a story having been asked, while listening, not to think about the story they might tell. They would find, it would have been explained, that a story would "well up" or come to them as they listened. As a social scientist with a particular interest in research methods including narrative elicitation techniques, I am intrigued by the story circle process. The example above, and the stories that might accompany it in a story circle, would by the nature of the process influence each other [what Pat Hill in this volume refers to as the "chaining" or "cascading effect" (from Lindlof and Taylor 2002; see 182)].● The story circle method is a form of group interview, but it appears that the stories are less powerfully influenced by the voices of others in the group than occurs; for example, in a focus group where a few dominant voices can determine the direction of discourse and emerging themes.✦

●**Donna:** This concept introduced by Pat seems to me to be a very important aspect of the experience of story circles. It not only describes the emergence of related stories during specific story circles, but I expect that it could also describe the possibility that those stories that do emerge are just the "tip of the iceberg" and that stories about the stories continue outside the story circles.
Bill: Agreed. The stories and storytellers influence each other, in part because story circles are structured to encourage behaviors central to democratic citizenship like active listening, rejecting "either/or" thinking, and remaining open-minded...learning through cascading give-and-take with and through others. In this sense, story circle participants may be more influenced by those gathered as a whole and more insulated from the distorting influence of a "few dominant voices."

Pat: I am reminded of a story circle from one of my classes that began with a prompt asking participants to tell a story that dealt with an issue of race. The first storyteller (an African American male) began with a discussion of the continued significance of race to his everyday experiences as well as many African Americans he knew. As his story progressed, the teller included vivid examples of how a beloved grandfather taught this student important lessons and strategies for survival. The teller indicated that he wanted to share his story to honor his grandfather (who was recently deceased). I witnessed a chaining-like process developing in which other storytellers also wanted to share stories to honor their grandparent(s) and other family members, who for them also passed on valuable lessons.

Jim: This improvisational aspect of the story circle sometimes gets forgotten and it is, for me, the essential community-making aspect of the process. Not planning which story to tell, but instead allowing the circle to dictate the story, makes the story circle a very alive experience. I like Pat's term, "chaining," because it makes me think of storytelling as a craft, creating links between each person in the circle and fashioning a chain of connections. The process of chaining, this subtle improvisation and exchange of breath and vibration, even takes precedence, for me, over the content of the stories themselves.

*Donna: Each of us have experienced the chaining or cascading effect of stories bringing to mind other stories; however, in story circles, all stories have a right to be heard and no one is asked to consider giving up their story to help create a group consensus. We can get "swept along" during a story circle, but we are never asked to renounce our authentic story because it does not agree with others in the group. The influence wielded by the group on the individual is not lessened in a story circle; it is a different kind of influence, however. The stories flow together; they are not formed by opposition or argument.

Having participated in and facilitated a great many story circles with a variety of prompts, I can say that the story circle is a useful educational device. Story circles have helped me open dialogues on uncomfortable but important social issues with participants. Because they offer participants the opportunity to hear and be heard in a structured and "safe" environment, they are very effective for group bonding. Lyons' chapter in this volume exemplifies this. Story circles also generate narratives which, as Webb, Hill, Lyons, and Slowiak demonstrate, are themselves important pedagogical tools. These narratives or first-hand accounts breathe life into the process of engaging with scholarly texts, especially when as teachers we encourage our students to explore some of society's more complex and important puzzles like the intersections of race, class, and gender as they shape human experience. Beyond using these narratives to facilitate student learning, the stories generated by the story circle method are data for social science research. As faculty who teach research methods for studying human behavior and experience in the social sciences, Sandra Spickard Prettyman and I have become intrigued by the possibilities of this approach to narrative data collection and choose here to explore what kind of contribution this may make to the social science toolkit.*

> *Bill: This was one of the most important strengths of using story circles in my classroom. First, hearing real world stories from peers or other participants in an intimate circle privileges exploration over familiarity. Second, a willingness to hear more, engage more deeply, with each other and with otherwise routinely dismissed scholarly texts cascades from here in a process of community building. Third, students in the class (and later other students working on Honors Projects) analyzed these stories as valuable primary source data, sharpening their analytical skills and deepening their understanding of race and politics.
>
> Donna: I agree that story circles facilitate student learning and that story circles generate data for social science research. In addition, I think that story circles are an answer to the question, "What is the Story?" In my work in Cascade Village, story circles provided insight into how residents viewed themselves and their world in a far more revealing way than the questionnaires that I distributed. For example, asking "what kind of public art would you like to see in Cascade Village?" did not result in helpful answers. Stories about growing up in Cascade Village revealed a rich history of topics that were great inspiration for community art.

This chapter starts from the position that the story circle method and the data it produces will hold significant appeal for many researchers in the social sciences. Why? It is relatively easy to use, participants generally enjoy participating, and the data are rich. However, to make good use of this new tool, there are questions we need to answer. What are the qualities or attributes of the narratives that this method elicits? What approaches might we take to analyze them? How are they different from information garnered from other sorts of techniques that ask people to share their experiences? These are the questions we explored with our undergraduate (Behrman) and graduate (Spickard Prettyman) social science research methods classes in the Fall of 2012.•

> •Donna: The story circle experience is safe and easy to use, if participants follow the rules, but it is also democratic and unpredictable.

Pat: Although, some students may find the process problematic. Our stories are not always pleasant to recall. Additionally, it can be difficult to work through to awareness of one's own biases. I am also remembering the white female student (I believe I shared this with the group) who shared in the story circle her experiences of being sexually molested by a black man, which subsequently "caused her to hate all back men"—the telling of (and reliving of) this story in the story circle caused emotional distress.

Carolyn: Pat's comment here is important, we need to be aware of the vulnerability of participants. We are asking people to tell stories that are close to the heart and to lived experience. There is real potential for anxiety although the intimate nature of the circle generates a relatively safe space, it seems to me. For me it connects to Bill's comment below about how the story circles help us individually and collectively engage with and struggle with the important issues of our time.

Bill: The data are amazing and our students loved the participatory and inquiry-based nature of story circles. At the same time, I struggled at first because I did not find it easy to prepare myself emotionally for the charged and layered dialogues that emerged. It becomes easier and it is certainly a very easy to understand process, but it demands a deeper and more vulnerable openness on my part, as the facilitator-participant. That is my sense of what "relatively easy to use" means here.

Donna: In class discussions we normally ask people to share their observations. We want them to use their objective self and to be aware of cause and effect in their environment. We then compare our observations to get a composite view from many directions. In story circles we ask people to share a lived experience. We want them to use storytelling skills to emphasize what has been meaningful to them. As listeners we are allowed to participate in that meaning through our imaginations. In some cases the meaning comes alive for the listeners and becomes a shared understanding.

Amy: My experiences with story circles and focus groups are widely divergent. In a previous career as an evaluation research consultant, my focus group research brought together persons with common interests or careers who found opportunities to network and discover common interests in the groups. They tended to be pleasant experiences. However, story circles brought together persons with no obvious similarities to speak about race. Participants discovered that, although they and the stories told were quite different, the experience of sharing itself created a bond, sometimes a strong bond. These were amazingly profound experiences and some storytellers expressed the opinion that they were life-changing.

Other chapters in this volume show ways this technique can be applied outside the classroom. The authors connect classroom to community on issues like race and demonstrate how participation in story circles enriched dialogue and enhanced understanding. In each case, the process also led to intellectual and professional development of students. In this chapter, we keep the tool "in the room": examining it, comparing it to another method, comparing its data to other data, and, in the end, reflecting on its potential usefulness in specific study situations. By focusing on the method itself, we are not engaging a wider community; however our classes were small communities, and we created a slightly larger community by combining the classes for three weeks during the semester. Beginning and advanced students came together in mixed-level groups to experiment and discuss their findings. Master's and doctoral students brought with them their plans, already in progress, for theses and dissertations. For them this was an opportunity to consider the story circle method pragmatically. The undergraduates tended to take a broader, more abstract, and less immediately practical approach to the exercise. Challenging each other as they worked side by side to collect, analyze, and critically compare their results, each group facilitated the intellectual and professional development of the other. This chapter recounts the process of working with students to explore the nature of the method and the data produced by story circles for social science research.

A. The Appeal of the Method

In this chapter, and generally this volume, we use the term *story* to mean personal narratives of lived experience. Broadly speaking, stories are important to teaching and to social science. In social science we search for effective ways to elicit and record people's experiences so we may analyze them and come to more complete understandings of the human condition. In the classroom we work to help students find linkages between scholarship and lived experiences—their own or those of others—so they may come to more complete understandings of the complexities of social life. Brene Brown, in her TEDx Houston talk observes that human beings are by nature "imperfect and wired for struggle." (https://www.ted.com/talks/brene_brown_on_ vulnerability?language=en) She considered the degree to which our stories allow us to see ourselves in context, to situate our experiences as we articulate and share them. This process of exposing, exploring, and accepting our vulnerabilities leads us to greater self-awareness and empathy. Brown's is a clinical, therapeutic perspective and as social researchers interested in understanding human behavior and the reasons for the ways we act, such a perspective creates a broad connection. As teachers interested in the intellectual and civic development of our students, there is also a more specific connection between the use of stories and social and intellectual engagement.

◆Donna: From the perspective of the arts, it seems that one of the goals of social science is to find solutions to the problems of human societies. In the collection of stories about growing up in Cascade Village there were stories about important issues in the community, such as a young man's first job, experiencing the community at night in a positive way, and enjoying neighbors who are different than you. It may be that stories contain important community wisdom that can be shared to provide benefit to the group. In each case the story did not tell the listener how to get a job or how to enjoy eccentric neighbors or how to enjoy the neighborhood at night. The story only demonstrated that individuals had engaged in these situations and had emerged richer and livelier for having done so.

Jim: The preponderance of "passive culture" in our world today makes us hungry for the experience of "active culture" that storytelling gives us. So often we watch stories on television alone and detached, or receive music through cables plugged in our ears. We are just consuming culture, but not participating in the creation of it. Story circles make us active participants in creating culture, hands on, and that brings us closer to the source of our humanity.

Donna: The ways we are "imperfect and wired for struggle" seem more likely to emerge in story circles than in focus groups, which seem to me to be structured to find consensus and often create their own hierarchy. This hierarchy is formed as those who are successful at making their opinions known rise to a position above those who are less successful.

Carolyn: Donna, I think you have intuited one of the concerns that haunts focus groups as research tools.

Bill: This struggle theme is important. Story circles allow us all to engage more directly and deeply with the struggles of our age. Story circles provide us with opportunities to help ourselves and our students to learn not to fear conflict or conversation about controversial topics. Instead, in story circles, we experienced these as opportunities to learn, listen and scrutinize with others *who disagree*, have different lived experiences, or bring competing perspectives to the table. Katherine Cramer Walsh (2007) concludes that because story circles are a game where listening *becomes* a virtue, participants learn to balance "unity and diversity, listening and scrutiny, and dialogue and debate." Walsh concludes that the "results suggest a rethinking of the place of conflict in deliberative democracy and an acknowledgement that it is the ongoing *struggle* with difference that provides unity in contemporary civic life" (14; italics added). We are both different and *united in the struggle* to balance civility and contestation, listening and speaking, diversity and unity in the stories we tell. Successful deliberative storytelling is civil contestation designed to help us all "face the reality of different realities" (8) as a democratic and deliberative pathway to achieving unity, building community, and advancing our understanding of, and appreciation for, both our shared struggle and the diverse resources we bring to that struggle.

Pat: In her book *The Development of Emotional Competence* (1999), Carolyn Saarni defines emotional competence as the ability to recognize and understand what someone else is feeling, the kind of emotional experience they are having, and why. She notes that the development of empathy is so very critical to emotional competence and the development of a moral society. She goes on to argue that only with emotional competence can one "care"—take action to reduce the negative experience of the other. Story circles create spaces for the development of emotional competence and possibly greater empathy.

B. An example...

At the University of Akron we have an annual event known as Rethinking Race (see Slowiak's introduction and Dreussi's chapter in this volume for more information). Among the nearly two weeks of talks, performances, and Face2Face conversations⁺ of Rethinking Race 2008 was a story circle event. Relying on our training from John O'Neal and Theresa Holden the previous year, the authors of this volume facilitated the gathering. Participants were invited to tell stories of their own experiences with race and race conflict. In my circle several stories were told that highlighted the danger, fear, and harm that racism had caused in the lives of non-white Americans. There was a young man in the circle with hair so fair that you could see his scalp redden when he blushed. When his turn came in the circle he told the following story which was, sadly, not recorded, so I retell it here from notes.

He came from a small town in southern Ohio and was the first in his immediate family to go to college. He had attended a high school in which there was almost no racial diversity. He had, he said, never really spoken to an African American. His first year at the University had been life changing for him. His assigned roommate was African American. His parents wanted to request a change but he said he'd give the arrangement a try. The roommates became friends and this friendship led to others for the storyteller, shaking many of his preconceived notions and radically altering his world view. Home again the following summer he went on a "hunting trip" with his male relatives and family friends. The term is in quotation marks because he explained that these trips really involved loading up pick-up trucks with camping gear, food, and beer and then finding a suitably secluded place to spend the weekend hanging out. There was always some hunting or fishing but most of the quality time was spent around big fires talking, eating, and drinking into the night. One evening talk around the fire turned to politics with some very unpleasant terms used to describe Hillary Clinton and Barack Obama who were then vying for the Democratic nomination. Perhaps, he said, his judgment was beer-impaired, but he responded to this banter by commenting that he was thinking of voting for Obama. He said it was as if he'd gone deaf at first—all sound seemed to cease. Then it was as if someone had thrown firecrackers into the fire as everyone was scream-

ing at him at once, rising up and threatening him as they did so. He said "I thought, 'I'm going to die here, tonight. They're going to kill me and bury me and tell my mother it was a hunting accident or that I'd run off'." His eyes filled with tears and he stopped talking. We all sat in stunned silence.•

✦Carolyn: There is a description of these small group conversations focused on specific questions that foster what Bill calls "difficult dialogues" in chapter one of this volume.

•Donna: I can't imagine this story being told if there had not been a story circle, unless the young man had grown up to be a poet or novelist.

Amy: Horrifying. It's hard to imagine another public venue in which this story would be told. How wonderful that he was able to share this, which I would hope and imagine would be healing for him. And, how insightful for those who heard this to have a glimpse into that mind-set. I generally sense a strong streak of denial about racism among young people.

Pat: This story clearly reinforces the need to create a space for open, honest, and critical reflection on pressing issues in our society.

Carolyn: Peggy McIntosh was recently interviewed in the *New Yorker*. She was talking about the importance of college and university settings for building opportunities both for individuals to express their experiences and for them to put those experiences of others into the context of systems and structures that define privilege.

The colleges and the universities are the places where you get a hearing. They're where you learn to see both individually and systematically. In order to understand the way privilege works, you have to be able to see patterns and systems in social life, but you also have to care about individual experiences. I think one's own individual experience is sacred. Testifying to it is very important—but so is seeing that it is set within a framework outside of one's personal experience that is much bigger, and has repetitive statistical patterns in it (McIntosh quoted in Rothman 2014).

Storytelling experiences like this can be profound and transformative for the teller and the listeners. Choosing to tell a specific story to a specific audience involves taking a risk, becoming vulnerable and sometimes allowing that vulnerability to be recognized as courageous.✦ Linking Brown's therapeutic point to pedagogy, this forges bonds between people and is a learning, or perhaps a growing, experience for the participants.

✦Amy: It must be a huge help in building community in the classroom as well.

Carolyn: Yes, I think the fact that participants are exposing themselves in this process but also being recognized as they do so really does build stronger ties within the classroom than we often see otherwise.

At the classroom level, the bonfire story is one I often recall for students as a way to help them understand what we mean in the story circle instructions by telling a story not offering "political theories or arguments or opinions or analysis." More importantly, in class the story serves as a primary resource students can use to help illuminate issues of race, class, and the patterning of urban and rural diversity that we focus on with articles such as Aldeman and Gocker's (2007) study of racial residential segregation in the US. For the social science researcher, it can be imagined that a series of stories like this would provide a good foundation for exploring the ways we talk about and make sense of human diversity in American culture. Specifically, through a collection of stories we could explore salient categories of diversity (i. e., what counts as a story about race and race conflict such that the participant would choose to tell it), patterns within storytellers' shared and divergent responses to experiences with diversity, and shared themes that comprise our cultural understandings of difference and how human differences relate to each other (intersectionality) and to the human condition in terms of success and suffering.[+]

> [+]**Donna:** The bonfire story demonstrates that racial conflict may be the price of group solidarity. The bonfire group maintained their identity by excluding and rejecting those identified as different from them. Skin color is such a simple and shallow way of identifying someone as "other."
> **Bill:** At the same time, the bonfire story suggests that engaging in story circles might also create, or allow us to re-imagine and enact together, new stories about new forms of group solidarity.

II. BEHRMAN AND SPICKARD PRETTYMAN—STUDYING THE STORY CIRCLE METHOD

Working with story circles in the undergraduate course Human Diversity[•] across many semesters, Behrman found, as Lyons did in his Law and Society class, that they were useful for illustrating and enriching course content. One student evaluation of the use of story circles in this introductory class commented that: "the stories, *our* stories, sometimes reinforced the points of the readings which was great but sometimes they actually added a dimension the article or chapter didn't include and that was the best because it was us doing the analyzing then." Success with story circles in the classroom lead us (Behrman and Spickard Prettyman) to a conversation about the how we might document the utility of the method for research. We decided we wanted to better understand story circles as a narrative data collection technique. Before designing a plan to do this, we asked ourselves what attributes or qualities could already be ascribed to the story circle method as a teaching and research tool.

> •**Carolyn:** This is a general education course filled with a mix of students from majors and colleges across the campus. Many are first years but some are seniors who have put off fulfilling their distribution requirements.

As a teaching tool, the story circle method changes the dynamic among students in the class. One student in Behrman's Human Diversity pointed out that "it was easier for me to understand the data [from a class reading] and believe it when there were real people, people like me, describing it to me. The data gave me a starting point for seeing what is really going on in the world. The stories gave me real examples that I am able to understand a lot more and made me think about the students in my circle in fresh ways, made me see them differently. . . ." They also change the student's associations between course content and the outside world. A student observed "after doing the story circles I really wanted to talk about race to everyone, and when I did, I realized how blind most people are to the implicit racism that still permeates society." Story circles conducted at Rethinking Race events, in classes, and research projects over a number of years have allowed us to amass a fairly large archive of stories. Recorded and transcribed, these stories were being used by classes and for individual and collaborative projects including student Senior Honors projects and collaborative works like the *Color Line Script* and production (Slowiak, this volume). In sum, we could see that, for teaching, this method quickly creates connection and trust among participants while focusing attention on a topic as both personally experienced and academically approachable. For research, this method was generating data but the process of data generation needed systematic exploration.◆

> ◆**Donna:** Is there research to support our experience that rather than creating conflict or a gulf between people, story circles come close to being shared experiences and therefore create connection and trust?
>   As Pat brought up in an earlier comment in this chapter, it is important to note there are times when a story circle has been troubled. In October at Cascade Village, "Pam" told a story about picking up the phone extension as a child and hearing the caller tell

her mom that her grandpa had murdered her grandma. This was a moment when it was difficult to be a part of a story circle. This is of course similar to Pat's experience with the young woman who told a story about being raped.

It is also worth noting such incidents are not common and that participants choose this time and place to share difficult experiences for their own reasons. They may be infrequent because the democratic nature of the story circles combined with a guideline of taking about three minutes to tell a story tend to naturally "tether" the story within the boundaries of the circle.

Carolyn: Donna, I do not know of research on trust and the story circle method although models from psychological therapy suggest our observations are valid. Considering your points about troubled stories, it seems to me, and Amy's data from Rethinking Race suggest that the dominant experience of participants in story circles overall is positive but we know that the stories often are not. Truly troubling stories calling for some response that steps outside the protocol have arisen for some of us. Do we need to develop a plan or share strategies for handling these?

Donna: My experience at Cascade Village was as a facilitator with adult participants. The story of hearing about the murder of her grandmother came from an adult who came voluntarily to a story circle knowing that she would be telling a story about growing up. I agree that when young people are asked to tell a story in class at the request of a professor, more care might be required to safeguard vulnerable students.

Bill: One of the reasons story circles are experienced as real is because it is immediately clear that the nature of the stories has been placed outside the control of the instructor; this is a key component for building trust. Most of the stories collected had positive and negative aspects and the power of the circle is that we are handling these together. Other than the same facilitation techniques we use in class discussion, I wonder if focusing on additional strategies for handling these weakens story circles.

Donna: Bill, I'm trying to think about what John O'Neal would say about this. He did caution for example that no one tell a story about engaging in illegal activities lest they put story circle members in the uncomfortable situation of knowing that a crime had been committed. Other than that I can't think of any ways that John safeguarded participants. Does anyone else remember anything?

Jim: This kind of situation is probably much more common for those of us who work in theatre. Very often in acting classes or during rehearsal or voice/movement work, an actor might touch some kind of personal experience or association that provokes an emotional outburst or episode. At these moments, I try to provide a safe space for the emotion to run its course without any kind of judgment or over-sentimentalization of the situation. Sometimes it's just a question of listening and waiting and then continuing the work to channel the newfound openness into something productive.

Because we both teach research methods classes in the social sciences, Behrman in an undergraduate anthropology program and Spickard Prettyman in a graduate education program, we decided to build an examination of the story circle method into our Fall 2012 classes. Behrman's class, Introduction to Anthropological Data, introduces students to a range of data types, data collection techniques, and data analysis tools, of which narrative data collection forms just a portion. Spickard Prettyman's graduate class is the first in a sequence of two Qualitative Data classes in which she trains graduate-level researchers in preparation for their dissertations. We decided to introduce our classes to two narrative elicitation techniques—the story circle and the focus group—through readings and in class training.✦ We did this separately in our respective classes but then combined the classes for three weeks to work in mixed class teams. In these weeks, the students would create a story circle prompt and a focus group protocol on the same topic and then use those tools to gather data which they would transcribe and then compare.

> ✦**Pat:** The comparison of these two methods is apt since they are applied in similar ways at times. Although focus groups have their origins in marketing research, as Kamberelis and Dimitriadis (2011) point out, focus groups "involve collective engagement designed to promote dialogue and to achieve higher levels of understanding of issues critical to the development of a group's interests and/or the transformation of conditions of its existence" (546). I think that this is clearly in line with story circle method. Moreover, they note uses of "Focus groups…have a long history for promoting social justice agendas…" (550). Again, a clear connection between the two.

The combined class elected to use the topic of discrimination for their undertaking. They felt it was close to the most common story circle prompt used by the Akron Story Circle Project but still allowed for a wider exploration of social conflict than a prompt with a primary emphasis on race would. The students each produced a few prospective prompts and spent a long class meeting comparing and discussing in specific detail the variations among their prompts. This is not a trivial issue. The wording of the prompt, they concluded, was akin to writing poetry; a slight difference might call forth utterly different stories. For example, when personnel from the Akron Story Circle Project worked with middle school teachers, we found that there is an important difference between the stories that will be told starting with the prompt "tell a story about a time you felt left out" and those elicited with the prompt "tell a story about a time when someone was not included."• Below is the list of forty-six prompts the research methods students explored that day. Note the similarities between, for example, numbers 23 and 27 and consider how the slight difference might yield different sorts of stories.

•**Bill:** Agreed. It is not trivial. Some of the most illuminating conversations to emerge from the Akron Story Circle Project work have grown out of conversations about developing a prompt. In a more recent conversation, we explored the benefits of a prompt like "tell us a story about your first job," because the prompt will certainly feel less controversial and yet still likely to bring out stories that allow us to more deeply examine the intersections of race, class, and gender subordination.

Jim: I agree that the prompt is vital for the story circle to yield its fruit—along with the basic rules. However, I also feel that like anything else, story circles take practice. I think that groups that engage in story circles over a period of time gain an extra dimension and deepening of the process that doesn't occur as easily with first-time doers.

Bill: Interesting. "Tell a story about a time someone was not included" seems to encourage stories about others where the first focuses on oneself. The former emphasizing feelings and the latter activities or choices. What differences did the teachers highlight?

Carolyn: You are right, Bill. The stories eliciting personal experience were very powerful and vulnerable. The teachers in the workshop demonstrated strikingly nuanced understanding of their own emotional development at the ages of their students, which is not surprising since it is their professional and intellectual home turf. The stories asking for stories about someone not being included sparked more strategic and professional conversation during the cross talk portion of the story circle I facilitated.

STUDENTS' PROPOSED STORY CIRCLE PROMPTS

1. Can you describe an instance where you, or someone you know, were discriminated against? Did that moment affect you? If so, how?

2. How do you feel we can combat the proliferation of discrimination?

3. Do you feel discrimination is an issue that persists today? If so, can you give some examples of modern forms of discrimination?

4. Tell a story about what you know about discrimination.

5. Tell a story about how you have come to know about discrimination.

6. Tell a story about your experience with the issue of discrimination.

7. Tell me about what you know about discrimination.

8. Tell about an instance of discrimination that you know about.

9. Tell me about discrimination in the US.

10. Tell me about how discrimination is being handled.

11. Tell some ideas that you may have when dealing with discrimination.

12. Tell me a story about an incident where you witnessed discrimination but were unable to stop it.
13. Tell me a story about an incident of discrimination that was directed towards you which caused you to feel powerless.
14. Tell me a story about your first experience with discrimination.
15. Tell about a time where either you or a person you know was affected by discrimination, whether being the victim or the individual discriminating against another.
16. What was your first memorable run in with discrimination?
17. What do you know of the advances in today's society to end the various forms of discrimination?
18. What are some of the other forms of discrimination that somebody can be subjected to other than just racially?
19. Tell a story about a time you witnessed a form of discrimination.
20. Tell a story about how discrimination has had an effect on your life.
21. Tell a story about a time you have intervened on someone's behalf to prevent discrimination.
22. Tell a story about how an individual act of discrimination has changed your attitude toward a friend, coworker or loved one.
23. Tell a story about a time when you felt discriminated against.
24. Tell a story about a time when you discriminated against someone.
25. Tell a story about how discrimination changed your life or a specific event in your life.
26. As a teacher, tell a story about a time you've seen discrimination affect outcomes in your classroom. (I guess this could be applied to any profession.)
27. Tell a story about a time you were discriminated against.
28. Tell about a time when someone in your family was discriminated against.
29. Tell a story about a time when you were involved in or witnessed discrimination against someone from either a higher or lower SES (could be changed for any type of discrimination).
30. Tell about a time when you were a positive influence or stood up for someone who was being discriminated against.

31. Have you ever experienced bullying, either as a witness, victim, or participant?
32. Do you believe today, popular culture is calling attention to bullying more than in your past?
33. Are you familiar with hate crimes legislation?
34. What do you believe it does for people?
35. Do you think it makes a difference in the way people treat others?
36. Have you judged others upon how you perceive their appearance?
37. Do you believe some biased beliefs and practices associated with discrimination are justified? i.e. Should anyone over the age of 75 be allowed a renewed driver's license?
38. Tell a story about a time you personally experienced discrimination.
39. Tell a story about a time you witnessed an act of discrimination toward another person.
40. Tell a story about your feelings toward discrimination.
41. Tell a story about a time you discriminated against someone else.
42. Tell a story about a time when you experienced a specific form of discrimination.
43. Tell a story about a time when you were in a situation and you realized that race mattered.
44. Describe a story about being in a work environment and realizing that you or someone you work with was being discriminated against.
45. Tell a story about a situation in which you or someone you know was denied an opportunity because of their individual difference.
46. Tell a story, describing a time when you unintentionally discriminated against a person, but did not realize it until it had already occurred.

As you can see, some of these prompts would elicit a one-word response, some are very similar to others in the list, some do not really ask for a story so much as an analytic disquisition, and some are overly restrictive, leaving open the possibility that some participants in the story circle might not have an experience to offer that fit the prompt. Consensus among the students was that debating options for the story circle prompt was a very valuable

exercise from a researcher's point of view because they were forced to scrutinize the connotations of words, imbedded assumptions, and the ways that
statement or question construction can lead or direct the participant and
potentially obscure or highlight themes that the question-writer may inap-
propriately anticipate. In the end, the class chose the following prompt: *Tell
a story about a time you experienced discrimination.* The process by which the
story circle prompt is operationalized was created by O'Neal and Holden
and slightly modified by the Akron Story Circle Project. The history of
O'Neil and Holden's work and the full story circle process are set out in the
introduction to this volume. We repeat the process here purely so the reader
can see the highlighted similarities and differences between the story circle
and focus group processes we operationalized. The combined classes relied
on the process as it appears below.

> *Bill: Some prompts are also more likely to make it easier for storytellers to avoid engag-
> ing with often uncomfortable controversies. It was not uncommon, for instance, to hear
> very short stories (prefaced by pointing out that they do not know any African Amer-
> icans) from white suburban students describing themselves or their families as racial
> heroes because they "just don't see race at all."
> Pat: Knowing the makeup of the class would help me to conceptualize the meaning of
> "experience."
> Carolyn: The combined classes encompassed a lot of human variation. Several of the
> graduate students were in their thirties and one was older while most of the under-
> graduates were around twenty years old. A number of participants had children. The
> classes were pretty balanced by gender. There were two international students who both
> happened to be Islamic, non-native English speakers. We had one student who was
> vocal about dealing with gender identity issues and one student who was particularly
> engaged with Jewish diaspora concerns. There were three African American students
> out of the roughly thirty participants and no Hispanic or Asian students.
> Jim: Many of these prompts will not elicit stories, but rather opinions or commentary.
> The real trick is finding the prompt that strikes to the core of storytelling.

THE STORY CIRCLE PROCESS

Let me explain briefly what we will be doing...

1.   We will sit in circles of six to eight people. A circle, not an oval or
     square, because being in a circle is important. In a circle everyone
     is in an equal physical space.
2.   The cofacilitators will introduce themselves and then move
     clockwise. Each person will simply tell the group their name and
     where they're from.

3. There will be a "Story Circle Log Sheet" on a clipboard in each circle to allow our research team to match up all the parts of a story that may emerge at different times with the one storyteller. There will be a Log Keeper and the circle will decide on a way to keep time.

4. As we move clockwise around the story circle, anyone can pass when it is their turn to tell a story. Do not take notes. Do not hold books or papers in your lap. Concentrate on listening.

5. After brief introductions, the facilitator will remind the group of the ground rules. Once the first story has been told, we will proceed clockwise around the circle, with each person taking approximately three minutes to tell an actual, personal story or passing.

6. Story circles are primarily about *listening*. Listening is more important than talking. Do not spend time thinking of your story. Instead, listen actively to all of the stories and trust that the circle process will bring you a story when the time is right. If several stories come to you as you are listening, reach for the deepest story that you are comfortable telling.

7. Each person just listens to the stories...no interruptions, no commentary, no body language other than active listening. We do not need to like or agree with anyone else's story, but just as we have a right to tell our own story, we need to respect the rights of everyone else in the group to tell their own story.

8. Tell stories...not political theories or arguments or opinions or analysis. A story can be something that happened to you or it can be the story of a family member, friend, or acquaintance—a story you've heard.

9. Silence is always acceptable. If you need to be silent a moment after a story, be silent.

10. When the stories have been told, the facilitator will ask if anyone who passed wishes to tell their story. They can pass again if they choose. Once all stories have been told, the facilitator will invite "cross-circle questioning," where you may ask clarifying questions about the stories you heard. The facilitator will allow about five minutes for this.

11. Then the facilitator will ask each participant to think of an image or "snapshot" for each story they heard in the circle, allow for a couple of minutes to think about images, and then ask participants to share the images that came to their minds as a way to identify themes that emerged in the circle. *Sharing these images should flow into a conversation about the themes they reveal.*

12. If the circle you are in will be joining a larger group, then your circle needs to decide on how to report back on the essence or themes that emerged from your circle. This should be a collaborative undertaking, and can be as creative as the group desires. Again, you need to keep to the allotted amount of time for this phase of the circle. Finally, join the larger group, and report on your story circle.

C. We are ready to begin…

The highlighted areas deal with analysis and allow participants to interact directly.

After creating the story circle prompt, the teams turned their attention to the challenge of constructing a formal focus group protocol based on the same topic: discrimination. The two teams, combining undergraduates and graduate students, worked to create focus group protocols independently and then brought their drafts to class. All together, we edited and reworked the rough drafts into a single, final protocol (below). There is not enough space in this volume to share the full set of draft protocols from which this final version was derived, but a process of detailed scrutiny and valuable argument among the students, similar to the one used on the story circle prompt, went into its development.

FOCUS GROUP PROTOCOL

Introduction

Thank you for agreeing to participate in this focus group. Today we will be considering the topic of discrimination. We are eager to hear about your knowledge and experiences regarding discrimination.

Our interests in facilitating this focus group include: understanding the ways you define discrimination, learning about ways you have experienced or witnessed discrimination, hearing what you consider to be patterns of discrimination in contemporary culture, and hearing about avenues you think can be taken to disrupt or change those patterns.

We have some specific questions for the group that will guide the discussion, but we are especially interested in your ideas, opinions, and experiences. Please feel free to share as we go through the evening. That said, it is your decision when and how much to share with the group. Your participation is voluntary; you should feel free to not answer or to stop at any time. In addition, the data collected here will be rendered anonymously. Nothing recorded today will be transcribed using names or other identifying details, and recordings will be destroyed after transcripts are complete.

There are a few rules that we would like to establish before we start:

1. Please be thoughtful in your use of language. Refrain from offensive tones, gestures, and words with reference to others in the group.
2. Please try not to interrupt when others are speaking. This demonstrates respect and also will help ensure that your points come through clearly in the transcript.
3. If you agree or disagree with someone, please let us know *how* and *why* (as opposed to just saying: "I agree"). This will help us understand your response.

Let us know if you have any questions or concerns as the focus group process is underway—we want you to feel comfortable with the process and in your participation.

Are there any questions before we begin? So, let's get started.

Area One: Knowledge of Discrimination (20 minutes)
(Numbered questions that must be asked)

1. How would you define discrimination? *(consider types?)*
2. A slightly different way to ask this is to ask, what behaviors constitute discrimination? *(consider overt and covert behaviors?)*
3. What would you say are factors or circumstances that lead to discrimination?

Area One: topics for consideration (NOT TO BE READ ALOUD. Topics may already have been be covered in the answers to questions 1–3. If they have not been covered, prompt participants to consider them.)

In addition to types of discrimination and varieties of behaviors that reveal discrimination already mentioned, participants may consider:
SOCIAL Context
How race, class, gender, sexuality, disability, age, cultural background, relative access to resources, and/or other attributes contribute to their perception of discrimination
POLITICAL Context
How de facto and de jure policies have influenced their understanding of discrimination
HISTORICAL Context
How historical shifts and social movements have shaped their understanding of discrimination

Area Two: Experiences with Discrimination (25 minutes)
(Numbered questions that must be asked.)

1. What experiences have you had with discrimination as a witness? (how did you respond?)
2. What experiences have you had with discrimination as a victim? (how did you respond?)
3. What experiences have you had with discrimination as a perpetrator? (how did you respond?)
4. What types of discrimination have you ignored? (discuss)
5. What are your thoughts about the impact discrimination has on others?

Area Two: topic for consideration (NOT TO BE READ ALOUD. Topic that may have been covered by the answers to questions 1–4. If they have not been covered, prompt participants to consider.)
SOCIAL Context
How specific people in their lives have shaped their understanding of discrimination

Area Three: Patterns of Discrimination and Change (15 minutes)
(Numbered questions that must be asked verbatim)

1. What factors prevent people from intervening in discrimination?
2. How might these factors be mitigated or overcome?

Area Three: topic for consideration (NOT TO BE READ ALOUD. Topic that may be covered by the answers to questions 1–2. If not covered, prompt participants to consider.)

Patterns

Thinking about the experiences related, do they see patterns in discrimination that help us understand the concept and its implications more broadly?

As with the story circle process, we have highlighted the places in the protocol where participants are specifically asked for their analysis of their experiences and those they have heard in relation to the focus group's topic. It should be apparent just from examining the protocols above that focus groups are unlike story circles in structure but like them in that they ask the participants to recall stories of their experience. Both methods also ask participants to offer their analyses, although to different degrees and at different points in the elicitation process.

To fully compare the two methods, the students returned to their teams, and executed first focus group and then story circle protocols. Teams used each other as participants, a choice we would not make again as it resulted in fatigue of the topic. These sessions were recorded, transcribed, and then compared. Below are four examples of data from these sessions.

An exchange between students in a focus group on the subject of experiences witnessing discrimination . . .

Undergraduate 1: Thinking about high school, like, I know ageism happens a lot. Like, seniors just harassing. I witnessed that in high school pretty often. I went to a big high school that was a suburb with fifty thousand or so people. There was a lot of students; there was a lot of social interaction. But not all of it was pleasant.

Undergraduate 2: Yeah, speaking of ageism, that reminds me of another story. I think last semester I was taking a class on the Incas, or whatever, and all like, you know, early twenties, mid-twenties, taking this class on the Inca, and there's this . . . there's an, uh, you know, a non-traditional is what I've been told is what you're supposed to call a someone who's a student who's, like, in their sixties. But, this guy was like, he had just turned sixty and he announced it to the class and, like, people were snickering and, I'm like, I remember every once in a while in class, like people would make fun of him because he was sixty and going to college and getting his bachelor's degree and it was just, like, I mean, he comes from a different generation and so, I mean, who am I to judge why he's coming back to get his education and here these kids are just mocking him because he's so late to the game, is what they consider it.

Undergraduate 1: Hmmm... that's interesting because I remember I had a class with Dr. Shott, Native Americans, and there was, I think he might have said it was the oldest student in the University in the class. It was an old woman. She was in a wheelchair, but yeah, yeah, yeah, she never experi—... like, no one ever made fun of her. She was pretty well respected. That's an interesting difference.

An exchange between students in a focus group on the subject of ignoring discrimination... ✦

Graduate student: I think it's hard to remember because we ignored it. Not to be smart but that's why it's hard.

Undergraduate: I guess a lot of times I'll, like, thinking back to high school again, types of discrimination, that I would see, I would just think oh, it's part of the whole experience and go about my day. Let the discrimination keep happening.

Graduate student: The younger you are, the more you ignore. You know, I mean, we've probably all been sitting with friends when someone was making fun of somebody else. Or laughing at something, really inappropriate and you kinda ignore it because, I think the younger you are the more, the more you know the people that you're around, probably the more likely you are to tolerate it because you know you're scared to be that guy or that girl.

Undergraduate: Right, right.

Graduate student: Because I know I've done that, I mean, I know I've sat there when people are making fun of someone.

Undergraduate: Oh, yeah definitely, I have too.

Graduate student: Or make a comment because (inaudible). Yeah, you don't feel good about it, but I know I've done that. ●

✦**Donna:** It is interesting to me that the story circle prompt involves telling a story about being discriminated against and the focus group chose the point of view of the observer, removed from the direct experience of being discriminated against.

Carolyn: Yes, Donna. The classes discussed this problem which could be seen as a limitation of the story circle. The single prompt focuses down on a specific experience where the focus group protocol casts a wide net, allowing people to consider the variety of positions an individual can have in relation to something like discrimination.

●**Bill:** In this focus group it almost feels like the graduate student is correcting the undergraduate, stifling storytelling?

Carolyn: In my experience outside this class-based comparison, a big distinction between the two methods is that the focus group protocol can ask the participants to assume a range of roles or perspectives from narrator of first-person experience to more objective analyst, while the story circle really limits the participant to narrating personal experience and then allows the group to consider analysis together. By pursuing so many angles and allowing so many types of perspective, I have found focus group participants sometimes gloss and shorthand experiences. This is noticeable in this example.

Jim: Yes, Carolyn, but let's not forget about the "after" part of the story circle process. I think there is a part of the process that even goes beyond the group's analysis of the stories to some kind of action plan. What are we going to do with these stories now that we've told them? How are we as a community going to integrate these stories into our story? Through art or some other kind of social action? So the stories don't just remain as artifacts, but they become tools to arrive at new understandings. That's what we're doing with this book. That's what the performance project was all about.

A Story Circle Story...

I have a story. It was when Tom and Mark and I were out [gathering a survey for another assignment in an anthropology class]. We went to one house and Mark went just across the street. And we were talking to, um, an older woman who answered her door, she lives alone. She lived there twenty-something years. She's an owner and she had a big problem with renters she said. She wanted more people in the neighborhood to own and get rid of the renters. And she was saying the neighborhood was really quiet, not a lot of crime until "those people"—looking at the people that Mark was talking to, which was an African American family—moved in. So that was really awkward. Mark was on the porch, talking to them and doing the survey and we were on her porch with her, hush-hush. And she was the one whose house got broken into at Christmas and everything under the tree was stolen. The "worst Christmas ever" she called it. She kept looking across the street. It happened after they moved in. She kept going into more instances of other houses being broken into, cops being called, she was just sure it was this family across the street. They were African American and they were renters and she was discriminating against that family for all of the problems on her street
—an undergraduate student

Another Story Circle Story...

If I were... there are many instances of discrimination. If I were to pick one, it would probably be incredibly difficult, but it's just having different experiences based on my gender, particularly in academia, um, and a lot if it is very covert and it's very under wraps and it's very benevolent in nature and

it seems like they're trying to be nice to me, and by being nice ... as an example, my neuropsych. teacher, um, in his effort to be nice, when the women presented in his class, he didn't ask us any questions, he didn't probe us, he didn't challenge our assertions, or challenge anything we had in our presentations; but when the men presented, he would ask them several questions. So, actually, the two men presented first in that class, and I was like, "Oh, crap! I'm going to really have to be on my game!" if this is how it's going to be. And so, I was really on top of things. I studied the assessment. I was doing really well. I was ready to go. And he asked me nothing. And I was ... and I thought ... you've got to be kidding me. And so, then I thought that was really interesting. And so I watched how he was with the rest of the women in the class. He asked no questions of any of the women, but asked several questions to the men. And I was speaking with one of my cohort mates about that in my program, as a man, he said that that wasn't true. That it didn't happen. And that I must have been looking for something. And so, I was really discouraged to hear that. And, uh, yeah. Telling me I'm looking for sexism because I want to see it. Because everyone wants to see sexism, right? (sarcastic) And so, I thought that was kind of horrifying, but I've had it in different instances. In one of my other classes now, with um, I have a female instructor, and she will do the same thing. We have a very small class; there's only six of us, two men, four women. And there are two individuals who really dominate the discussion, a man and a woman. And when she wants to pull somebody in, she doesn't pull the three women in, she pulls in the other man. She'll look at him and say, "Jim, what do you think about this?" And, every time, I'm thinking, you've got to be kidding me! There are three other women here; you are a female; why do you keep asking him what he thinks. Like his opinion is so much more valuable than my opinion and what I would have to say about it ...
—*a graduate student*

As you can see, the focus group examples are exchanges between participants while the story circles contain uninterrupted monologues. Neither of these approaches leaves the speaker free from the possibility of influence from other participants, however, as the focus group participants are responding to each other overtly and the story circle narrators are potentially responding to the content of a preceding story.

III. THE ANALYSIS

This section begins with our (Behrman and Spickard Prettyman's) general observations about the methods and then turns to the specific analyses presented by the students.

Focus groups and story circles are both forms of group interviews that elicit narratives from participants. Group interview data are complex. They are hard to transcribe as people often talk over one another or respond to cues the recorder does not capture. Carey, quoting Silverman, indicates that the goal of analyzing group data like the transcripts of focus groups is to understand participants' "interpretation of reality" (Carey 1995, 448). What researchers ask for and how the group responds constrains the version of interpreted reality available for analysis. As we saw above, focus group protocols emphasize unfettered interaction among participants and participant analysis of the topic at hand. Story circles privilege participants' personal perspectives, constraining dialogue in favor of the individual narrative and postponing group analytic dialogue until after narratives are shared.♦ Focus group protocols attempt to control interaction by structuring the parameters of the exchange content; story circle prompts clearly do not do this sort of structuring, but the story circle process does dictate behavior in the group and actually limits the types of free interchange that focus groups encourage.

> ♦**Donna:** Do participants in story circles talk over one another to the same extent that those in focus groups do?
>
> **Jim:** They shouldn't, if they're respecting the rules that have been outlined. However, I think we've all found that some groups behave rather anarchically and, in that case, you may just have to throw up your hands and let the group's energy take over. Even in those cases, though, you must be vigilant that no one is being left out or asserting their point of view over the whole group.
>
> **Bill:** There might be another dimension to this difference. Focus groups appear to be more like what Barabus (2004) calls discussions and story circles more like what he calls deliberations, where the rules of the game move participants from exchanges likely to reinforce stereotypes and deepen divisions to exchanges that are more likely to result in social learning and movements toward achieving agreement. This seems related to the description that follows, where you distinguish between constraining content versus behavior.
>
> **Carolyn:** Thanks, Bill. I find that distinction helpful.

Despite the differences just mentioned, there is a key, cautionary similarity of which researchers must be aware. Both methods produce data which are non-probabilistic; they cannot be analyzed statistically. Each group is a unique combination of individuals interacting in a specific context so, in effect, each focus group or story circle is not an n of 8 or so individuals but an n of 1 group of individuals. An individual personality may dominate; an individual might feel their position was approximately represented, or unwelcome, or too different or difficult to express. This means that the groups are not representative of the sum of the participants. Although they *cannot* give the researcher an understanding of the range and distribution of experiences, nor the ability to draw reliably representative generalizations of larger groups, the data these group interviews offer are valuable because they can offer dominant themes related to the topics, components of those themes, and an understanding of dynamic relationships among those themes.*

> *Bill: This seems very important. This data helps us unpack and contextualize themes that emerge in the stories, placing an emphasis on the intersubjectivity of experience and communicative action.
>
> Jim: I love this comment. In creating a performance and an ensemble, these are essential guiding principles. One cannot do *Hamlet* as it was done one hundred years ago. And certainly a *Hamlet* created in Akron should behave in a very different fashion from one created in London or Los Angeles. Unfortunately, this kind of rootedness does not appear often enough in our arts, and we end up with a lot of generic works masquerading as universal or popular.

There is a real issue of data loss through censoring and conformity among participants in focus groups that Carey (1995) explores. Some researchers have argued that these problems can be managed to a degree by asking participants to write out answers to the questions based on the protocol before the focus group—sort of cementing their internal opinions and warding against groupthink pressure. The story circle method seeks to acknowledge differences within the group and in the prescribed process therefore asks participants as a group to explore the issue together by looking at stories' themes as well as common and countervailing threads that emerge in the themes.• A further avenue of research would be to explore the ways participants in story circles experience pressure to conform or self-censor in light of preceding stories and others' opinions during the analytic discussion.

> •Amy: This self-censoring is one of the reasons why I discourage entire classes attending Face2Faces together. F2Fs, as another form of group exchange, has the potential to work like these two methods to couch difficult dialogues and can be more open than a classroom because it is a one-time gathering of individuals of whom few, if any, know each other or will meet again.

Recognizing that focus groups have been used and critiqued as a data collection method for many years and that there is no corresponding literature for story circles yet, we will bring up one last concern from the focus group literature. Carey observed a trend across a small number of focus group studies completed before 1995 that she found troubling. When there was a discrepancy between survey and focus group data, researchers consistently privileged the focus group data as "real," but these data were without exception negative or socially critical in nature. So, she asks, is it the case that researchers are primed for critique and that the nature of focus groups result in data that meets expectations? This, Carey pointed out, could be a serious flaw in the method. Kitzinger and Barbour (1999) in their work found some confirmation of this and suggested structuring focus groups to balance opportunities for positive and negative comment. Interestingly, the concern seems to have dropped out of the literature since then. It might be useful to compare story circle and focus group findings on a similar topic to see the degree to which negative or critical themes dominate in their respective data.♦

♦**Bill:** Perhaps unrelated, but I see two challenges here. First, rather than compare positive to negative it seems more useful to compare comments that advance our understanding to those that reinforce tired intellectual trenches. If we do this, then we might, second, wonder if story circles help us overcome a tendency to be *merely* critical by challenging negative-sounding critiques with stories that embed these into a shared struggle for unity within diversity, to community-building, common aspirations, and learning to overcome obstacles to achieving agreements.

Donna: My experience is that story circles produce more positive than negative stories. That is more examples of people behaving in an admirable way than examples of people behaving in hurtful of destructive ways. The stories have more "hope" than "dismay." This may have something to do with the history of "story" which can include adventures and danger but most often emphasizes overcoming adversity. Focus groups tend to come out of business or academia which can include a "bottom line" that is negative or a critique of the system which is seen to be for the improvement of the system whatever that is. Jim should speak to this. As I remember he and his students were concerned that so many of the stories that they consulted in making the Color Line Production described their experience with race as positive. As I recall Jim and his students felt that perhaps the whole story had not been told.

Jim: I don't think that it was so much about whether the stories themselves were positive or negative concerning racism. In fact, most of the stories revealed aspects of racism in Akron that shocked us all. However, it was our own attitude about what we were doing that had a rosy, unreal, aspect to it. Obama had just won the Presidency and, as a group, we were in a kind of euphoria that quickly evaporated once we were able to distance

> ourselves a bit from it. The second version of the performance allowed us to take a more
> critical view of the topic, not the stories. We didn't tell the stories differently, but we
> framed them differently and, for me, that made it a more honest performance. I will
> say that this change of "frame" came about naturally from the group. It was not some-
> thing that I imposed.

Group sizes for story circles and focus groups differ slightly. An optimal story circle is six to eight individuals; focus groups are generally larger, ideally between ten and twelve participants. The question of how many groups one needs to convene in order to feel that one has sufficient information to claim a degree of understanding is important in qualitative analyses. Twohig and Putnam (2002) address how to assess the representativeness of the data when a statistically representative sampling model to research cannot be employed. As they indicated, researchers generally watch for saturation or a point when no new themes or information seem to be emerging from repeated group interviews. Judging this saturation point is much harder in story circles than in focus groups in part because focus groups' protocol dictates a predetermined field of legitimate themes far more strictly than the story circle process.

Another important difference between the two methods is revealed when looking at research design and participants' attributes. Focus groups call for homogeneity within the groups (ideally a group of strangers who are likely to approach the topic in question from roughly similar perspectives, e.g., separating mothers and non-mothers when exploring the topic of childbearing) finding that this promotes rapport during the interview process (Hughes and DuMont 2002). Story circles, on the other hand, call for heterogeneity of experience within the group—ideally a group of strangers who are likely to approach the topic in question from dissimilar perspectives.* Focus groups seek to get people of relatively similar backgrounds in groups to get richness or depth in their data.• Story circles consistently avoid this seeking of uniformity within the groups, with one effect being to maximize exposure of group members to variation in experience. Importantly, both methods encourage participation from vulnerable populations including people who cannot read, people who are reluctant to be interviewed alone, and people who feel they have nothing to say. Finally, both methods call on text and/or content analysis techniques (Miles and Huberman 1994, Bernard, Ryan, and Bernard 2003) in order to identify themes; both techniques place a high value on emic categories[*] and both privilege the perspective of the participant over that of the researcher, although to different degrees.[+]

[*]**Bill:** Important beyond research, since democracy depends on us learning to engage respectfully with those who hold differing views.

[•]**Amy:** Absolutely. Pleasant and positive but not as profound as shared stories in story circles.
Carolyn: I agree, Amy. I have found that both methods leave some participants feeling they have gained or grown through the experience. A possible distinction I would like to explore is that story circle participants seem more often to indicate feeling a new connection to others in the group than I have noticed in focus groups.

[+]**Bill:** Emic?
Carolyn: When thinking about analyzing human social experiences, *emic* refers to the insider's point of view. It is contrasted in anthropology with the *etic* perspective which is the outsider or observer's point of view. The emic perspective is informed by a long and deep involvement with the rules, categories, and ways of thinking that characterize a social group, while the etic perspective is informed by only what can be observed or learned by asking about the group and comparing that to knowledge of other groups and existing theories about group practices. The former is of course more subjective but also rich while the latter offers greater potential for empirical analysis.
Donna: Thank you for introducing the word *emic*. I was not familiar with it and it is a great word for describing the nature of story circle data.

[+]**Donna:** In a room of one hundred people we would quickly exhaust the number of war stories unless the room was full of vets who had seen active duty. It would take much longer to exhaust the discussion of opinions about war. People can have opinions about a far wider range of topics than they have had direct experience with the ideal story circle group is one what contains individuals who have experienced personally the topic of the prompt.
Jim: I'm not so sure about this, Donna. Do we need veterans to tell war stories? Surely, a veteran's experience of war is very different from someone who has never known the battlefield, but the mother of a soldier has a version of war and the son and even the person who stayed home. As a teenager during the Vietnam War who turned eighteen just in time for the final lottery, with an older brother who declared himself a conscientious objector, a mother with three brothers who served, and a father who didn't, I have many war stories of my own.

The students in the combined class worked in their teams and also submitted individual statements regarding the comparison of the methods. Addressing the two methods in terms of how they felt as participants, there was disagreement among the students. Many preferred the focus group experience, which they saw as providing the researcher with ample and more concrete information. It is noteworthy that this perspective was especially strong among the graduate students who were focused on designing their own dissertation research and saw this method as more effectively moving them towards a workable dataset.● "Focus groups are carefully planned and a facilitator keeps them on topic; story circles have more of a general topic, and are very unstructured."◆ They also concluded that focus groups were more effective at building relationships among the participants because they explored more facets of the topic together. They were not discomfited by the possibility that some participants' voices were dominant and others less often expressed in the group.✚

●**Amy:** And a recognized technique more readily acceptable to their dissertation committees?

◆**Bill:** Which means they are a whole lot more like real conversations, capturing a richer picture of how we actually interact, listen, and tell stories.
Carolyn: Bill, I think this is an interesting point. Digging a little further, the students found story circles unstructured when they are actually both structured and constrained, but their structure opens spaces for individuals to speak without interruption, which invokes civility and aligns with our sense of respectful, genuine interaction despite the contrived situation.

✚**Pat:** The variety of forms that the "report back" aspect of the story circle can take is worth noting here both because it calls on different parts of our brains asking for creativity, and because it demands cooperative interaction from the group. I recall during the creative singing of a song as a mode of reporting back (where I learned that Carolyn can really sing and Bill really can't (oops)) that this portion of the story circle protocol created a space for self-disclosure and relationship formation.
Jim: Exactly, Pat. We can't lose sight of this part of the process or we end up putting too much emphasis on the product as the stories themselves. But the product is something else entirely—it's community, compassion, and courage. Human values that are rapidly disappearing from our daily lives. Forget the piddly political discussion about family values. Let's talk human values. It's in family values that fear and racism lurk. They don't exist in human values.

Interestingly, spurred by the graduate student's story about gender discrimination, we, the authors, did a count of the average number of times that individuals spoke as recorded in the full Focus Group 2 transcript by gender. These data indicate that there was a large difference. No corresponding difference appears in the same group of students' story circle transcript.●

> ●Bill: Wow!
> Amy: Yikes!
> Donna: Wow!
> Jim: Triple wow! So it seems that story circles are a feminist tool!

Gender	Undergrad/Grad	# of separate contributions
Female	Grad	10
Female	Undergrad	12
Female	Undergrad	16
Male	Undergrad	32
Male	Grad	43
Male	Grad	44

Some students felt that the story circle experience was more pressured for each participant and "forced" creativity from participants in an "uncomfortable" way.◆ Others found the story circle process more comfortable and satisfying.

> *I thought the story circles were interesting. It reminded me that I was really experiencing "authentic" interaction. The focus group was okay…some of it was okay. Most, I can't even remember. This may be due to the fact that this was my first anthropology class. I also thought the S.C.'s were more intimate.*✦
> —*undergraduate reflection*

> ◆Bill: It is uncomfortable and it should be. I wonder if the feeling of being forced is just another way to express the feeling of being out of one's comfort zone, because passing and silence are highly—and explicitly—respected aspects of the story circle protocols.

> ✦Donna: The emphasis on listening makes "not remembering" less of a problem in story circles.
> Amy: Plus, hearing someone's personal experiences is simply more memorable than hearing one's opinion, don't you think?

Bill: Unless it is my opinion. ☺

Examining the relationship between process and content for the two methods, one team observed that "the value of the focus group discussion often relates directly to the skills and background of the facilitator; in story circles the facilitator can use a primer story and other memory prompts to stimulate the group but it is an open discussion; honest, open and simple stories, you don't even think about it as you talk about it." The same team observed that the methods differ in terms of loud voices and silences. "The people in story circles have a set time that they talk for their story, in a focus group there are those that are dominant talkers and those that do not talk much. In the latter case the facilitator may need to try to get the ones that don't talk much to make their opinions known. In a focus group the facilitator will try to get people to talk when there is a prolonged silence; in story circles silence is good, they can use that time to process information." Finally, they observed that "story circles use emotional data but focus groups try to stay away from hot topics that produce extremely strong feelings."•

•**Bill:** I see this as a strength for story circles then in this comparison as, for progress toward civil society, we need to address hot topics more productively and with those who see things differently.

IV. SUMMARY AND CONCLUSION

Summarizing the key points of comparison from the teams' analyses in chart form below, you can see that these methods have strong similarities and obvious differences as well as clear uses and limitations.

Focus Groups

Useful for identifying dominant themes at the start or during research
Useful for confirming/refuting findings of dominant themes from other data collection
Researchers' protocol frames and guides discussion, guaranteeing that certain topics will be addressed allowing for reliable comparison of groups
Not useful for statistical analysis (each focus group is an n of 1)
Cannot be used to understand range or distribution of experience
Assumes participants are informants

Story Circles

Story Circles
Useful for identifying dominant themes at the start or during research
Useful for confirming/refuting findings of dominant themes from other data collection
Prompt is very open and does not frame or guide stories strongly
Not useful for statistical analysis; but because individual stories are solicited with equal time for each story-teller, is it really an *n* of 1?
Cannot be used to understand range or distribution of experience
Assumes participants are collaborators
Generative and potentially transformative in nature
Participants leave wanting to do it again!

Overall, the balance of preference from the students tipped in favor of focus groups as a research method, especially among the graduate students who, as noted above, felt researcher control over structure was a primary advantage. An example of the opposite opinion comes from an undergraduate, quoted below. In this comment the student hones in on an aspect of story circles, addressed earlier, which might be called its "generative and transformative capacity." Ochs and Capps (2000) identified something like this when they wrote about the difference between telling a story *to* another person and telling a story *with* another person. What they were referring to when they wrote *telling a story to* was performative storytelling or polished storytelling with an intent to teach through the tale. When they wrote *telling a story with* they were referring to the ways we tell stories to others when we are still working things out for ourselves, trying to determine what to make of the story and using the listener actively to help us situate and explore experience we seek to understand.

> *A big difference for me is the fact that focus groups seem to be built to get something from people. It assumes a sort of static state for them—they have experienced or they know something about how they will behave if they do experience something and the researcher just needs the right questions to get it, walk away with it, have it. The story circles seem to be built around the idea that we are all trying to understand something in our world together. The researchers and the participants all want to consider and understand the thing so they explore it together and since listening to each other is likely to move us—maybe closer to each other—we are trying to come to a shared understanding of the thing that respects our different angles on it. I can see*

that analyzing the focus groups is quicker and easier but it also has less dimension because it is sort of pre-determined in a way.
—Undergraduate reflection•

•**Donna:** Reading this chapter has been another turning point (one of many in our work together). I am hooked on the ambiguity, intimacy, and rawness of the story circle experience. I am equally enthralled by the democratic nature of the exchanges. I have been somewhat reluctant to bring it under too much academic scrutiny. But this chapter makes me realize that story circles can take it. They are not delicate flowers that need protection but robust varieties that simply need more light and space.

Jim: Nice analogy, Donna. It comes back to the difference between active and passive culture, participatory democracy, interactive theatre, para-theatre, civic activism, call it what you will. It is what the community needs. Sharing stories connects us to our sources and creates webs of contact that can't be reproduced in any other way.

Bill: Right on Jim and Donna.

REFERENCES

Aldeman, Robert M., and James Clarke Gocker. 2007. "Racial Residential Segregation in Urban America." *Sociology Compass* 1, no. 1: 404–23.

Barabas, Jason. 2004. "How Deliberation Affects Policy Opinions." *American Political Science Review* 98, no. 4: 687–701.

Bernard, H. Russell. 2011. *Research Methods in Anthropology: Qualitative and Quantitative Approaches.* Lanham, MD: Altamira Press.

Brown, Brene. 2010. "The Power of Vulnerability." TEDx Houston, YouTube video. https://www.ted.com/talks/brene_brown_on_vulnerability ?language=en.

Carey, Martha Ann. 1995. "Concerns in the Analysis of Focus Group Data." *Qualitative Health Research* 5, no. 4: 487–95.

Walsh, Katherine Cramer. 2007. "The Democratic Potential of Civic Dialogue." In *Deliberation, Participation, and Democracy,* edited by Shawn W. Rosenberg, 45–63. United Kingdom: Palgrave Macmillan.

Hughes, Diane L., and Kimberly DuMont. 2002. "Using Focus Groups to Facilitate Culturally Anchored Research." In *Ecological Research to Promote Social Change: Methodological Advances from Community Psychology,* edited by Tracey Revenson et al., 257–89. New York: Springer.

Kamberelis, George, and Greg Dimitriadis. 2012. "Focus Groups: Contingent Articulations of Pedagogy, Politics, and Inquiry." In *Collecting and Interpreting Qualitative Materials,* edited by Normal K. Denzin and Yvonna S. Lincoln. Thousand Oaks, CA.: Sage.

Kitzinger, Jenny, and Rosaline S. Barbour. 1999. "Introduction: the Challenge and Promise of Focus Groups. In *Developing Focus Group Research: Politics, theory and Practice,* edited by Rosaline S. Barbour and Jenny Kitzinger, 20. London: Sage.

Lindlof, Thomas R., and Bryan C. Taylor. 2002. *Qualitative Communication Research Methods*, second edition. Thousand Oaks, CA: Sage.

Miles, Matthew B., and A. Michael Huberman. 1994. *Qualitative Data Analysis: An Expanded Sourcebook*, second edition. Thousand Oaks, CA: Sage.

Ochs, Elinor, and Lisa Capps. 2001. *Living Narrative: Creating Lives in Everyday Storytelling*. Cambridge: Harvard University Press.

Rothman, Joshua. 2014. "The Origins of Privilege. An Interview with Peggy McIntosh." The New Yorker online blog. May 13, http://www.newyorker.com /books/page-turner/the-origins-of-privilege.

Ryan, Gery W., and H. Russell Bernard. 2003. "Techniques to Identify Themes." *Field Methods* 15, no. 1: 8109.

Saarni, Carolyn. 1999. *The Development of Emotional Competence*. New York: Guilford Press.

Silverman, David. 1993. *Interpreting Qualitative Data: Methods for Analyzing Talk, Text, and Interaction*. Newbury Park, CA: Sage.

Twohig, Peter L., and Wayne Putnam. 2002. "Group interviews in primary care research: advancing the state of the art or ritualized research?" *Family Practice* 19, no. 3: 278–84.

Once Upon a Time

Story Circles and Public Art in Cascade Village

Donna Webb

*Once upon a time I was a student at Chappell Elementary School. The white
and black kids walked from different sides of Recreation Park, to school. I
remember the names of Susan, Charles, Herbert and Geraldine. Susan was
white and Charles, Herbert and Geraldine were African American.*

*Beginning in seventh grade I attended the consolidated Ypsilanti High
School. One day near the end of the school year, I was walking home when
I saw Geraldine ahead of me. I think that I was walking with Susan. Geraldine was a sinewy girl, a little taller than I. She came up closer and asked
aggressively, "What did you say about me?" I honestly had nothing to report
and said so. She asked again as though she was sure I had been making comments about her and then abandoned her cause, striding away.*

*The next year my dad enrolled me in a small laboratory school for
normal school teachers. That school provided private education for local residents. I never saw Geraldine again. Over the years I thought about Geraldine more than anyone else that I knew at Ypsilanti High School. I wondered why I still remembered her. I sometimes considered using the story of
my encounter with Geraldine as a way of telling about the white experience
of race but it somehow didn't really seem like a story. One day, while listening to a story that included violence, I realized that I had not been afraid
of Geraldine. I became aware that I didn't think that she was planning to
beat me up. I would say "fight" with me but I had never been in a fight with
anyone. I would definitely have been beaten up, if she had chosen to do that
but I didn't remember feeling afraid. That made the experience even more
perplexing.*

*In May of this year, probably an anniversary of my encounter with
Geraldine, it struck me that Geraldine had been reaching out to me. It*

seemed to me that she was challenging me, not with the question of what was I saying about her but with the question of why I wasn't saying anything about her. Why wasn't I noticing? Why weren't we walking home toward Recreation Park together?

According to Dr. Martin Luther King, during the time I was in seventh grade, blacks had half the income of whites. There were twice as many unemployed blacks and the rate of infant mortality among blacks was double that of whites. One-twentieth as many blacks as whites attended college; of the employed blacks, 75 percent held menial jobs. Geraldine, no doubt noticed. I did not.

This story has come to end but there is still story to be told.

I. INTRODUCTION

The preceding story is one that might be told during a story circle. It is an example of a story that provides the opportunity for new awareness. Today, I can imagine Geraldine asking me, "What are you saying now?" I am answering Geraldine through my project, Cascade Village Public Art, and dedicating this chapter to her.

Broadly speaking, my goal here is to describe how I used stories gathered during story circles to create a vibrant public art plan for the Cascade Village community. As you will see, story circles conducted by the Akron Story Circle Project contributed greatly to Cascade Village Public Art (CVPA). The plan for art in Cascade Village came about as the result of a cascading effect typical of story circles. A simple story will sometimes gather momentum and pull us along with it (cascade) to create a larger sense of meaning and urgency.

What follows is a story about a place, a fifteen-month-long project, the interactions of an artist and a community, and some of the meanings and urgencies that spun out or became clearer because of all this. It begins with some background on place (section II). This leads to a description of the Cascade Village Public Art project and an illustration of the interplay of storytelling and art production (section III). I then turn to the importance of story circles for Cascade Village, the ways we specifically used stories as prompts for art, and a consideration of the value of a community illustrating its stories (section IV). This section ends with a particularly important historical story, Miller Horns' story that ties this community into the racial and historical fabric of the wider place that is the city of Akron. I close the chapter (section V) with a few thoughts on story circles and public art, including the work Jim Slowiak and I did with story circles and my recommendations for public art in Cascade Village. Finally, I include a few thoughts about the way this chapter fits into the collective effort of this volume.

II. CASCADE VILLAGE BACKGROUND

The history of Cascade Village has not been written. We suffer from a lack of knowledge that would put the situations faced by current residents into historical perspective. The little information that is available confirms the suggestions made by residents in their stories: the neighborhood was built for local industry and lost ground as this industry declined. It has always had a low-density population. Slum conditions have been recorded at the location of Cascade Village three times during the last one hundred years (Olin 1917, Maples 1974, Endres 2013).

Cascade Village is located in the Elizabeth Park Valley neighborhood, which grew up around the Ohio & Erie Canal in the mid-nineteenth century. Though the area is within walking distance of Akron's downtown, many people still have old canal locks in their back yards. The neighborhood includes a part of the Cascade Locks Historic District and is the site of the restored Mustill Store, which served the needs of canal boat passengers from the 1820s until the end of the nineteenth century. The Towpath Trail running through the neighborhood will one day stretch to one hundred miles, from Lake Erie to New Philadelphia. Even now it brings thousands of hikers and bikers to the area each year. The presence of four railroad track beds, the Little Cuyahoga River, and the old Ohio & Erie Canal help to create a low-density population and a park-like setting in the neighborhood.

Though Elizabeth Park's success as a neighborhood was linked to the growth of population and the economy in Akron, Elizabeth Park did not flourish in equal measure. Akron's population more than tripled between 1910 and 1920 (City of Akron 2016). As early as 1910, industrialists Harvey Firestone and Frank A. Seiberling realized that the housing shortage was detrimental to local industries. They founded Goodyear Heights and Firestone Park as model communities for middle-class white workers. Elizabeth Park Valley remained a neighborhood of poor people. One of the first projects there and the one that resulted in the naming of the neighborhood took place in 1911. Frank Mason, successful Akron businessman, found that a children's playground planned for the North Side along the Little Cuyahoga River did not have adequate funding due to poverty and slum conditions in the neighborhood. Mason purchased the property and improved it to make a playground for the children at a total cost to him of $35,000. Mason then donated the twenty-five acre site to the City of Akron. It was named Elizabeth Park after Mason's daughter, who had passed away (Olin 1917). Two years later the great flood of 1913 destroyed most of the improvements that Mason had added, but the use of the area as a park continued. As migration into Akron increased due to the rubber boom, the African American population rose to 5,580 in 1920. The next year the Akron Ku Klux Klan formed. By the mid-1920s the Klan's membership had grown to 52,000 members and was the largest Klan chapter in the United States (Maples 1974).

In 1944, Mary Peavy Eagle (1909–2003), founder of the Akron Council of Negro Women, heard about a slum clearance program, one of President Franklin Delano Roosevelt's WPA projects. Eagle contacted her councilman, Ray Thomas, and asked for help in getting the project started. He agreed, and the blighted area located near North Street in the area along the little Cuyahoga called Elizabeth Park and inhabited largely by African Americans were replaced by barracks-style, brick residences built by the Akron Metropolitan Housing Authority and called Elizabeth Park Homes. It contained 275 units which rented for from $16 to $19.50 per month (see *Figure 1*). Elizabeth Park Homes was an example of war-time, government-built, multi-family, rental housing property. It was racially mixed and offered housing to the African American workforce.* By the 1990s the rubber industry was all but gone from Akron, and Elizabeth Park Homes had become the new "North Street slums." Elizabeth Park Homes was believed to be the site of criminal activity and was considered beyond repair, needing to be torn down. For example the two-story Elizabeth Park shelter house that was the site of many social events for residents was destroyed in 1993 by "a fire of suspicious origin" (Endres 2013).

*Amy: It's surprising that the housing was racially mixed. Unusual for the time and, given Akron's Klan history, no doubt controversial.

Pat: This was likely an outcome of US poverty during that period.

Bill: Neighborhoods where the *powerful* reside are less racially and economically mixed when compared to *power-poor* neighborhoods.

Akron civic leaders saw opportunity to improve conditions in the Elizabeth Park Neighborhood in 1998, when the HOPE VI program was formally recognized by federal law to revitalize the worst public housing projects in the United States and to create mixed-income housing developments. Mixed-income developments create neighborhoods in which those who receive public assistance live next to those who pay market-value rent and those who own their own homes (Scearce 2009). In 2003 the Akron Metropolitan Housing Authority and experienced HOPE VI partner, The Community Builders (TCB) out of Boston, secured funds to demolish and replace Elizabeth Park Homes, by then a sixty-five-year-old public housing site. TCB was designated as the developer, property manager, and community services provider in the HOPE VI application. The result was that in 2006, Cascade Village (see *Figure 2*) replaced the obsolete Elizabeth Park Homes with 242 newly constructed mixed-income rental and owner-occupied units and became home to 281 residents. The new community featured improved natural and recreational amenities and expanded economic diversity and opportunity for residents. It was constructed at a total development cost of $35 million (The Community Builders, Inc. n.d.). Today the average household income in Cascade Village is $11,988.38. Most of the residents live below the poverty level, either because of disability or lack of jobs (Fisher et al. 2012).•

•**Pat:** Recent statistics note that of the forty-six million US residents who now live below the poverty line, nearly 60 percent are socially marginalized populations. This is despite the fact that all racial and ethnic oppressed populations combined comprise just 37 percent of the US population. Cascade Village mirrors similar communities nationwide.

Bill: Cascade Village is a microcosm of larger stories, a uniquely rich compilation of stories illustrating many aspects, positive and otherwise, about the great American experiment. Your work there, Donna, put story circles into a larger community context, and I wonder how being so deeply embedded within a mixed race, power-poor, brand-spanking-new community context highlighted things about story circles we did not see as clearly on campus or at the Urban League or Belcher House?

Donna: That is a good question! I was always aware that I was not in an academic environment at Cascade Village. My relationship with residents had a very different power dynamic. I was not offering residents money or grades to participate in any of the activities that I offered. I was not even a part of the power structure at Cascade Village. I had no say as to whether they could be evicted or provided with any service that they might expect from staff there. The relationship between me and residents began with and depended on verbal exchanges. So the introduction of story circles may not have been seen as such a leap as it may be seen in a classroom setting. Revealing personal stories in the presence of a professor may be a new experience for students.

Figure 1. Elizabeth Park Homes, 1941. *Photo by Carl Pockrandt, 1941. Courtesy of The Summit County Historical Society of Akron, OH; housed at Akron-Summit County Public Library.*

The background of Cascade Village provided me with both a context and inspiration for the art projects undertaken through Cascade Village Public Art. The stories told by the current residents confirm the recorded history and add a new chapter. They affirm the history of low-density population and the working-class roots of the neighborhood. The neighborhood of hastily constructed buildings and residences located on the Little Cuyahoga River near the Ohio and Erie Canal in the 1820s was transformed in 1912 into Akron's first park for the working class, Elizabeth Park. In the 1940s construction began on the site to house the rubber workers who made the tires for airplanes and military vehicles needed to win World War II. Today 31 percent of the residents of Cascade Village are in the category of ages forty-five to eighty-five. Born between 1929 and 1969, they experienced some of the peak decades of the rubber industry and its decline. They saw first-hand the effects of the Urban Renewal project that leveled the African American businesses along Howard Street near the present Cascade Village. They have stories to tell. Half of the households have children under eighteen. They are the ones I think will benefit from the stories. You will see how this history connects to

Figure 2. The Little Cuyahoga River running through Cascade Village, 2007

a resident of Cascade Village who attended a story circle and told a story about his first job. The storyteller was one of many Cascade Village residents who have struggled in recent years to be part of the workforce. The children hearing this story will soon be attempting to enter the workforce.◆

◆**Donna:** This background information helps remind us that the problem of poverty in this neighborhood is long-standing. The neighborhood was new once before when Elizabeth Park Homes was built. This suggests that story circles which introduce and circulate community information from the bottom up might be an important addition to top-down government-sponsored initiatives like public housing.

III. THE CASCADE VILLAGE PUBLIC ART PROJECT AND THE INTERPLAY OF ART AND STORIES

As I developed what became a fifteen month plan for Cascade Village Public Art (CVPA) activities and projects, I asked: "what kind of public art would be welcome at Cascade Village?" Instead of proposing that a specific piece of public art be made there, I set out to explore the Cascade Village community and its relationship to art in as many different ways as my resources would allow, with the hope that more specific long-term solutions would become apparent in the process. My strategy was to look at the landscape, people, and history of the community as being capable of inspiring art, and to

look at residents of Cascade Village as artists. I was motivated by the opportunity I saw everywhere at Cascade Village to include an artistic perspective.✦

> ✦**Pat:** Donna, this is a wonderful strategy. It reminds me of a discussion we have in my
> Qualitative Research Methods class where I use the metaphor of a "sidewalk" to facil-
> itate their comprehension. I tell my students that I am building "Hill University" and
> ask them "when should I put down the sidewalks—before or after the students arrive?"
> We discuss that while sidewalks are frequently a necessity, they sometimes are con-
> straining. Wouldn't it be great to first discover what emerges from an investigation of
> where people choose to walk to get to certain locations before putting down the side-
> walk? You clearly did not put down a sidewalk first here.
>
> **Jim:** Donna's project makes me think of *creative placemaking*, which is a term that is currently
> being used to describe projects that involve artists in creating community in a variety
> of ways. ArtPlace America (ArtPlace), a long-term collaboration among several founda-
> tions, federal agencies, and financial institutions, defines *creative placemaking* as "projects
> in which art plays an intentional and integrated role in place-based community plan-
> ning and development." *Creative placemaking* brings artists, arts organizations, and artis-
> tic activity directly into the community development process keeping it "locally
> informed, human-centric, and holistic."
>
> **Donna:** In response to Jim's comment, I very much identify with creative placemaking. It
> does not seem to me that public housing is the ideal place to practice placemaking. The
> goal of the staff at Cascade Village is to move people along and out of Cascade Village
> if they are receiving public assistance to pay their rent. It did not appear to me that the
> staff or the residents see Cascade Village as a long-term residential community in the
> way that many of us view our neighborhoods.
>
> **Bill:** Building on Jim's comment.... Just last night, Donna and I participated in a "Com-
> munity Conversation" hosted by the Akron Art Museum. A participant at our table
> suggested a great idea from Milwaukee where the boards used to board up doors and
> windows on vacant property (to be demolished in most cases) are painted by local artists.
>   I thought this was a very cool idea. Clearly Donna's work bringing art and an artis-
> tic perspective to Cascade Village is designed to work upstream, to strengthen a com-
> munity rather than provide a band-aid, but these are all illustrations of using art and
> an artistic eye to create and strengthen community life.
>
> **Donna:** I attended two community meetings that week. One at the Akron Art Museum
> was 90 percent white and the second at the Second Baptist Church was 90 percent
> African American. I believe they would both have benefited from a joint meeting. As
> Theaster Gates said in the opening remarks of his exhibition at the Milwaukee Art
> Museum in 2010 regarding his inclusion of a gospel choir at the museum, this was
> "temple swapping" and "When the museum and the church conflate, boy is that sexy"
> (Gates 2010).

The CVPA project, funded by the Knight Foundation (through Community Builders Inc.) for 2012–2013, was designed to strengthen the com-

munity at Cascade Village through art. In addition, the award of a Faculty Improvement Leave from the University of Akron gave me time to explore my interest in the intersection of community, art, and science. Two faculty initiatives to which I belong, Synapse and the Akron Story Circle Project, also provided resources to this project.

Synapse is an initiative at the University of Akron to encourage collaboration between artists and scientists. Faculty members in art, design, biology, polymer science, engineering, and computers have worked together since 2009 on a variety of exhibitions, lectures, and residencies as well as classroom projects. This group has provided me with new ways to engage with social change through science and art. The Akron Story Circle Project gave me access to an expanded personal experience of race and a glimpse into the diverse research conducted by my colleagues in the group. The Akron Story Circle Project values stories because sharing individual stories can, among other things, contribute to community history. Stories told in organizations reveal deeply held assumptions. It has been said that the images and metaphors that are used in organizational storytelling influence our individual world view (Kaye 1996). These functions can be expanded by bringing in new story-tellers and by "revisiting old stories" (Boje 1995, 1117). As Forster et al. point out, stories "act as both mirrors and windows on the human experience, showing people either how to look at reality in a different way or suggesting alternative realities" (1999, 14). Storytelling as described here is an important and credible aspect of art making.

Bill Traynor, of Lawrence Community Works and a consultant to TCB, has much to say about working with the residents at Cascade Village. He had several meetings with the staff there during my sabbatical project. Traynor believes that when creating programs to expand social and economic opportunities for residents of public housing:

> *The forms of engagement are shifting.* We're shifting away from highly structured forms of long-term commitment to looser, more flexible forms of engagement. We need to find the forms of engagement that feature—rather than fight—these trends. One of the ways Lawrence Community Works has embraced this shift is by offering many different doors of entry to the network and by creating more provisional, flexible, action-oriented forms of engagement....(in Scearce 2009, emphasis mine)

Using my experiences with Synapse and Akron Story Circle; my knowledge
of ceramics, public art, photography, drawing, and storytelling; plus the
support of colleagues in the social sciences, hard sciences, and the arts, I was
able to offer residents of Cascade Village *many different doors of entry* to community awareness and participation. My goal was to create experiences that
would allow residents to explore the landscape, history, and people of Cascade
Village, combining the observational techniques of artists, biologists, and
social scientists to tell their stories. For example, on one of the first CVPA
events, young people at Cascade Village participated with a biologist on hikes
along and into the Little Cuyahoga River to measure water quality. The young
people took photographs and made drawings of this experience which we
displayed where the children and their parents could view them. On another
hike we walked with a City of Akron engineer to look at the future site of an
$8 million sewer improvement project at the edge of Cascade Village property.
Not only is this project the first of an $870 million project with the potential
to create jobs for those living at Cascade Village, but it lies adjacent to a small
wetlands that will be preserved by the city as part of its environmental effort.
It is also the area of the local woods where the Pig Man is said to live—more
about that later. Calling attention to the landscape at Cascade Village is in
keeping with a long tradition with which art looks to nature for inspiration.•

•Bill: Story circles are an amazing tool for helping us to see our world differently. We see
connections between statistical and narrative data that we did not see before. Story
circles allow us to see and understand both types of data more deeply, by integrating
two ways of seeing. In the same way, artists and scientists in collaboration both share a
profound appreciation for the importance of careful observation and bring two complimentary ways of seeing into a single conversation.

I organized ceramics classes in which residents made many pots, as well
as classes for children in which they drew and painted and took photographs
and sewed on buttons they had made by hand. I helped children plant seeds
in the community garden and allowed them to create paintings of the
garden and its produce. These and other activities that I will discuss later
in the chapter, according to Jessica Russell, Senior Community Life
Manager at Cascade Village, "gave residents of Cascade Village opportunities to explore various art mediums that will ultimately enrich and enhance

their lives" (Russell 2013). As successful as the art activities were in general, in my opinion, the most universal and iconic art forms to emerge during the year were the stories told and illustrated by residents of Cascade Village. Critical to this process were the story circles with residents led by the Akron Story Circle Project. The prompt given during the two story circle sessions described here was to "tell a story about growing up."♦ Since many of the participants in the story circles grew up in Elizabeth Park, the stories were a part of the history of Cascade Village as well. As I will describe, we passed on some of the stories told by older storytellers to younger listeners who illustrated the stories. The stories contained perspectives on race that seemed to have been tempered by time and by wisdom.✦ The story circles and the process of illustrating the resulting stories reveal the residents of Cascade Village to be unique and creative individuals, as evidenced both by their storytelling and their ability to illustrate those stories.

♦**Amy:** The prompt is so important. It must be broad enough to allow everyone to participate but narrow enough to provoke specific stories.

Pat: I agree on the importance of the prompt to the direction of the conversation. But I have noticed in several story circles that a particular story told early on totally shifted remaining stories to a different direction.

Carolyn: This phenomenon is something we grappled with when we compared focus groups to story circles. It seems to me that the impact of a dominant story on a circle is less problematic than the impact of a dominant personality on a focus group, but there is room for argument here and this is a discussion worth having.

Jim: This makes me think that there is an aspect to story circles that we haven't yet touched upon, which is the conflict resolution aspect. For example, I remember John talking about resolving a problem of the "use of the kitchen" in an office environment through story circles. I imagine we would each tell a story about how our lunch was stolen one day or how we had to clean up someone else's mess or get stuck day after day doing the dishes. Keeping it in the story mode, not the "whining" or "bitching" mode—keeping it on this level makes us realize that the power of story circles is not only historical or sentimental or archival. It really is a placemaking tool.

Bill: Placemaking and peacemaking, which are, of course, intertwined.

✦**Bill:** The students in the first class I worked with as a part of this project, when John came to my class and ran story circles, felt strongly that future storytelling would be even better with multi-generational participants. For this reason, the next class—the one my chapter in this volume focuses on—partnered with the Urban League. And the students were right, confirmed again by your insight here.

A. First Story Circles at Cascade Village

June 2, 2012 was Community Day at Cascade Village. Various organizations such as Youth Excellence Performing Arts Workshop (YEPAW), the Cancer Society, and Akron Public Schools were in attendance. Ferris Brown, executive director of the Cascade Locks Association was present, making balloon animals for the children. It was a beautiful day and several hundred residents turned out. The CVPA table was located near the Community Center. There were sign-up sheets for pottery classes for adults and children. Two art students from the University of Akron gave demonstrations of throwing on the potter's wheel, which drew many observers. The Akron Story Circle Project members were in attendance as well to facilitate story circles that day and to promote a second round of story circles later in the fall. My husband Joseph Blue Sky acted as barker, calling people over to the Akron Story Circle Project table by extolling the virtues and adventure to be had within the story circle.• We had a youth circle and an adult circle at noon and again at one. Participants were asked to tell a story about growing up. The youth focused on the various ways it was possible to be embarrassed and to fall down in public, leading to peals of laughter which spilled over into the adult circle.

•**Pat:** I remember that day so clearly—experiencing so many wonderful stories. But Joe's "barking" was particularly memorable.

Jim: I remember thinking that day about the importance of neighborhood. Previously, we had done story circles in apartment complexes, on campus, or in churches or other institutional settings. This was the first time that I recall being in a neighborhood environment and the feeling of belonging, roots, and home was very strong.

Bill: The feeling of excitement, kids running in every direction, games being played, clay being formed, painted faces smiling and singing made the story circles feel less fragmented and more integrated, like a calm moment in storm of hubbub where some took a moment to reflect and listen.

Donna: I remember that day as being a perfect mix of academic gravitas (thanks to the Akron Story Circle Project) and community joy (thanks to the weather and to the Cascade Village residents.)

Carolyn: In addition to the joyous sounds and colors of the day, I particularly remember a quality to the circles. They were a little more unruly than other story circles in an exuberant sort of way. We all went with the mood and loosened the format/structure a bit. In the adult circle, some people slipped in after it started, some had to leave before it was done. Some stayed and stayed and the Pig Man stories were told collaboratively at the close. The adolescent group was giggly and loud but sincere in their participation before breaking apart to bubble out the door and rejoin the celebrations outside.

The adult stories included those that described the crime in Elizabeth Park Homes as well as those that described joyful events. One story was about the youth gangs that permeated the old neighborhood. It emphasized that gangs, while violent, could also provide help and protection. Another story was told by an elderly doctor who did house calls in Elizabeth Park in his youth. He was sometimes not paid for his services and considered Elizabeth Park a dangerous place. Other stories stressed the fun of growing up in a close-knit community where young residents built forts and play houses out of pilfered cardboard boxes. Several people told stories about a local boogeyman called "the Pig Man" who was evoked by parents to convince young people to be at home before dark.♦ The Pig Man and his equally dangerous family allegedly lived in the woods east of Elizabeth Park Homes and later, in Cascade Village. The story of the Pig Man and his family was repeated later in our October story circles as well as during storytelling on camping day.

♦**Bill:** The stories collected by my students in the Law & Society class described in chapter one also focus heavily on crime and punishment. Like your storytellers, we heard a more nuanced reading of the nature of criminal activity in contexts where powerful agencies like the police clash with and within power-poor communities. Despite mass media depictions of these communities as entirely unlike those more powerful Americans are familiar with, these communities—as shown in your stories—also have family doctors doing house calls, colorful local legends, and more.

Carolyn: This is one of the things I love about really engaging with the wider community. In my work on the other side of town with a student using story circles to study something called "nature deficit disorder," we encountered tales of the Pig Man. This is an example of this story circle enterprise illuminating a facet of regional or local knowledge that history, anthropology, or folklore students might want to pursue.

Jim: I wonder why "Pig Man"? Perhaps there was a wild pig in the woods at one time that had escaped from someone's farm? In any case, it reminds me of the story of the neighborhood witch. She was an old woman who lived alone in a decaying house on the street, and the rumor was that she could make potatoes fly. I laugh now when I think about it because clearly one day, when some kids were bothering her, she threw some potatoes at them. That's how the potatoes flew!

B. More Cascade Village Public Art: Many Different Doors of Entry

Many of the stories told in the story circles at Cascade Village were positive and were the result of activities that bought people together. So it must also be true that activities that brought people together could result in new stories and might be described as story-building activities. I think of story-building as the conscious constructing of opportunities in the hope that stories may result. Opportunities to engage in story building by creating *provisional, flexible, action-oriented forms of engagement* seemed to be everywhere. A brief and incomplete list of CVPA projects and events that I hope will result in story-building follow.

During the Summer Youth Program I moved three potters' wheels into the café in the Community Center. Though it was a bit awkward to teach pottery with no real working space, storage space, or utility sink and only three wheels, each of the thirty children made several pottery projects over a two-week period and a small group of adults made pottery for more than a month. This adult group became "Cascade Creates," which met throughout my sabbatical year and is still meeting today. Members of Cascade Creates bring their expertise to the group by teaching and learning; first pottery, then jewelry, crocheting, and sewing. The children and adults, who like to make things, became an ongoing source of friendship and support for Cascade Village Public Art.✦

✦**Pat:** Donna, I think that you gave these residents a valuable gift by creating this space for the sharing of common concerns and interests. It reminds me of the many conversations that Carolyn and I have had about the valuable role that our book clubs play in our lives. We meet monthly to discuss not just the books we read, but also to enjoy the company of other women. We share personal experiences and offer emotional support. We also offer personal and practical advice and tips to help others cope with their situations. I can just imagine that the Cascade Creates group value their time together and find it helpful just getting to talk with others who are in the same boat.

Donna: This might be the place to say that the Akron Story Circle Project has also created a space for the sharing of common concerns and reminds me of all the generosity and warmth I experienced within this group.

When the Summer Youth Program director planned a field trip to the Cleveland Zoo, CVPA asked to go along and provided the children with drawing materials to do sketches of the animals. It was a hot day at the zoo. The kids were dispersed in small groups with other adults. I did not see them for most of the day. I did not expect evidence of much drawing. It was very exciting to find that fifteen children created more than one hundred drawings of the animals that day. These drawings are contained in a self-published book, *Cascade Village Goes to the Zoo* (see *Figures 3* and *4* for examples).

The success of the drawing project at the zoo led to a plan to have the children illustrate the stories about growing up told by adults in story circles.

PoLerBear

Figure 3. Polar Bear by Antwoan Lollis, Age 10

In an effort to get kids out of the air conditioning and into the July land-scape of Cascade Village, CVPA organized a day-long camping experience. The older kids prepared "hobo" dinners. We set up tents in the morning and built a campfire with supervision from the Akron Fire Department. The kids went in small groups down to the Little Cuyahoga River to explore the water under the supervision of Scott Thomas, a graduate student in biology from the University of Akron. The kids cooked lunch and later a snack over the campfire, did drawings and watercolors of the aquatic life they found in the river, and got to see a snake, frog, toad, salamander, and turtle close enough to touch. At the end of the day we told stories about what happens at Cascade Village at night. These included stories of the mythical Pig Man and Pig Family that live just north of Lods Street in the woods. The chil-dren who chimed in to tell the story of the Pig Man revealed that it was most dangerous to be near the Pig Man's house at night.•

•**Pat:** I recall being very intrigued with the Pig Man stories as an "insider" legend or "pos-session" retained and re-transmitted through generations of residents.
Bill: I recall the same, as well as wanting more. Where did this story come from? How did this story play out in the community? Was it used to scare kids so they would stay away from a dangerous location—like the pond at the end of my street growing up, which was forbidden—or to marginalize a family or section of the neighborhood? Does the story have multiple versions? Is it rooted in reality in any way—that is, is there a pig

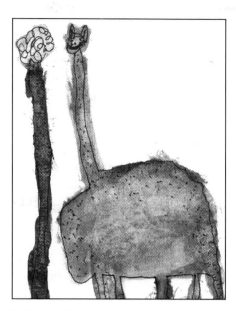

Figure 4. Giraffe by Montajsia Nixon, Age 9

man or pig family and, if so, who are they and where are they now and how did they come to be seen as the pig family?

In the summer of 2013 the Senior Community Life Manager at Cascade Village asked CVPA to repeat the camping experience. The tents, trip to the river, drawing, painting, and cooking-out were repeated, and in addition the kids planted two Bing cherry trees and learned to care for them. Kevin O'Shea, the tree expert, also hooked his tree trimming harness to a swing-set and let the kids hoist each other several feet off the ground. This was their favorite activity.

Other sources for the interplay of stories and art arose from the cultivated environment. In 2012, the Akron Urban Gardeners[1] wrote a grant to create a garden in remembrance of people who had lost their lives by jumping off the Y Bridge that passes over Cascade Village. Included in the memorial garden is a community food garden. The grant allowed the gardeners to plant tomatoes, mustard greens, peppers, squash, and many herbs in the garden. By August no one was going to the garden and most of the produce went unpicked. CVPA took the children from the Cascade Village Y Summer Program and

Figures 5 and 6. Photos by Annalisa Duncan, age 9

then the After School Program, to the garden, first to weed and then to pick
the produce. The children offered the produce, as well as watercolors they had
created of the garden, for sale at the Community Yard Sale at the end of

Figure 7. Weeding the Garden

August 2012. The children really enjoyed going down to the garden and often ask when they will be able to go again. In the summer of 2013 CVPA invited the children in the Y Summer program to plant tomatoes, peas, and carrots in the garden. The program can give the children only pre-packaged food as part of their effort to provide safe food for the children. Seeing peas blooming and forming pods and carrots being pulled from the ground was a brand new experience, one that I hope to hear about in a story circle years from now.

C. More Story Circles at Cascade Village, October 2012

In October of 2012, the Akron Story Circle Project invited residents of Cascade Village to a second round of story circles. An invitation was included in the October *Cascade Village Voice* newsletter. A dozen residents arrived at the Community Room in the Midrise Building, in Cascade Village.

We made two circles, one led by Bill Lyons and Carolyn Behrman, the other led by Pat Hill and me. The participants were prompted to tell a story about growing up "back in the day." When the first round of stories was completed we stopped to eat chili, chicken and rice, corn bread, salad, and cider. Then the second group began arriving and the two groups ate together and socialized. We then did a second round of stories with eight residents.

The stories told in October 2012 by adults at Cascade Village were collected and stored in our archives at the Active Research Methods Lab (ARM Lab)

Figure 8. Photo by Fred Stuckmann, Photographic Fellow at Cascade Village

at the University of Akron. My plan to retell these stories to children who reside at Cascade Village came from a number of converging ideas. John O'Neal and Theresa Holden have always encouraged creative use of stories collected about race.♦ The theme of "growing up back in the day," while not always yielding stories appropriate for children, is bound to yield some lessons learned and worth passing on. This was the case at Cascade Village. Themes of the first job, the neighborhood at night, and the value of eccentric neighbors emerged with potent and entertaining messages for children. The demographics of Cascade Village show a relatively high proportion of young children and single mothers and so the number of adults who might be available to tell stories to children may be low, compared with families in which there are two parents. The low ratio of adults to children in families made the sharing of stories all the more important. So it seemed reasonable to survey the collected stories to find those that might be interesting and appropriate for children.

♦Jim: John and Theresa encourage using the stories as a pretext, a kind of runway, to put lots of other projects into flight. While the stories have a value in and of themselves, we really need to consider how to incorporate the stories into the larger cultural landscape. Performances, like *The Akron Color Line Project Performance* contained in this volume, are one possibility. Artwork, storybooks, research projects, political action, exhibits, festivals are some other outcomes from story circles that communities might consider.

A goal of Cascade Village Public Art is to encourage the use of local experiences as inspiration for art. The children had already been successful at illustrating animals they saw at the zoo. In order to encourage the continued use of drawing to enhance experience, I asked children in the Cascade Village YMCA After School Program to illustrate the stories about 'growing up' gathered from the October story circles.

IV. IMPORTANCE OF STORIES AT CASCADE VILLAGE

As described earlier in this chapter, stories not only tell about individual experiences, they also consolidate opinion and confirm values. The reputation of Elizabeth Park Homes (the housing project torn down to make room for Cascade Village) is for the most part negative. Public discussion leading to the tearing down of Elizabeth Park Homes described the area as blighted (City of Akron 2005).* Nevertheless, the first story circles on Community Day 2012 about growing up there 'back in the day' revealed that there were also many positive memories. It is especially important to highlight these positive memories because Cascade Village is still commonly referred to as Elizabeth Park by longtime residents of the city. For example, residents report that when they say that they live in Cascade Village they are often asked where that is. They respond that they live where Elizabeth Park used to be. The Elizabeth Park explanation clears up the mystery. Though some residents grew up in Elizabeth Park and are aware that people in Akron have a negative opinion about the place, story circles revealed that people also flourished in Elizabeth Park. This coexistence of opposite points of view can be heard in LeBron James' autobiography.

> I biked up the north side into a section of the city known as the Bottom•
> and went past the Elizabeth Park projects—my own home for a time—
> two-story apartment buildings in unsmiling rows, some of which had
> been condemned, some of which had been boarded up, some that had
> screen doors with the hinges torn off or the wire mesh stripped away. I
> headed back west and biked along Portage Path, a wealthy section of
> town with sprawling houses of brick and stone and shiny black shutters
> all perfectly aligned. (James and Bissinger 2009, 6).

*Amy: In my graduate courses in Urban Studies at the University of Akron, we often utilized Elizabeth Park as case study in blight and potential renewal.
Bill: Donna is now working in, living within, that renewal process.

•Bill: Story circles go to rock bottom, raising us up by grounding us in experience as Pat argues, and teaching us how to navigate a world where our experiential frameworks can be so remarkably different. Donna's storytellers were describing a place and communities that many see as on the bottom, geographically and socioeconomically in the Akron area. In a story circle we all come down to the bottom, grounding our interactions in our stories. This started as something, but now I am not sure where I was going with this bubble! Just struck by the image of Bottom here.

Donna: In talking to my students about Cascade Village I heard several of them refer to it as the Bottom. So that term has not disappeared.

Carolyn: In my research over on the other side of town, I found material on employment and residence patterns in Akron in the 1800s and early 1900s. Employers and the city were anxious to create a vibrant city here. There were several waves of successful industry here before the rubber tire industry took firm hold so even before the rubber boom, there was money going to infrastructure and city services. One of the most important were the neighborhood schools. The neighborhood schools concept, which originated in Akron, was meant to allow children easy, walkable access to schools. Income-linked school taxes paid for these schools but black children were not permitted to enroll. (Small consolation but the school tax was not deducted from their parents' pay.) The poorest workers and all black workers clustered in the least desirable locations where schools were not built. These areas included the low-lying, easily flooded areas like the site of Elizabeth Park. These sorts of areas are often referred to as Bottoms.

James goes on to say this about Akron later in his book:

> Whatever I went through, I always loved Akron. Even back then, growing up in the 1980s and 1990s, there was one thing that always bothered me. In school, whenever I looked at a map of the United States—because you know how schools are, there is always a map of the United States in every classroom—the first thing I did was look at Ohio. There was Cleveland, of course, because everybody knew Cleveland, former home of the legendary Browns and Jimmy Brown, home of the Indians. On some maps there might be the state capital of Columbus. Or even Cincinnati. But where was Akron? How come there was never Akron? (James and Bissinger 2009, 8).

The stories included in this section were collected during the October story circles. They deal with important aspects of growing up: landing that first job, getting to know our local landscape at night, and the richness added to life by getting to know neighbors. These stories tell very different narratives than those I heard from adult residents outside the story circles. The difficulty of getting a job seldom is discussed with the light touch provided by Mr. Eddie Turner. Though the night time is often frightening to both adults and children, Miss Val Moss's story helped the children to see night as a lovely and poetic experience. Finally, Miss Val Robinson's story of her eccentric but generous neighbor illustrates the possibility that neighbors can enrich one's life in ways that have nothing to do with money.✦

> ✦**Donna:** All three stories are in the ARM Archive but they are difficult to sort out from the other stories. It would be a good idea to put the three stories in one file so that they can be accessed. However, the text included with this chapter is identical with that of ARM Archive for each of the included stories.

A. Illustrating the Stories

We brought the children of Cascade Village together on three occasions to create illustrations for the stories collected in the October story circles.✦ Illustration of the first story took place on January 19, 2013 (see *Figures 9* and *10*). This was a day off for the Akron Public Schools so nearly twenty children took part in the YMCA day care program that day.

> ✦**Amy:** What a fantastic idea, Donna! Such a creative way to allow the children to relate to the adults. The results that you've included in this chapter are wonderful.

Mr. Eddie Turner was scheduled to arrive at three to retell the story of his first job. Mr. Turner had not arrived by three. Since the children were ready and waiting, I showed them our book, *Cascade Village Goes to the Zoo*, illustrated by children in the summer of 2012. We could all see how well the drawings illustrate the trip to the zoo many of these same children took the previous summer. I wanted them to be confident that they could illustrate a story.

I explained that they could use the same technique used in the zoo drawings. The children drew the animals with a pencil or magic marker as a way of planning out the illustration. Watercolor was applied in a second process to provide color and a sense of atmosphere and place. Since Mr. Turner was still not present and it was not clear if he was coming, I told the story of his first job which I had heard during the October story circle and read a second time by consulting the ARM archive of stories. I like the story very much and was able to tell it with enthusiasm, if not with the authenticity of Mr. Turner.

Like all story circle stories, Mr. Turner's story was short, about three minutes. After the story was told the kids asked questions. They wanted to know if Mr. Turner got in trouble with his parents at the end of the story and if he ever got paid for his first job. I asked the kids to provide "snapshots" of their impressions of the story.• I asked them how they would have felt in Mr. Turner's situation. They were then asked to create a drawing of something that happened in the story. When the drawing or mapping out of the events of the story was completed the kids were offered watercolors to enhance the drawings as seen in *Figure 10*.

•**Donna:** The "snapshot" is a story circle technique or stage in the process that happens immediately after the last story has been told. Participants are invited to describe the image that came to them during a story. As these "snapshots" are shared participants are helped to remember the stories they have just heard.

Pat: I love the "snapshot" aspect. It is always interesting to me to discover the participants' interpretations of what they learned from these stories—filtered through the lens of their own lived experience.

Jim: Yes, and it's interesting to notice through which "channel" they have been absorbing the stories. In Performance Ecology, we use some terminology from process psychology. We each have a primary channel through which we tend to perceive what is happening around us: visual, aural, proprioception, movement, relationship, or the world. Sometimes to suggest that someone change their channel of perception allows for a breakthrough in how he/she navigates life.

Bill: Snapshots are powerful. I struggle with attaching an image to a story, but the struggle was always worth it, because it did re-channel my own perceptions of the stories and what I was hearing from the stories.

At this point in the process, Mr. Turner arrived. I invited him to tell his story. He asked for a chair and began to tell the story with enthusiasm. He included details that I hadn't known, since they were not included in the transcript of his story from the story circle. These included his discussion with the police and with his parents afterwards. The kids seemed to enjoy hearing the story again. For me it was not ideal because the children continued to work on their paintings during his telling of the story and may not have been able to respond to some new aspect of the story since their drawing or outlines of what had happened had, in some cases, already been completed. Even though things did not go as I had expected, the story itself was so engaging that it seemed effective when I retold it and was received enthusiastically in the re-retelling by Mr. Turner.

The success of Mr. Turner's story reminds me of what Claude Levi-Strauss said about the difference between a myth and poetry. He felt that poetry relies

Figure 9. Mr. Eddie Turner telling the story, My First Job

on the exact nature of, and precise use of, words to be effective. Myth, on the other hand, can be told in many ways by many different people and still remain potent (Levi-Strauss 1955, 210). I feel that Mr. Turner's story operated like a myth in the Cascade Village community, where it was retold powerfully—in words and pictures—by many. This story is worth telling many times.◆ The illustrations that the children did are charming and show promise in terms of both their aesthetic quality and ability to communicate. One interesting thing to me about these illustrations is that the children all drew the house very large and Mr. Turner very, very small.✦

◆**Carolyn:** I especially like the ways that resilient variations from the core story circle method have been arising as we have moved out into our fields to pursue our work. In this case, reiteration is vital. Like poetry or other symbolic literature, retelling becomes the linked chain that connects the basic method to Donna's discipline's many forms.

Donna: Each of the three storytellers included in this chapter retold their stories at a Slide Jam event at the Akron Art Museum in March of 2014. A Slide Jam allows many different presenters to share ideas very quickly with the audience. My three storytellers misunderstood the request to tell their stories in the same way they told them originally. They each thought that our groups' ten-minute limit belonged to them alone! The result was three much longer versions of their original stories. They had no problem retaining their original spontaneity and charm in the longer versions, each speaking without notes and delivering an expanded version of their story.

Carolyn: This story or retelling stories makes me think that we should consider how stories change as they are retold and how we change peoples' stories when we retell them.

⁺Bill: As an artist, does this say something to you? Can you elaborate? It would be great to hear more. Does his absence (from the first telling) impact the size in the illustration because they were less able to imagine him in the flesh?

Donna: Children from ages five to ten may draw people of different sizes in the same drawing. The choice of scale probably relates to the perceived importance of the person to the child. In this project there is only one small figure in each drawing. In each case the figure is small relative to the very tall roof upon which the figure stands.

Text of Mr. Eddie Turner's Story, "My First Job":

I'm Edward Turner, known as Papa and I was born in Georgia, right in Georgia, but I moved to Ohio when I was like five years old but I was raised up in north Akron right down in the Elizabeth Park area which is known as Cascade Village now (laughs).

Though my name is Edward Turner, everybody call me Eddy but the people that know me in Cascade Village call me Papa.

I remember a time when I was back younger, a lot younger... on the north side. I was going to junior high you know back in the days it was called... junior high school.

Yea it was... and I meet this pastor, I met this pastor and we was talking and stuff and he told me, he said, I was looking like a promising young man and he wanted to teach me some trades. You know so first I said I needed to talk it over with my parents and everything and see what they, you know, have to say about it. And so he said, "I can go with you and meet your parents and everything. I'm a pastor. My name is John...." and I'm like, "John... is kind of an odd name for a pastor" (laughs) you know "well you said you're a pastor, ok."

So I took him home, met my parents and he talked to my parents and everything, so he told my dad that he's going to teach me how to do roofing work, you know stripping down the shingles off of the roof and laying down new shingles and everything. So you know I was very interested in that 'cause you know I like to do all kinds of work with my hands and stuff, you know. And so once he got finished explaining and everything to my parents I spoke up and said, "How much I'm gonna make?" you know. And he said "Don't worry you're going to be paid real swell! Real swell!" I said, "Ok." I said, "Yea, I'll go along with you and you know and I didn't mind." You know and so that day came and he came and got me early in the morning. Came and got me and we went to the location where we were supposed to be working doing the roofing job. And I didn't see nobody at home you know and everything. So I figured well you know, it's a vacant house, somebody probably getting ready to buy it and move in, you know. He didn't tell me that the owner of the house had left to go to work early in the morning and

Figure 10. Illustration for My First Job by Lauren

wasn't going to be there until evening, so to make a long story short we hook up the equipment, put up the ladder and stuff and everything, got up the roof so we could start stripping the roof, ok.

    So when it came time to start stripping the old shingles off the roof to put down the new shingles, the pastor told me, he said, "I have to make a run, ok? I'm going to leave you up here because I've shown you what to do; you know what to do and everything so I'm going to leave you in charge." Quite naturally, I'm the only one up there on the roof; I'm going to be in charge you know (laughter). He goes down the ladder over there and I'm just stripping the roof and tearing up roof and the next thing I know I hear some "ReaaaBoom!" you know. Like, "Oh!" So I go over to the other side of the roof to see that ladder fell down (laughter). Now, I'm stuck up here on this, way up, on this roof (laughter) and ain't a soul passing by nowhere, you know. And I'm wondering "How am I going to get down from here?" You know the pastor gone; he said he'll be back. So I said, "Ok, I'll take a squat." And I sit down on the roof and waited, and I waited and I waited (laughter) and I waited. No pastor and didn't see nobody pass by so after a while it started to get dark, you know.

    All of a sudden I hear this car pull into the drive way, I looked over and it's some lady getting out of the car, you know. So I yell, "Hey Miss! Hey Miss!" And I scared the living daylights out of her 'cause she ran straight

Figure 11. Bats by Jakai Mills

into the house and called the police, ok (laughter). Cops get there talking about, "What are you doing up there on that roof?" (laughter). And I'm like "I'm stuck!" (laughter) "I'm stuck, can you help me? Can you help me?" And the officer finally pulled up the ladder you know and I got down off the roof and they still arrested me. They saying I tried to break in this woman's house and she so scared. "That man up there on my roof I don't know anything about him (laughter) and he trying to come in." And I'm like, "Oh lord, where is the pastor, where is the pastor?" (laughter). Finally the officers put me in the car and everything and they talk to me and I explained my story to them so they took me home right. Next day come, here come the pastor you know, I was so heated and frustrated, but I had to remember, "pastor, pastor." I said, "Why did you leave me stuck up on the roof?" He said, "You know what brother, I forgot all about it I had to go to work and I forgot about you was up on the roof." "Well I'll tell you one thing, I will never work for you again." (laughter) And that's what happened.

Illustration of a second story took place on March 1, 2013. Ms. Valerie Moss (see *Figure 12*) arrived at the Community Center in the afternoon after the children arrived from school. She had the printed text of her story from

Figure 12. Val Moss

the October story circles and also brought some images of bats so the kids could imagine the story more vividly. None of the children had seen a bat at Cascade Village, though they are common in Akron. They liked the idea of the bats and saw them as positive in light of the superhero, Batman. As she told her story, Miss Valerie Moss allowed the children to imagine a night sky full of bats. (See *Figure 11*)

Text of Valerie Moss's Story, "Creatures of the Night: A Bat Tale"

I was trying to decide what story to tell first. There are of course, there are so many of them. The one that keeps coming to mind is something that happened while I was living in West Virginia. I was brought up in West Virginia. At that time, of course, we had outhouses and had to pump our own water and we had to get the wood from the shed. And of course, the place I lived at in West Virginia was just one road. It was called The Holler. I don't know if you're familiar with that (laughter). And of course in that holler it's just black, know all black people in the holler on just one big dirt road.

But the most fun I had living there was swinging on the porch swing, of course, not wanting to go to the bathroom at night 'cause I didn't want to go out there 'cause the snakes were out there . . . in the back yard. But, one of the fun things that we had was waiting for it to get dark 'cause we didn't have street lights, only thing we had was the moon. Might have been one light in that holler and depending on where you lived you couldn't, you know, see it in that holler. But the most fun was when it got dark, the bats came out and they would swarm over, you know, and fly over our heads and that was what I loved (laughs)... we would chase the bats, the bats would chase us. They would, would come down and they would come down and we would run (laughter) and so that was one of my fondest memories (laughter). It was...

...It was called a holler, called a holler; it's what's called a holler....A holler, a holler is where you go, it's like a, a gully type thing. It's like a valley.

Yea and it's just called a holler and it was like this: the mountain was there and on the other side was the railroad tracks and, just you know, just another bunch of woods and so we'd have to walk down pass the railroad tracks, tracks to the springs and get our water or we had to pump it you know from, from a well.

Illustration of the third story took place on June 8, 2013. Ms. Val. Robinson arrived at about three at the Community Center. She had the manner of a delighted child as she told her story about her childhood neighbors and their animals (see *Figures 13* and *14* above). The kind and numbers of animals varied from her original text which suggested that the story was an ever-changing and expanding one. She had a wonderfully robust speaking voice.

Test of the story by Val Robinson, "Felix the Cat":

I've got another childhood memory to share. I had four younger sisters. We lived in a neighborhood where this young lady that I went to school with lived right near. Her house was right across the backyard which we called the alleyway and she used to have a whole lot of animals. For some reason her family liked cats, and dogs, and rabbits and so she had a variety, like going to the zoo. She had a variety of domestic animals and I noticed that I couldn't wait to go, get home, so that I could go over and see her and play with my favorite thing: a pet that she had and that I called Felix the cat. Felix the cat would, soon as I would come in door, up her driveway, he would meet me at the driveway and jump into my arms (laughter) and uh, uh that was my first experience.

My, I took him home and my parents said, "Oh no, no cats! No cats!" (laughter) Because they were dog lovers and so they said, "Get out of here! Get out of here with that cat! Take that cat back home with those people with the farm!" (laughs) My dad, my dad used to call them farm people and so I would take the cat back and then I would sit on (laughter), sit on the back porch with my friend and she would introduce me to all the animals. But my favorite animal was Felix the cat. Yes, so that's a childhood memory that I wanted to share. When I, when I had a friendship with Felix the cat, yea!

Figure 13. Felix the Cat by Alciya

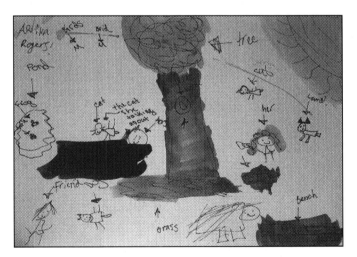

Figure 14. Felix the Cat by Andrew

B. *The Value of Illustrating the Stories*

The storytellers in the previous section are describing a time in their lives when getting a job, staying out at night, and dealing with eccentric neighbors were not as ominous as they seem today. When the children heard these stories they could experience a more positive side of the kind of events that are often problematic for them and their families. In addition, illustration of events from a story can increase any benefits it may provide. Recent research confirms the value of drawing in processing emotionally charged experiences such as those in the stories included in this chapter. Children aged five through twelve years old were asked to recount details about an emotionally charged experience. One group was simply asked to describe details of the situation, the other group was asked to draw the experience prior to providing the details. The group that drew recounted twice as many details of their experience as the group that did not draw (Driessnack 2005).

If the children are more likely to retain the experiences that they respond to by drawing, then drawing important parts of stories told by adults has the potential to address a common complaint made by adult residents at Cascade Village that children who are misbehaving don't listen to them (Fischer et al. 2012). This perceived need for improved intergenerational communication is not limited to Cascade Village. Storytelling is an age-old remedy for this problem. A number of the stories told by older residents about growing up centered on a time when they misbehaved. One story which I did not present to the children was about a young man who drove his mother's car into a stream after he had been repeatedly told to stay on the front porch and not get into the car. The children showed interest in what happened to the story-teller when he or she got into trouble. For example, Miss Val Robinson tried to take Felix the cat home to her parent's house and was told, "Get that cat out of here. Take it back to those farm people." Mr. Eddie Turner's parents were very angry at him when the police brought him home from his first job. When Eddie Turner described his parents' anger upon his being returned home by the police, conversation with the participating children turned to how parents worry about their children.

C. *The Story of Miller Horns*

Another example of the power of storytelling comes from local artist, Miller Horns. Mr. Horns graduated from the Cleveland Institute of Art even though he could not read or write when he entered the school. He went on to be awarded the prestigious Rome Prize and spent three months making his art in Rome. Back in Akron he was inspired by local history. He designed a monument to tell the story of local African American entrepreneur, George

Figure 15. Miller Horns. *Courtesy of the* Akron Beacon Journal.

Mathews.[2] Mr. Horns related the following story on the historic marker attached to his most ambitious work of art: the *Matthews Hotel Monument*, located on Howard Street just two blocks from Cascade Village.

Howard Street District

The center of African-American culture in Akron during the mid-twentieth century, Howard Street, was home to many of the city's black-owned businesses and entertainment establishments, and provided an atmosphere in which minority businesses could thrive. Attracted to the vitality of the neighborhood, entrepreneur George Mathews (1887–1982) established a barbershop here in 1920 and in 1925 opened the adjoining Matthews Hotel. The hotel quickly became the anchor of the Howard Street District. Mathew's success allowed him to endow a scholarship fund at the University of Akron in 1964.

Though Miller died before he could participate in story circles at Cascade Village, this is a story that is still ours to hear.

In some ways the memorial held for Miller Horns at the Summit Art Space in October of 2012 was like a very large story circle. Several hundred of Miller's friends and relatives gathered. It seemed we were there for the sole purpose of telling the story of his life. Stories flowed out from every part and time of Miller's life and began to form a mosaic of his achievements. After an hour and a half, Miller's uncle Otis Beecher closed the "story circle" and still the people remained standing in small groups continuing by doing "cross talk" and "snapshots." The stories that everyone knew were the ones that Miller told over and over again in a sixteen-year period during which he was consumed with turning stories into public art.

One story that Miller told us during his life was that of John Malvin, the black canal boat captain who carried both black and white passengers and is reputed to have helped a number of slaves to escape along the Freedom Trail that ran through Akron very near to Cascade Village. Another story and the one most applicable to this chapter was the story of George Mathews. In 1925, Mathews saw a need for a hotel on Howard Street to serve the African American community as well as the visitors who came to perform in the hotels downtown. African American performers such as Duke Ellington, Elsa Fitzgerald, Red Foxx, and Cab Calloway were welcome to perform in Akron's Main Street venues, but could not stay in the segregated hotels. The Matthews Hotel welcomed them and also housed a barbershop and the Cosmopolitan Club on the second floor where people of all races met to gossip and socialize and hear the great performers play after hours. Though Miller Horns passed away before he could participate in a story circle at Cascade Village; his commitment to his story of George Mathews and the monument that he left to us describing the story, show the power of stories and public art to bring community values to life.•

•**Bill:** The Miller Horns case is a fantastic illustration, in his life and work, of the link between storytelling in words and in pictures. And in the ways that this brings people together into communities. Your kids, illustrating stories told by adults in their own community, is like a remix of Miller Horns' life, extended across many lives, young and old.

Pat: I agree. The stories are a wonderful way to celebrate the memory and life of Miller Horns.

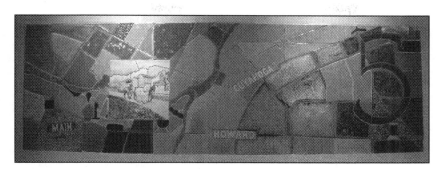

Figure 16. Lauer Building, ninth floor mural

D. Conclusion: Story Circles and Public Art

In 2009, I completed a commission with the architectural firm Braun and Steidl for the refurbishing of the Martin P. Lauer Apartments, a low-rent senior public housing development operated by the Akron Metropolitan Housing Authority. The theme of the project was the history of Howard Street. My friend, Miller Horns had already been bending my ear about Howard Street and the architect had lots of new information from her research which fit right in with what Miller had shown me. I was also working at the time with Jim Slowiak, who was using story circles in his theater class. In the class, students used material from story circles to write a play.

The Akron Story Circle Project helped Jim to gather stories at the Akron Metropolitan Housing Authority's Belcher Building as well as the Akron Urban League. The stories that we gathered were mostly about Howard Street. There was a great synergy in which the stories became the script of Jim's play (chapter 7 in this volume) as well as being the inspiration for a series of nine tile murals that I made for the Lauer Building. (see *Figure 16*) The play produced by Jim's class was presented twice at the University of Akron, once with an audience of nearly three hundred people. My nine murals introduce a different Howard Street theme on each of the nine floors of the Lauer building.

John O'Neal, cocreator of the story circle process believes in having as few rules as possible. His last rule, number 11, for story circles says, "Make some kind of follow-up activity that's viable for the particular group." This rule leaves the door open for a wonderfully wide range of possible results, including public art like my tile murals or Jim's play.◆

Amy: What other social science research method has such open-ended results? Your tiles and Jim's plays are such wonderful products of data-gathering. I remember when you mentioned the tiles the first time. I was—and still am—so impressed. And, as I discuss in my chapter, the response to Jim's play was outstanding.

The stories collected in story circles and told to the kids in the After School program at Cascade Village suggest that looking closer at the various kinds of stories told by residents may yield positive directions and models for revitalizing the culture of the community. If this is true, some solutions to ongoing problems such as poverty, joblessness, and lack of identity in the community may already be present and available to the community through the storytelling process.

Because the stories told by Eddie Turner, Valerie Moss, and Val Robinson reveal such core issues as getting a job, feeling safe at night, and appreciation of neighbors different than us, I believe that stories are a key to finding solutions to long-standing problems experienced by residents in public housing.✴ The answers to these problems may be in the wisdom of the community. Following John O'Neal's eleventh rule, "Make some kind of follow-up activity that's viable for the particular group," will allow fuller expression and dissemination of that wisdom. Therefore I propose an artist-in-residence program housed in one of the housing units at Cascade Village so that it is located within the community. I propose this program as both a first step in the development of a public art master plan and as one of the elements that will help ensure that the art making remains community (public) oriented and flexible to the needs of this public.

✴*Bill:* Is it stories that do this or is it in the interactions, in the space created to be real, is it learning to listen and tell stories, experiencing the passion or humor of another's story that suddenly feels familiar and closes a cultural gap, the moments where we are all present and willing to open our minds and hearts to friends-in-waiting?
Donna: YES!

Like the Mathews Hotel, an Artist in Residency Program would provide a place where creative artists could interact with the people who live nearby. The residents of Cascade Village would choose what kind and which artists to include. These could include all kinds of creative practitioners: playwrights, musicians, composers, painters, sculptors, creative writers, photographers, and storytellers.•

> •Bill: What a fantastic follow-up activity.
> Jim: Donna, this should be part of a Creative Placemaking grant. We need to get together about this. Perhaps we can put something together that involves Balch Street and Cascade Village in one grant?
> Donna: YES!

Artists could come and stay in the artist-in-residence space, called the Miller Horns' House, for periods of from one week to one year. While living at Cascade Village, they would set up the Miller Horns' House as a working studio, do creative work, and invite residents to participate. They could do things as diverse as offering classes to children and adults and putting on plays and musical performances with the participation of residents. In a sense and as described here, all of these artists in residence can be thought of as storytellers and as participating in story building. While living in Cascade Village they will be telling the story of Cascade Village and helping and encouraging residents to tell their stories as well.

An artist-in-residence program would provide the opportunity for stories to be told, to unfold in many different ways, and to be captured in many media. Each time an artist in residence tells the story of Cascade Village or allows residents to tell their stories, there is another opportunity for a follow-up activity. Story and follow-up activities should begin to create versions of the "chaining" or "cascade effect" that members of the Akron Story Circle Project have experienced and described in these chapters.

Bill Traynor (2008) says the following about interactive spaces:

> In a network approach, building place-based community shapes new places and forums for "bumping up" time. In a network, you want to create as many opportunities for people to bump up against one another as possible. This is advantageous to information sharing and relationship building. The problem is that opportunities that are too contrived or controlled diminish our critical ability to choose. But we can redesign the spaces and interactions that exist to be more conducive to peer-to-peer connections. Informal time can be programmed into meetings and events. Spaces can be redesigned to encourage intimacy.

Though Traynor is not talking about a community-based artist studio and artist in residence, my own experience suggests that working together to create a project such as a tile mural, community garden, theatre production, musical concert, poetry reading, etc. is a good way to create "bumping up" time. I believe that an artist in residence should be at the core of a vibrant public art plan for the Cascade Village community.

V. SOME FINAL THOUGHTS ON OUR COLLECTIVE EFFORT IN THIS VOLUME

The Akron Story Circle Projects described in this volume provided a remarkably flexible and effective collaborative experience for its five members. We have all collaborated in the past with other colleagues and recognize that the core question is whether or not something was accomplished by the group that no one person could have done on their own. This, we would all agree, has been our experience with story circles. There is no project described in this volume that was done without support from others in the group. Trust has been critical to these accomplishments. The five members of the Akron Story Circle Project began to understand the importance of this trust during our training with John O'Neal and Theresa Holden. We trusted in the process they taught us.♦

> ♦**Pat:** Story circles brought us together. In a society characterized by hate and distrust, it is a joy to find others who share common ground, and who can truly trust each other, cocreate, be spontaneous, and contribute to each other's wellbeing.
> **Carolyn:** I'm with Pat. Thinking about, writing about, teaching about diversity using a technique that brings out connection as it highlights differences in experiences has been a wonderful intellectual, pedagogical and personal journey.

The clarity and simplicity of the story circle process was transformative.♦ We each experienced a personal commitment to it and what is more, we understood that the other members of the Story Circle Project were committed as well. Knowing that the members of our group would show up and participate was a great advantage when creating an experience for a group of people who have never done story circles and may have little affection for speaking in a group. Introducing my colleagues to the residents at Cascade Village created a sense of sureness and inevitability of the success of the process that is difficult to describe. The call to tell stories will only be successful when the potential

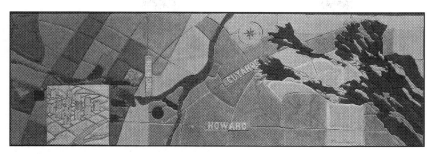

Figure 17. The Boogie Man of Howard Street by Donna Webb

storytellers have trust. Trust can be developed over time between friends and family members but is more difficult to accomplish in the academic and community environments in which we work. My colleagues provided what felt like a safety net for Cascade residents who came to the story circles.

> *Jim: I find Donna's work and energy so exciting and inspiring. I don't have a lot to add to this chapter because I feel that it reaffirms everything that we have been saying throughout the volume in a very "in the trenches" manner. Donna is practicing everything we are preaching and doing it as part of her daily work. For me, she is the consummate teacher and artist and storyteller. Thank you, Donna.

I also participated in the story circles and discussions that my story circle project colleagues arranged as part of their research. My experience with gathering stories from Akron teachers, public housing residents, and University of Akron students with the Akron Story Circle Group, discussing the projects of my colleagues, and reading their research has broadened my own experience with race and with collaboration in general. My new understanding of theatre, communication, political science, and anthropology has strengthened me as a teacher, colleague and artist. (see *Figure 17*)[3] Jim's plays and directorial skills, Bill's course materials and agility in dealing with controversial subjects in the classroom, Carolyn's writing skills and wide world view, Pat's empathy and her ability to express that in the academic world where critical thinking places so many limits on personal warmth; these and much more, have been my reward for showing up and participating with them in story circles related to their disciplines. For example I am particularly struck by the chaining or cascade concept introduced by Pat, echoed in the responses of Bill and Carolyn and exemplified in Jim's theatre project.

The Story Circle training enabled us all to share ideas and experiences through what Lindlof and Taylor (2002) describe as "chaining" or "cascading" effect—talk links to, or tumbles out of, the topics and expressions preceding it" (p. 182). As we progressed in the training, we quickly experienced a profound depth of one another's everyday experiences. (I think this is from Pat's chapter; see 60.)

The five of us have worked together long enough to have experienced this effect in many ways. A simple story will somehow gather momentum and pull others along with it to create a larger sense of meaning and urgency. The story about Geraldine that I used to open my chapter came into being as a result of the jostling, probing, and momentum caused by many other stories.

NOTES

1. This group was formed in 2010 in order to establish the Memorial Garden below the Y-Bridge which would facilitate community involvement on issues such as mental health and suicide, food access and environmental literacy. The Memorial Garden is located along the Little Cuyahoga just next to Cascade Village. The garden is shared with Cascade Village residents.

2. Inexplicably, George Mathews' name was not spelled the same as his Matthews Hotel.

3. *The Boogie Man of Howard Street* was made in response to stories about the wonderful night life experienced by story-tellers before the business district on Howard Street was razed as part of an urban renewal project. These stories were collected with the Akron Story Circle Group and used to create Jim's play as well. The author feels that the pressure to support the urban renewal project came at least in part from a fear of night life. The dark figure is the hero of the art work, casting a large shadow visible to citizens who worked and shopped further south in the Akron city center.

REFERENCES

"About ArtPlace: Introduction." 2016. ArtPlace America. Accessed March 24. http://www.artplaceamerica.org/about/introduction.

Boje, D. M. 1995. Stories of the Storytelling Organization: A Postmodern Analysis of Disney as "Tamara-Land." *Academy of Management Journal* 38, no. 4: 997–1035.

City of Akron Department of Planning and Urban Development. 2005. "Elizabeth Park Urban Renewal Area Eligibility Report and Urban Renewal Plan."

"Cascade Village." 2015. The Community Builders, Inc. Accessed May 3. http://www.tcbinc.org/what_we_do/projects/cascade_village.htm.

City of Akron. 2016. "Facts." Accessed June 7. http://www.akronohio.gov/cms/site/3037e0093496c8d5/index.html.

Driessnack, Martha. 2005. "Children's Drawings as Facilitators of Communica-
    tion: A Meta-Analysis." *Journal of Pediatric Nursing* 20, no. 6: 41522.
Endres, Kathleen. 2013. "Mary Peavy Eagle, 1909–2003." *Akron Women's History.*
    Summit County Historical Society. February 13. Last accessed June 6, 2016.
    http://blogs.uakron.edu/womenshistory/2013/02/13/mary-peavy-eagle
    -1909-2003/.
Fischer, Rob, Mark Joseph, Mark Chupp, April Hirsh, Taryn Gress. 2012. "Evalua-
    tion and Learning in Community Change: Insights from a Community
    Survey at Cascade Village." *Cleveland: Case Western Reserve Center on Urban
    Poverty & Community Development.* Unpublished report.
Forster, Nick, Martin Cebis, Sol Majteles, Anurag Mathur, Roy Morgan, Janet
    Preuss, Vinod Tiwari, and Des Wilkinson. 1999. "The Role of Story-telling in
    Organizational Leadership." *Leadership & Organization Development Journal*
    20, no. 1: 11–17.
Gates, Theaster, and Dave the Potter. 2010. "To Speculate Darkly." Opening night
    lecture, Milwaukee Art Museum. April 16. video, 12:38, posted as "Theaster
    Gates–Opening Night Lecture, Milwaukee Art Museum," posted by
    "objectlab," May 25, 2010. https://www.youtube.com/watch?v
    =2QWXC36fHNc.
Horn, Miller. 1992–2000. Conversations with Donna Webb. Various places.
Kaye, Michael. 1996. *Myth-makers and Story-tellers: How to Unleash the Power of
    Myths, Stories and Metaphors to Understand the Past, Envisage the Future, and
    Create Lasting and Positive Cultural Change in Your Organisation.* Sydney:
    Business & Professional Publishing.
Maples, John Lee. 1974. "The Akron Ohio Ku Klux Klan, 1921–1928." Master's
    thesis, The University of Akron.
Olin, Oscar E. 1917. *Akron and Environs.* Chicago: Lewis Publishing.
Russell, Jessica, Senior Community Life Manager, Cascade Village. Personal
    conversations, 2013.
———. 2013. "Comments on Cascade Village Public Art Prepared for Provost
    Sherman, University of Akron." Unpublished report.
Scearce, Diana. 2009. "Net-centric Organizing: Learning from Bill Traynor and
    Lawrence Community Works." November. Working Wikily.
Traynor, Bill. 2008. "Community Building: Limitations and Promises." In *The
    Community Development Reader,* ed. James DeFillipis and Susan Saegert,
    209–20. London: Routledge.
Webb, Donna. 2012. *Cascade Village Goes to the Zoo.* Akron: Donna Webb.

Story Circles

A Powerful Tool in the Multifaceted Toolkit for Addressing Race in University Cocurricular Programing

Amy Shriver Dreussi

Engaging individuals in difficult dialogues* focusing on volatile issues of race is an act of faith and bravery. At the University of Akron, a group of faculty, staff and students took on this challenge and, as a result, affected change in individuals, the university and the community at large.

*Carolyn: This term, which seems so central to all of our goals, is also the name of an initiative promoting "civic engagement, academic freedom, and pluralism in higher education" out of the Thomas Jefferson Center for the Protection of Free Expression in Virginia.

Bill: "Difficult dialogues" is frequently used in conflict management literature and appears as a subheading in my chapter. The authors of *Getting to Yes* wrote another book later titled *Difficult Conversations* (great book). Much of the material in that book was later the basis for a very popular book called *Crucial Conversations*. The phrase captures one of the cores of what we are doing as educators here: assisting our students and ourselves to become more skilled at discussing the sensitive and controversial topics where we can learn the most from each other, but tend to shy away. Teaching in this area is absolutely an act of faith and bravery; to do so successfully we need to be fully present and vulnerable, ready for our own language or perspective to become a text for analysis.

Pat: Dialogues of race continue to be "difficult" for many educators. As Cornel West wrote in *Race Matters* (1997): "Race is the most explosive issue in American life precisely because it forces us to confront the tragic facts of poverty and paranoia, despair and distrust. In short, a candid examination of race matters takes us to the core of American democracy. And the degree to which race matters in the plight and predicament of fellow citizens is a crucial measure of whether we can keep alive the best of this democratic experiment we call America."

From a communicative perspective, reflecting on the notion of "bravery" is significant as conversations about race tend to unleash that which we have been socialized to bury and leave unsaid. "Rethinking Race" events have demonstrated to me that many students are indeed "brave" and are willing to risk moving beyond boundaries to learning about and engaging in interracial conversations about race (in many ways more than educators leading their classrooms).

Jim: A lot of my comments will come back to the theatre as a double, a kind of reflection, of life itself. Difficult dialogues imply conflict and conflict is what produces action in the theatre. When Bill talks about being fully present and vulnerable, he is also using "acting" terminology. This is the "state of readiness" that actors must always seek. When we engage in story circles, we are connecting to some kind of rooted, human behavior that allows us to enter into the difficult dialogues or explain the unexplainable. Theatre director Peter Brook talks about theatre (or storytelling in this case) making the invisible visible. Our story circles on race have given students permission to speak the unspeakable and make the invisible visible.

Donna: This might be verified by looking at faculty research begun as a result of Rethinking Race and any resulting community projects.

Story circles came to the University of Akron as part of a series of events which ultimately became Rethinking Race: Black, White and Beyond but was initially informally referred to as simply Race Week. The first Race Week was held in 2007 in honor of the ten-year anniversary of then-President Bill Clinton's visit to the UA campus to begin a national conversation on race. In the intervening years, these endeavors have traveled parallel tracks, engaging the University community and the community at large in efforts that purposefully and boldly explore issues of race and ethnicity. This chapter reports assessment data gathered at intersections of those paths.

The original Rethinking Race: Black, White and Beyond was quite modest and, along with the Akron Story Circle Project, has grown and changed into undertakings that have had a profound and lasting impact on attendees from the student body and the community at large. The data tell the story.•

•**Bill:** I regularly hear from former students that their experiences in the early years of Rethinking Race were the most memorable parts of college for them, often insisting that everyone should be required to participate in story circles and cocurricular events like Rethinking Race.

Donna: The data and student responses are very important. They indicate that Rethinking Race is a successful event. I am curious about the impact of Rethinking Race on faculty research. Rethinking Race has impacted the research of faculty members of the Akron Story Circle Project. The members of the Akron Story Circle Project have also brought students into their research projects. This is no doubt impacting student educational experience.

Jim: Rethinking Race and the Akron Story Circle Project have certainly changed how my students think about theatre and its place in the community. Although the allure of Broadway musicals, movies, and television will always be present, I have found my students much more receptive to the notions of Theatre of Place and working with one's community as an artist. This kind of collaborative community effort has made my job more enjoyable and has sparked several other productions and artistic projects in Akron.

Carolyn: Jim, I think it has changed the way anthropology students involved with the method think about the discipline. Because this work involves academic skill development as well as community engagement and introspection, I think it has broadened and deepened their appreciation for higher education. I have had students say that they now have a better way to answer their parents who question the value of a major or minor in social science and an answer for what they personally find meaningful and useful in the endeavor.

I. RACE WEEK: SUCCESS, GROWTH AND TRANSFORMATION

Organizers deemed Race Week 2007 sufficiently successful that they decided to make it an annual event. These early organizers, including the authors of this text, sensed that there was a genuine need and appreciation for opportunities for race-focused informational events and open discussions. Although assessment was not as formalized in the initial year as it became in subsequent iterations, the organizing committee repeatedly heard comments from attendees reflecting a sense of gratitude and even relief to be able to address these difficult topics in a straightforward, open manner.

Additionally, our experiences in the classroom revealed to us that many of our students had little personal interaction with people of other races and lacked information about and understanding of racial issues.♦ There is as well substantial research indicating that education in the United States is now more racially segregated than it was in the past. Nationally, 7.9 percent of white students attend schools whose student populations are predominantly comprised of racial minorities, as compared with 65 percent of African American students and 72 percent of Latino students (Orfield 2009, 12).

♦**Bill:** This experience gap makes already difficult dialogues even more challenging.
Amy: ...and more indispensable!

Pat: Again, the importance of "Rethinking Race"—enabling educators to explore ways to create a hospitable and productive learning environment that addresses the history and everyday experiences of a racially diverse population.

Jim: For me, the challenge comes in creating the possibility to grow and develop what we have accomplished. Too often the tendency is to try to repeat and institutionalize successful efforts. This leads to atrophy and eventual defeat of any movement. How can education in this country be more segregated now than in the past? Easy. The movement has atrophied. One of the goals of John O'Neal's Color Line Project is to reinvigorate the movement, and this should also become a goal for all we do as educators, scholars, and artists. Another important website is Animating Democracy, which "inspires, informs, promotes, and connects arts and culture as potent contributors to community, civic, and social change."

Bill: Jim is right, as I see it anyway. In our work on the volume we have often returned to the question "what will Story Circles 2.0" look like? That question articulates our desire to, as Jim put it, grow and develop rather than just repeat and institutionalize something that, by doing so, inevitably becomes stale and lifeless. We should not underestimate the value of adventurousness and uncertainty. Without suggesting any of us have gotten stale, I am sure we all recall clearly the excitement and sense of adventure that permeated everything we did in the early years of what was then called the Akron Color Line Project. To grow and develop we need to find ways to recapture this energy and vulnerability, this sense that our students picked up on right away, that we were on a journey with our students and, just like them, we did not know where the path would lead us.

Carolyn: Hear, hear, Jim and Bill. Working on this volume is inspiring some nostalgia for that early energy. But it is also making me realize that the evolution to 2.0 is going on although it may be going on in our own alleys. Perhaps it is time for a group dinner so we can catch up! Some of us have talked about designing a collaborative course that applies lessons we've learned, move beyond them in terms of the dimensions of difference we focus on, experiment with the ways we use the story circle method, and the sorts of products that might come from the work. This morning I worked with new faculty members on designing research with students. We are planning on exploring how the story circle method might be adapted for use with our city's growing international refugee community.

Unique programming like that of UA's Rethinking Race provides a venue for all students, minority as well as majority, who lack direct and personal exposure to persons of different racial groups to learn about and frankly discuss difficult issues faced by persons of different races.[+] As noted in Ropers-Huilman, R., Winters, K. T., & Enke:

Just as institutions consciously respond to the needs of students with different levels of mathematical knowledge or those who face different developmental challenges, institutions would benefit from being more thoughtful about the types of experiences they facilitate for students to think about their own racial identities. Students are not identical in their racial understandings, and they need different types of conversations, programming, and interactions to facilitate their racial identity development. (48–49: 2013)

⁺Amy: We tend to view diversity events as primarily benefitting minorities, which is rather silly. Everyone benefits…and if we are speaking in terms of actual numbers, given the racial composition of UA, it is primarily majority students who benefit, right?

Donna: Since the University of Akron has about 13 percent African American students, it is very difficult to give the remaining 87 percent direct and personal exposure to African Americans. One of the issues we sometimes face with story circles is a majority of white participants who reveal through their stories that they have very little experience with racism and feel that in those instances where they have observed it they noticed and felt it was wrong.

Bill: In my experience, the impact of these events is greater on majority populations, perhaps because our privileged position insulates us from the routine need to understand other cultures and perspectives, making these events further from our comfort zones and more challenging…giving those white students who were open, a context within which they were given a gift, a permission to just listen, and those who were less open, a call to quiet the riot inside as a step toward listening.

Jim: Several times John O'Neal conducted story circles in my Voice and Diction classes. At first, I thought it was an odd activity for the class, but then I found that there was an immediate bonding that occurred and the story circles also gave each person in the class permission to speak. Those who had been shy or afraid to own their voice found that speaking was their right.

Pat: In these discussions of "difficult issues" I noticed that typically white participants resorted to silence in fear that their comments would be misconstrued as evidence of racist thinking, while many participants of color may have felt it futile to give voice to their inner thoughts. Our work with John O'Neal introduced a new paradigm to defy tightly held cultural expectations relating to race talk.

The University of Akron's commitment to diversity is embedded in the strategic plan, Vision 2020. One of the new initiatives launched as part of the strategic plan, The Akron Experience, is "a new initiative that provides every student with a unique in-and-out-of-the-classroom learning experience to strengthen the connection between campus and community," very much aligned with Rethinking Race: Black, White and Beyond. Indeed, the orientation of the Akron Experience is an expansion of the Rethinking Race model.

In terms of student racial diversity at the University of Akron, less than one quarter of the Fall 2012 enrollment of 28,771, including undergraduate, graduate, and professional students was comprised of persons of color. Table 1 provides a breakdown.

Table 1: University of Akron Fall 2012 enrollment by race

Race	% of total enrollment
African American	13.2
American Indian	0.3
Asian American	2.1
Hispanic American	1.8
Native Hawaiian	0.1
Nonresident alien	4.0
Two or more races	2.1

Source: UA Institutional Research

II. RETHINKING RACE: A DISTINCTIVE APPROACH TO COCURRICULAR PROGRAMMING

Most, if not all, colleges and universities have race-based programming during the month of February in recognition of African American History Month. Rethinking Race, while conducted in this time frame, is distinctive in that it is more extensive than most, encompassing two weeks of programming. Other distinctive aspects of Rethinking Race include:

- It is embedded in the coursework of classes across campus—from history to nursing, communications to economics, faculty develop specific assignments around the events of Rethinking Race.
- The organizational structure is decentralized. Individual faculty from around the campus identify appropriate and engaging speakers, find the funding to bring them to campus during the first two weeks of February, and make appropriate arrangements.
- It addresses issues of race broadly, expanding beyond the usual black/white focus to encompass race universally.
- It transcends boundaries in terms of the types of programming offered, including not only the typical keynote speakers, but also music, dance, plays, film, poetry, and two types of facilitated conversations, and another type which has become known as Face2Face Conversations About Race, which are less formal discussions typically facilitated by faculty, staff and/or graduate students•
- Story circles provided yet another distinguishing characteristic. Much like Face2Face conversations, story circles flipped the class-

room, treating students as colearners rather than passive consumers. Story circles brought Rethinking Race directly into classrooms (as described in other chapters in this volume) and added a deeply participatory component to other events in Rethinking Race to work with student on how to best apply classroom insights to real world problems, like engaging in difficult dialogues about race.

> •**Donna:** I am very proud of Rethinking Race at the University of Akron. It is an initiative that reflects the diversity of the faculty as well as the students.
> **Bill:** Ditto. Rethinking Race started out as a mostly grassroots effort of faculty and staff volunteering our time because our students were asking for help with difficult dialogues surrounding race in Akron. The early years were incredibly exciting and filled with invention and innovation. Nothing was fixed and we created new event-types on the fly, like Face2Face conversations, in response to constantly emerging student demand. We advanced efforts across campus to embed cocurricular events into syllabi, connecting Rethinking Race texts to meaningful course assignments, helping our students make connections between scholarly insights in the classroom and real world problem solving. And we built a still growing community of scholars from various disciplines, working with a large number of students to change the campus culture.

III. STRUCTURAL CHANGE

The year 2008 was transformative for Race Week. It had become apparent that the one-week format of the inaugural year was insufficient to contain the myriad events that UA faculty developed, planned, and executed. Additionally, planners resolved to broadly approach issues of race, expanding beyond the typical black/white dyad. As a result, the name was changed to Rethinking Race: Black, White and Beyond to reflect the expanded time frame as well as the broader focus on race. In addition, the effort received a $10,000 grant from the University's vice president of research, George Newkome.

Other changes implemented for the 2008 series included the addition of learning objectives and instruments to collect qualitative and quantitative data to measure them. The addition of a formalized assessment process not only provided rationale and guidelines for programming but also established a feedback loop between attendees and organizers. The data gathering permits enhancements that render events more meaningful to those in attendance.

The initial learning outcomes aimed at enhancing attendees' abilities to:
- Appreciate and respect diversity among people.
- Identify and analyze contemporary issues.

- Relate the contributions of groups and people to the history of ideas and belief systems.
- Engage more productively in difficult dialogues.
- Critically analyze one's own culture.✦

> ✦**Donna:** It would be interesting to revisit the learning outcomes to see if the participating faculty and other organizers see those outcomes differently after seven years of participating in the event.
>
> **Pat:** That is a good suggestion Donna.

The UA Office of Multicultural Development as well as the Institute for Teaching and Learning, the University's faculty professional development entity, became the primary sponsors of Rethinking Race: Black, White and Beyond.✦ These cosponsors reinforced two critical elements of Rethinking Race—the multicultural approach as well as the commitment to include Rethinking Race events as assignments embedded in faculty spring syllabi. In later years, a more direct faculty development aspect was added to Rethinking Race: Black, White and Beyond in the form of professional development seminars.

> ✦**Donna:** It is so appropriate that ITL is a primary sponsor. I believe that one of the most important outcomes of Rethinking Race may be a shift in faculty research.
>
> **Jim:** Yet I still feel a real lack of interdisciplinary thinking from the administration, especially concerning the arts, humanities, and social sciences. I think we need to come up with some stronger action steps for the future.
>
> **Bill:** ITL and the Office of Multicultural Development support were key. And sadly, we lost Helen as ITL Director and now ITL no longer exists.
>
> **Amy:** Yes, sadly, ITL ended its commitment to Rethinking Race in the fall of 2013. Helen is much missed. We hope that Rethinking Race is sufficiently embedded in the UA culture that this change will not dilute the cocurricular endeavor.

The involvement of the Institute for Teaching and Learning has paid off quite well. The number of faculty who embedded Rethinking Race in their spring syllabi more than doubled from 2007 to 2012, from 60 to nearly 130 (Qammar 2011).

IV. ASSESSMENT: INTEGRAL FROM EARLY YEARS

Assessment became an important element of Rethinking Race early in its tenure. Student participants have been the focus of this assessment, as planners primarily sought data to enhance the learning experience. Beginning in 2008, data were gathered from student attendees at events in two ways—through electronic scanning of student ID cards (to collect demographic and UA data, including college in which they were enrolled and their class standing) and through utilization of event surveys. Event surveys, distributed prior to events and collected immediately thereafter, were designed to gauge the effect attendance had on the students, as well as their motivation for attending the events (e.g. did they attend voluntarily or as part of a course requirement, either for full or extra credit) and the extent to which events challenged attendees' preconceived notions of race. These instruments gathered both quantitative data and qualitative data. In 2012, event surveys were modified to better align Rethinking Race's assessment with the previously mentioned University of Akron's strategic plan, Vision 2020.

Over the years, attendance increased from 3,500 in 2008 to 8,000 in 2012.•
In 2012, student participation in Rethinking Race came from every college within the university and included students in the university's early college program, undergraduate, graduate, and professional programs (Qammar 2012). Outreach to the greater Akron community resulted in an expansion of community participation such that in 2012, 30 percent of attendees came from the community (Qammar 2012). Although attention has been focused on assessing the student response to Rethinking Race, assessment of community impact has not been as well developed. This assessment has largely been gauged by attendance data. Demographic data is not available, as community attendees lack the ID cards such as those held by UA students which are run through card readers for a quick gather of demographic data. Some community members do fill out the event surveys which are distributed at all events, but their numbers are quite small. This is an area of assessment which planners hope to expand in the future.

•Pat: BRAVO!

V. RICH DATA: RICH EXPERIENCES

Over the years, the open-ended questions on event surveys provided Rethinking Race planners rich data about the impact events were having on our students. The questions have been modified somewhat over the years, but generally they have consistently attempted to measure what participants learned as a result of attendance and the extent to which attendees' perspectives were changed by the experience and prompted them to become more open to diversity.

Planners have been gratified by the extent to which students have found Rethinking Race events to be revelatory. Respondents have described in vivid terms how Rethinking Race events have introduced them to new ideas and realities that they had not previously experienced or, in some instances, imagined. Responses such as, "I never really looked at it that way" or "How did I get this far in my education without having learned this?" are commonplace.◆ "This represents what higher education is all about," wrote one student in 2011 (Qammar 2011).

> ◆**Pat:** This is so profound!! I think many participants of these events discovered just how racialized our own identities and viewpoints have been.
> **Amy:** Some students were downright indignant about this glaring gap in their education to date.

Some have even described life-affirming and life-changing experiences. "My faith in humanity has been restored," noted one attendee after an Akron Story Circle Project activity in 2012 (Qammar 2012). "Changed my life and career goals," wrote one student in 2011 (Qammar 2011).

The following is a small selection of responses to open-ended questions from thousands of surveys gathered over the years:

- *New discussions that I never heard before* (From a student attending a 2011 screening of excerpts of the cartoon *Boondocks*)
- *I never realized some of the very sly tactics that can be used to cause people to think in terms of race instead of actual issues* (Student who attended a 2009 lecture about race and the 2008 election)
- *It made me more aware of how much racial messages are used in political communication* (same)
- *This event helped me see race in a different light* (same)
- *I never knew that Mexicans were so discriminated against and that they were placed at the same level as dogs and blacks.* (Screening of a documentary about *Hernandez v. Texas* US Supreme Court decision of 1954)

- *I learned about how Mexican Americans were segregated and discriminated against. I didn't realize that this really happened since most of the segregation we hear about is regarding African Americans.* (Student in a Latin American history course who attended a screening of a documentary about the US Supreme Court's 1954 ruling in *Hernandez v. Texas*)
- *It really hit me deep. I myself am Mexican/American and seeing how my people fought for our rights today impacted me so much. It showed me a different view of my people and the United States of America I am part of. I was kind of disgusted with the government and proud of my people and our courage. Esta presentation es muy interesante! Muchas gracias por tu horas.* (Screening of a documentary about *Hernandez v. Texas* US Supreme Court decision of 1954)
- *It made me think more about the music I listen to and why* (Student in a Human Diversity course who attended a Face2Face Conversation about music and racial stereotypes)
- *I need to be a more open person, with myself and the world.* (Student in an introduction to political science course who attended a comedy event)
- *This event has made me more aware of the perspective of African Americans. I think from now on, I will be more conscious in interactions I have with members of the African American Community.* (Student comment after a comedy event)

For some students, events provided a new way of looking at topics with which they thought they were familiar, as well as a desire to expand their knowledge on the topic. Below are three examples of remarks from students who attended a lecture by Hari Jones, curator of the African American Civil War Memorial and Museum:

- *I learned about the Civil War from a more Afrocentric perspective. I learned about the contributions of Africans to the civil war.*
- *I thought I knew a lot on this topic. I did not. Dr. Jones was very good.*
- *I want to learn more about history of the mid 1800s to the mid 1900s. That time is so different from our world today and I want to know more about how things were back then. Not only with black history but as a whole.*

Four student attendees in 2011 expressed a desire to continue or redirect their studies as a result of attending Rethinking Race events:

- *It made me eager to take a class concerning the subject.*
- *I've always wanted to understand the demands and incentives that promoted global and foreign policies. Now I have a base to begin my own research on labor.*
- *I have much stronger desire to explore the issues addressed on my own and share what I have learned with others.*
- *I was debating whether I should continue with my learning of the Spanish language and Latino culture. Now I know I want to continue so I can better understand and communicate with those that are struggling with injustice.*

In addition to story circles, Face2Face Conversations About Race offered another type of facilitated conversation during Rethinking Race. These are typically facilitated by UA faculty, staff or graduate students. Face2Face discussions are very popular Rethinking Race events. They are typically well attended—occasionally too well attended to allow all attendees to participate. In cases of large attendance, facilitators have occasionally endeavored to locate a vacant space in which to convene a second conversation, as smaller groups permit more students to become actively involved. Despite valiant efforts on the part of facilitators to keep everyone involved, there are attendees who do not actively participate. Although 100 percent participation is likely unrealistic, even among those who are very interested in the topic at hand, Face2Face events generally seem to have lower rates of participation than do story circles.

Face2Face topics are generated by faculty and/or graduate assistants and reflect the broad base of Rethinking Race, both racially and academically. Previous topics have included "Talking Black in the Classroom," "Stereotypes in Children's Media," "Is Racism Inherited?" "From San Juan to Akron," "What Would Abraham Lincoln Say?" "White Privilege," "International Perspectives on Race in America," "Race and Politics," "Racism in Cartoons," and "Native American Issues."

Survey respondents have indicated that they welcome opportunities to discuss these topics with persons of other races:

- *Good to share information with other ethnic groups having different opinions on an controversial topic (Race and the 2010 Campaign)*

- *This event changed the way I think about different people and how to be sensitive. (Neither Black Nor White: Biracial Issues in America 2011)*
- *I found that some other race feel the same way I do on the topic (Guilt v Responsibility 2012)*

These remarks underscore the appreciation attendees have for the opportunity to interact on topics that are typically avoided or, at best, uncomfortable. Race, it seems, is an elephant in many living rooms—and classrooms.

VI. THE AKRON STORY CIRCLE PROJECT

The Akron Story Circle Project and Rethinking Race are a terrific match, thus the decision to invite John O'Neal to UA for Rethinking Race was an easy one.* Storytelling is a powerful mechanism for getting at what Rethinking Race does so well—what we have elsewhere in this volume referred to as "difficult dialogues" which Caruthers et al. (2004, 36) refer to as "undiscussables," or "those subjects that people choose not to talk about because they have been 'taboo' in educational settings." As one student noted after a 2012 story circle event, "It allowed me to see how far I've come as a person, especially since high school where there was no diversity" (Qammar 2012).

> *Donna: Jim's suggestion that we bring in John was brilliant. Their shared commitment to theatre was a catalyst for social change. This is a good example of the relationship between faculty research and Rethinking Race.
>
> Bill: Jim bringing in John was a dramatic and powerful turning point for our project, for Rethinking Race, and for our community. I would not likely have had the courage to integrate story circles into my course syllabi if John had not been here to work with us and then to lead circles in my class that first time. My students loved it and, while the theatrical reporting out part at the end still feels outside my comfort zone every time we do it, I continue to use the tool.
>
> Pat: I agree that bringing in John was brilliant. It certainly was a turning point. It enabled us to find each other.

Data gathered by surveys during Rethinking Race events over the years have underscored this. This chapter includes analysis of three different events that are linked to the Akron Story Circle Project—a 2011 play that was developed from story circles about Akron's civil rights history (see the introduction and script in this volume), a series of impromptu story circles hastily assembled in 2010 to accommodate an overflow crowd for a different Rethinking

Race event (as well as the planned story circle after the event) and a 2012 Akron Story Circle Project entitled Crossing the Line and Story Circles.

In 2011, one of the more popular events of Rethinking Race was the student production of a play written by students of Jim Slowiak. The script for this play is included in this volume, along with Jim's reflections on the creative process he and his students underwent to move from collecting stories in story circles about race issues in the local community to writing and ultimately performing this play.

Although not a story circle itself, the dialogue in the play was taken directly from story circle stories. The impact on students was powerful, as indicated from the survey data reported below. The data provide strong evidence of an effect noted elsewhere in this volume, a genuine bridging of that all-too-familiar town-gown divide.•

•**Bill:** Jim's students conducted story circles and transcribed and analyzed these as the basis for the first draft (and performance) of their play. Then, his students engaged with stories that were gathered and transcribed by other UA students during their process of finalizing their script for the performance analyzed here. As the script evolved other faculty on the team were brought into conversations with Jim and his students. I remain profoundly impressed by the work Jim's students did turning these stories into an entire performance, and with how Jim gently guided them through multiple layers of "difficult dialogues" from start to finish.

Carolyn: As an outsider to theatre and to creative writing/play writing, I was awestruck by the process I witnessed in this play's development. I attended a rehearsal early on in the process in which Jim and the students talked through, worked, and reworked material on several levels (basic communication, movement, spatial relationships, musicality, historical/ethnohistorical, thematic, and philosophical). Donna and Jim invited me and some of my students to an early performance and art display (of Donna's students' works inspired by the stories gathered) at a Metropolitan Housing Authority residence. At this event again I witnessed the lively process of evolution taking place as a group of people, led by or maybe I mean conducted (in the sense of an orchestra) by Jim, worked their creation forward together. We should perhaps sit in on each other's classes more often but I cannot imagine that there are many people out there who can work the magic of educating and creating on so many levels at one time. Jim, you rock.

Donna: As Carolyn just eluded to, many of the stories collected for Jim's play were from story circles conducted at the Akron Metropolitan Housing Authority residence, the Belcher Residence and at the Urban League. This is a great example of an activity that "affected change in individuals, the university and the community at large."

Bill: The very emotional reactions of the storytellers to seeing their stories performed (at Belcher and later in EJ) is strong evidence of a profound community-level impact.

Pat: I totally agree. Who would have known that the simple act of telling stories of everyday experiences (by the Akron Metropolitan Housing Authority residents and the

Belcher Residence) could lead to such an enlightening and transformative performance. Jim, you and the students were outstanding!! I remember facilitating the "talk back" session after the EJ performance and realizing that what everyone just experienced was a profound awakening of the devastating effects of injustice.

As evidenced in Table 2 (below), the data tell a compelling story about how well received and important the play and the brief discussion session that followed it were for attendees. The data below are derived from 87 surveys which employed a Likert scale assessment (1= strongly disagree, 2 disagree, 3 neutral, 4 agree, 5 strongly agree).

Table 2 : Mean scores; Story Circle play

Mean Score	Survey statements
3.76	Prior to attending my level of interest in participating in this event was high.
3.84	It is likely that I will participate in other Rethinking Race events during the next two weeks
4.21	This event gave me the opportunity to participate in an open and honest discussion.
4.36	This Rethinking Race event has made me think more deeply about the issues related to race.
4.40	Gaining an understanding of diversity and multicultural issues will help me succeed in the work place.
4.35	I felt comfortable with the topics discussed in this Rethinking Race event.
4.30	I agreed with most of the comments that were made during this discussion/lecture/event.
4.04	Some topics covered by this event challenged my preconceived ideas about the topic.

The data indicate that, although respondents were somewhat uninterested in the topic prior to attendance (3.76, the lowest mean score), their expressed willingness to attend future events increased during the performance. It should be noted that this lack of initial interest is fairly common among those individuals, mostly students, who complete Rethinking Race event surveys.♦ It is as well worth noting that the increase in engagement is also typical of story circles and Rethinking Race events in general. The play also provided a potent opportunity to learn, discuss and rethink preconceived ideas.

◆**Bill:** This was a common refrain from my students: At first I did not want to go at all, and almost dropped the class, but after I went to my first event I wanted to go to as many as possible.

Jim: So many of the students at UA enter the university having never attended a live theatre performance. How important is it that we provide engaging theatre events to initiate those novice students into the power of performance to explain and transform the world we live in? While theatre for entertainment is a whole lot of fun, theatre for social change can be so much more compelling, as we discovered from the comments on these surveys.

Their open-ended responses revealed how much they learned and how profound the play proved to be. Attendees were asked, "What did you learn from this experience?" Many respondents were surprised to learn the racially contentious history of Akron, a northern city. This sentiment, as we see below, was shared even by individuals who were life-long residents of the city:

- *I didn't realize there were so many activities of discrimination going on in Akron—a northern city.*
- *Akron culture: I am not a lifelong resident of Akron, OH. To hear these events that took place was shocking and interesting. I had no idea these events took place. I also learned how much talent UA has! The actors were amazing!! I will definitely try and support future events. The delivery/acting were excellent.*
- *The most significant thing I learned was that racism lives everywhere and to find out it was so deeply (embedded) in Akron. The history around Akron should be talked about more especially since I'm born and raised in Akron.*
- *The past is the past and that race has been institutionalized. I never thought about racism today and that blacks/whites can be so separated even in the twenty-first century.*
- *Akron used to be racist. You always hear about racism has affected the U.S. but you never know how close to home it is.*
- *How racist Akron used to be. I never knew racism that took place in my hometown. I was just saying how racism and discrimination has affected us as a whole.*
- *That racism was very big even here in Akron. I never knew that. I see why people are so picky and why history is so important.*◆

- *Before tonight, I honestly never knew that there was such obvious seg-regation in the north let alone Akron. The Firestone story really got to me because I didn't know that there were instances in Akron where people wouldn't work with others because of the color of their skin. History: I wrote three pages of notes!*
- *It was interesting to learn that racism was not just a predominately southern thing. While down south there were signs (etc.) to let people know about segregation. In the North, it was very prevalent, but more hidden. History classes teach you its normal (me good guys) vs. me south (me bad guys) that's not the case.*

*Carolyn: I love the use of the word "picky" here. The author of the comment simultaneously reveals a bias being overcome and that old lag we all have where our language reveals the hold our old attitudes have on us.

Jim: Isn't that interesting? How often in a story circle do we find ourselves telling a story and realizing that our "way" of telling the story has been inscribed by family and regional and generational codes that break down and begin to transform even as we are telling the story? This for me is one of the most exciting aspects of story circles. We actually see transformation taking place in the here and now. We live the change we seek in each moment of telling and listening.

Another survey respondent was not at all surprised and saw a reflection of him/herself in a character in the play.

I've always been an empathetic person but hearing the story of the African American fellow with a MS in Chemistry working in the elevator for twenty-one years really helped put things into perspective for me. I have a MS in Chemistry also was a very frustrated working as a lab tech due to the recession. To be reduced to even lower positions based only on color would make me feel like parts of the city looks now.•

•Carolyn: I want to say something about this generation of empathy that stories allow and how, as in this case, it can help us cross into a place where we understand intersectionalities of race, class, and gender in ways that go deeper than reading scholars like Patricia Hill Collins and at the same time make such scholarship enduring for us.

Jim: I'm not sure we should only talk about empathy or the generation of empathy here. Bertolt Brecht saw empathy as a negative force in the theatre. In Brechtian terms, empathy means an implicit acceptance of the situation or circumstances. If I feel bad, then I am excused from taking action. Just feeling is not enough. We must generate

action, not just empathy. I believe the story circles go well beyond generating empathy and actually, because of their performative nature, serve as a tool for change.
Carolyn: Good point, Jim. I do think that finding capacity for empathy is vital to community. The word acceptance here has two opposing meanings. Encouraging a participant toward acceptance of others' presentations of their experiences as valid is part of our goal. Acceptance of conditions of oppression is, obviously, not.

Asked to describe the impact of the event, survey respondents wrote that it provided a new perspective on the city and the experiences of its older citizens, made a lasting impact and inspired some to work for social justice and to learn more about their city's past and present:♦

♦Amy: I feel like this provides evidence that story circles accomplish several things—not only providing a meaningful experience for those in story circles who provide the data, but also providing powerful experiences for those who merely see the products of that data.
Donna: The rules for story circles included the last rule, number 11, "make some kind of follow-up activity that's viable for the particular group." In other words, as important as it is to affect the participants in story circles, it is also important that at least some of the stories begin to have a life of their own, that they move into the culture and cause change. This is part of the powerful, transformative roles that story circles have to play.
Carolyn: So, this event derived from story circle activities—which is not participation in a story circle as we have read about in some chapters in this volume nor the academic engagement with information from story circles, as we have read about in other chapters—had a profound impact personally and academically for viewers. I can't decide if that is further evidence that story circles have especially powerful transformative roles to play or evidence that lots of things can do what story circles do if they engage thoughtfully with genuine experience and share it with heart.
Bill: Perhaps both, but the tears of joy in the eyes of the storytellers who attended the performances tell me that the rootedness in stories matters a lot. Further, it was the real-world story characteristics of this data that made the biggest difference to my students, and the technique made it easier for them to access this data.
Jim: I don't think we should take too much away from the power of the theatre act itself. While other modes of delivery can also "engage thoughtfully with genuine experience and share it with heart" as Carolyn says, it's in the theatre, the most human of all arts, that we go to remember what it is to be human and what it is to take action. While I am also touched by the tears and initial outbursts of emotion in these comments, did seeing the story of Rita Dove's father enacted on stage move these spectators to take action in their own lives? And how? Those are the questions I want to have answered. But those answers remain unmeasurable…and that is the beauty and the frustration of the theatre's ephemerality.

- *It opened my eyes more to the racism that has existed in Akron.*
- *We need to work harder to respect one another and help each other.*
- *It made me look at the culture of Akron differently.*
- *The things I learned will always stick with me.*
- *Akron is rich with history and culture and I have a new found respect for the city.* *
- *It showed me more about how important my history is to my future.*
- *It made me want to learn more about my history.*
- *Makes me aware of the problems today.*
- *It hit deep.*
- *Inspirational to start change locally now.*
- *It made me think about the past and wonder if things have changed.*
- *I teach 7th/8th graders. I feel that I can relate more to what our youth are facing as far as race goes. I work my ass off for my kids. These are my students. Even though they are receiving the teaching to meet their needs, black/white students' futures will change because of society.*
- *I now have a new take on racism. I'm always nice to people in general, but now I've seen the other side of life and it has changed my opinion on things.*
- *This was very moving night. It made me rethink everything I've ever thought and assumed about race.*
- *It has opened my understanding of how blacks feel and what they go through still today here in our community.*
- *It had such a profound effect on my view of race and racism. It made salient the idea that there is a cultural struggle is still going on.*
- *The event was amazing! I'm glad I was required to attend because if not I might have missed out on a spectacular performance. I'm not even from Akron area and it was really insightful to learn about the history of African Americans in Akron Being of a person of many different races, I was oblivious to racism and to know that it exists at the level it does today is mind blowing.*
- *It makes me want to learn more about the history of Akron and how to promote change in attitude.*
- *This event made a major impression on me because I have always heard about the history of Akron through my grandparents and parents per-*

spective. My grandmother would always tell me stories of day trips to O'Neils and such but there were large holes in her description of the city (i.e. Howard Street). I have a better understanding of the subtly of the racism that occurs here. I did notice almost immediately upon my arrival at UA as an eighteen-year-old college freshman.

- *I understand how older blacks were treated.*

⁺Donna: As a result of preparation for this volume I discovered the 1974 master's thesis written by John Lee Maples, "The Ku Klux Klan in Akron: 1921–1928." The revelations about Akron history are staggering. I would not have discovered this important document if I hadn't participated in the story circles to collect stories for *The Colorline Play*.

Jim: I think all of us have found continued inspiration in the initial research and material we discovered during the early days of the Akron Story Circle Project. I'm now working on a performance involving Akron's history and its relationship to rubber. The stories of racism in the rubber industry in Akron led us to investigate the sources of the raw rubber and the horrific acts of torture and genocide that accompanied the harvesting of natural rubber in Africa and South America.

VII. IMPROMPTU STORY CIRCLES IN 2010

In 2010, Rethinking Race volunteers faced a harrowing experience. A comedy performance by Mark Cryer of Hamilton College entitled "99 Questions You've Always Wanted to Ask an African American but were too afraid for fear they'd break their foot off in your a**"● was scheduled for a campus theater with a capacity of 325. Comedy has proven to be a popular and effective vehicle for Rethinking Race. Story circles were planned after the performance, so a contingent of faculty and students trained in the story circle technique were present that evening.

●Amy: By the way, that is the official title, with caps on the beginning and no caps at the end and asterisks for the last two letters.

Bill: I remember at the time how difficult it was to tell people about the play without causing a pause or laughter or puzzled looks!

Jim: I think this performance was one of the most successful events for Rethinking Race. We even brought Mark Cryer back the next year! Unfortunately, I never got to see the performance because of the overflow situation. These story circles were among the most "charged" that I conducted on campus. It was truly a diverse population. They weren't already bound by the limits of a particular course or instructor and they were spontaneous. This gave the stories, for me, a resonance and truth that went beyond other stories told in classes by students.

The theater filled quickly to capacity and some one hundred additional students were clamoring to be admitted. Many, perhaps even most, of the students outside the theater needed to attend a Rethinking Race event for class credit, and some were required to attend this specific event. The excluded students demonstrated a range of emotion, from anger to tears, as it was near the end of the two weeks of Rethinking Race and students' opportunities to attend events were narrowing considerably. They were a formidable crowd. Happily, story circle veterans, including these authors, were able to defuse the situation. There was an on-the-fly decision to direct the excluded students to the rooms in the same building where the post-performance story circle were to take place.

In those rooms, we hastily gathered and ran what turned out to be some very compelling story circles with students who likely did not expect to be active participants in a Rethinking Race event that evening. The exact number of students and others who participated in these story circles is not known, but the evening had an obvious effect on those in attendance, as measured by the quantitative and qualitative data gathered in sixty-five surveys.

The data reported below were derived from not only the impromptu story circles, but also from the previously planned post-performance circle, at which Mark Cryer provided a meaningful contribution. One of the statements on the survey that students were asked to respond to was "This event gave me the opportunity to participate in an open and honest discussion." The mean score of responses to this statement, 4.62 (on the 1–5, strongly disagree to strongly agree scale), underscores the inclusive value of story circles. There was, as well, strong positive agreement (a mean score of 4.43) among respondents to the statement that the event caused the responder to "think more deeply about the issues related to race."

Table 3: Mean scores: Story Circles after and in lieu of "99 Questions"

Mean scores	Survey statements
3.94	Prior to attending my level of interest in participating in this event was high.
3.89	It is likely that I will participate in other Rethinking Race events during the next 2 weeks
4.62	This event gave me the opportunity to participate in an open and honest discussion.

Mean scores	Survey statements
4.43	This Rethinking Race event has made me think more deeply about the issues related to race.
4.21	This Rethinking Race event enhanced my interest in diversity and multicultural issues.
4.11	Gaining an understanding of diversity and multicultural issues will help me succeed in the work place.
4.36	I felt comfortable with the topics discussed in this Rethinking Race event.
4.23	I agreed with most of the comments that were made during this discussion/lecture/event.
3.77	Some topics covered by this event challenged my preconceived ideas about the topic.

In response to the open-ended question asking what they had learned that evening, respondents commented upon the universal themes of discrimination as well as the necessity and difficulty of enacting change:

- *That race issues are something everyone has some experience with. Everyone in my group had some interesting story to tell about their experience with being discriminated against. Hearing stories about others' discrimination or dealing with preconceived notions about race.*
- *We have all gone through struggles and discrimination, but we have to rise above ignorance and agree to make a change.*
- *To come out of your comfort zone and just listen.*
- *Change is possible, but it is still going to be hard work.*
- *Change is occurring and ignorance still exists. If we work together and talk, great things can happen.*
- *I learned about the many minority issues that arise throughout others' lives. I talked about the one time I learned what it actually felt like to be the minority. I was very nervous because I was not accustomed to the different situation but I very quickly learned to adapt because I was willing to meet others of different race and ethnicity and never wanted to judge others based on their physical appearance and characteristics.*
- *That racism is a form of ignorance. People do not think the same way and it is a misunderstanding between different people. Although there are many different races and a lot of diversity, thoughts on racism still haven't changed.*

- *How racism happens on more than 2, 3, etc. sides and my feeling that modern racism is more based on a misinterpretation of the majority of color/race belonging to a subculture that they do not like compared to the fact that a person is of a specific color/race. For example, I believe more people don't like a race, like the black race for the fact the majority are of the modern "ghetto" culture, but they may in fact talk to blacks that are of their own culture.*♦
- *Hearing how race has affected many different people in different ways, but now the people respond to race conflict and what they choose to do about it.*
- *How much racism still exists today (and that) racism goes both ways*
- *This event changed some preconceived notions about how far we had come as a culture when considering racism. I had assumed we were a great deal farther than we truly are.*
- *This was interesting. I wish he would have had time for another round of stories.*

♦**Carolyn:** Hey, fellow authors! How do you deal with students who are in this frame of mind in your classes?

Pat: I look forward to these teachable moments!! I find that many students in my classes are not equipped to discuss issues of race/racism, oppression, and bias. Like for example when students overlook or don't comprehend issues of privilege, and see racism as only existing "back in the day" with no connection to historical and/or current structural issues. I look to these instances as conversational starters to help scaffold these ideas and emotional roadblocks that interfere with students' ability to hear and understand viewpoints different from their own.

Bill: On the one hand, this comment invites me to connect the student and class conversation to the literature on race and place. That reframing usually sets a tone that makes it easier to be open and honest in the conversation. At the same time, shifting to focus on the tendency to conflate race and place leads some to find refuge in "see, we should not even be talking about race at all," and others to "it is all about how you are raised" in a Bill Cosby-like focus on individual behavior as if structure did not matter.

Jim: I have trouble reasoning with students about such matters as race. What I try to do is demonstrate as much as possible through the creation of teams or what I choose as material in class. For example, I had a MA student with a strong fundamentalist Christian background in class one summer. He was very afraid about "attempts to change his beliefs." I showed a film about the choreographer Bill T. Jones and his dance company which highlights the death of his gay partner, his bereavement, and the inclusive aspects of his company and work. At the end of the film, my student approached me and quietly thanked me. He had never seen an example of real love between same-sex partners and it made him rethink his attitudes towards gay relationships. His work for the rest of the course totally changed. He found a new creative freedom and even physically, he himself became more free. He lost some of his excess tension and physical blocks. Amazing. Unfortunately, it still didn't help his writing skills!

VIII. CROSS THE LINE

In 2012, the Akron Story Circle Project ran an event entitled Crossing the Line and Story Circles. It featured an activity in which participants were asked to walk over a line on the floor if they were in concurrence with various statements. The statements centered on behaviors and experiences, often of a very personal nature. This activity was followed by a series of story circles.

The purpose of the event was: "to provide a safe space for dialogue to occur around issues of collective importance that come from personal experience with race."*

*Bill: And the addition of the Cross the Line activity provided another layer of structure to the experience, highlighting silence and observation, self within communities and a dynamic and contingent picture of the intersections of race, class, gender, and sexual orientation. The story circles that followed felt particularly emotional and open-hearted to me.

Pat: I agree, the willingness to cross the line demonstrated the successful creation of a safe space to share.

The data gathered from 74 event surveys indicate once again a high level of impact on attendees, particularly when compared to the overall mean for these statements derived from 2,221 event surveys collected (Qammar 2012). The questions on the 2012 surveys were somewhat different than those from previous years, as mentioned, to more closely align assessment with the University's strategic plan.

Many students attended events because they were required to by faculty and therefore express a distinct lack of interest in advance. In 2012, 41.8 percent of attendees who completed surveys said that they were required to attend a specific event for a graded assignment; another 24.4 percent said they would receive extra credit (Qammar 2012). Interestingly, attendees at Akron Story Circle Project events express higher advance interest than the overall mean. The data provide a strong indication of the power of these events. Those completing surveys had a stronger than average responses (reported below as grand means) on every one of the key questions, assessing the learning that took place through attendance, having the opportunity to participate in frank discussion, thinking more deeply about racial issues, enhancing interest and understanding in race-based topics generally and so forth. Crossing the Line was no exception.

Table 4: Mean scores & comparison to grand means—
Crossing the Line 2012

Cross the Line	Grand means	Survey statements
3.21	3.37	Prior to attending my level of interest in participating in this event was high.
4.21	4.19	I learned something by attending this event.
4.53	3.76	This event gave me the opportunity to participate in an open and honest discussion.
4.21	3.96	This Rethinking Race event has made me think more deeply about the issues related to race.
4.00	3.85	This Rethinking Race event enhanced my interest in diversity and multicultural issues.
4.32	4.19	Gaining an understanding of diverse people, cultures or ideas will help me succeed in the work place.
3.95	3.64	This event has made me re-examine my views on a topic or issue.
4.32	3.90	This event contributed to my understanding people of other racial and ethnic backgrounds.
4.21	4.05	This event allowed me to better understand someone else's views by imaging how an issue looks from another perspective.
4.26	4.07	Attending this event was a good use of my time.

Some of the responses to the open-ended question asking how profound an impact the event had on participants are below. From these it is clear that the event raised awareness about the viewpoints of others, revealing both more similarities and more differences between attendees and others.

- *People have different attitudes toward each other, but people are suffering and we may not know that.*
- *Made me more cognizant of other people's desires and what they seek. Gave me a better alternating perspective of how those of other races view racism.*
- *Everybody cries male/females.*
- *All of us have to cross lines we don't want to.*
- *Issues about self-identification are challenges for all!*
- *Many people are in the same boat as me... more than expected.*
- *We think we experience things by ourselves when we are actually all in this together in terms of the emotions we share.*
- *It is important to listen.*
- *The term 'colored' is subjective.*
- *I think the 'boundaries' theme was the most profound for me. Breaking Boundaries! Understanding Boundaries.*
- *Everyone feels different about something.*•

•**Bill:** So many of these, more so than comments on other story circles, focused on empathy. I suspect this is a result of the addition of the silent line crossing activity before telling stories.

Donna: I am underwhelmed by many of the comments made by students about their experiences in Rethinking Race. They don't seem to me to be the comments of people who have undergone a transformative experience. On the other hand, the comments about Crossing the Line seemed to me to be heartfelt. At least part of the reason the participants seem more open and empathetic as a result of this event might be explained by the leadership provided by Pat Hill. I went into Crossing the Line knowing the questions that Pat would ask the participants and wondering if students would engage. Pat created a "place" in which all of us felt willing to cross the line. An amazing experience!

Jim: Again, I come back to the importance of action, performance, in stimulating transformation. Embodying the experience in a simple way can be much more effective than sitting at a desk and talking about it. I think the big takeaway from this activity is how to make each classroom assignment, even the most theoretical, a performative experience? I remember a dinner with some astronomer friends in Italy who spontaneously improvised a demonstration of the movement of the earth and the moon around the sun which has stayed with me much more clearly than any diagrams or illustrations ever have.

The parallel paths of the Akron Story Circle Project and Rethinking Race: Black, White and Beyond are remarkable to note. Both tread into human territory that is simultaneously universal yet remarkably sensitive. Everyone has stories about race and everyone can benefit from learning more about race, whether that learning derives from a comedy routine, a film, a lecture on history or genetics ... or from something as incredibly powerful (and as simple) as individuals coming together to share their stories with others in an atmosphere of trust and openness.

Both Rethinking Race and story circles continue to serve the University as well as the community at large, providing common ground and an open environment in which students, faculty, staff and community members can learn, discuss and become engaged in those topics that otherwise remain "undiscussable."◆

◆**Donna:** It is very helpful to see the kinds of data and feedback collected about Rethinking Race so far. It makes me realize how much work remains to be done in understanding why Rethinking Race and Story Circles in particular are such important experience for us all.

Pat: I agree with Donna. Amy, your findings are very revealing of the continued importance of the Rethinking Race programs.

Amy: These comments from attendees—and the struggles we see with our students—are exactly why we work so darn hard to do story circles, plan Rethinking Race, urge our students to move beyond their preconceptions ... on and on and on. It's all about getting beyond the "undiscussables." It's not easy. It's hard work, as they say, and well worth doing.

REFERENCES

"Animating Democracy: Fostering Civic Engagement through Arts and Culture." 2016. Animating Democracy. http://animatingdemocracy.org.

Caruthers, Loyce, Sue Thompson, and Eugene Eubanks. 2004. "Using Storytelling to Discuss the 'Undiscussables' in Urban Schools." *Multicultural Perspectives* 6, no. 3: 36–41.

Maples, John Lee. 1974. "The Akron Ohio Ku Klux Klan, 1921–1928." Master's thesis, The University of Akron.

Orfield, Gary. 2009. "Reviving the Goal of an Integrated Society: A 21st Century Challenge." The Civil Rights Project. University of California at Los Angeles.

Qammar, Helen. 2011. "Rethinking Race: Black, White & Beyond: A Unique Model to Enhance Essential 21st Century Skills." March 29. University of Akron Institute for Teaching and Learning.

———. 2012. "Rethinking Race: Black, White & Beyond." March 28. University of Akron Institute for Teaching and Learning.

Ropers-Huilman, Rebecca, Kelly T. Winters, and Kathryn A. E. Enke. 2013. "Discourses of Whiteness: White Students at Catholic Women's Colleges (Dis)engaging Race." *Journal of Higher Education* 84, no. 1: 28–55.
West, Cornel. 1993. *Race Matters*. Boston: Beacon Press.

The Akron Color Line Project Performance

(Drawn from the stories of people who live in Akron, Ohio)

Devised and directed by James Slowiak

in collaboration with The University of Akron Color Line Performance Team, including India Burton, Treviel Cody, Yulia Gray, Rosilyn Jentner, Kyle (T. J.) Josza, Erika Kinney, Christopher Laney, Avery McCullough, Benjamin Rexroad, Sarah Taylor, and others

The setting is an empty space with several chairs and coat racks with costume elements for quick changes. For Version 2, slides of contemporary Akron landscapes and neighborhoods were projected upstage. All photographs in this chapter are by Andrew McAllister and reproduced with permission of the Center for Applied Theatre and Active Culture and New World Performance Laboratory.

THE WALKAROUND*

> ***Carolyn:** Jim Slowiak and India Burton, an actor from the first and second casts to work with Jim on this play, sat down together one afternoon to talk about the production. Their words were recorded by Carolyn Behrman and form the core around which the other volume authors have commented here.

The walkaround starts upstage left and proceeds in the clockwise direction.•

> **•Jim:** Rehearsals and performances of the first version of the play took place right after Barack Obama was elected president and there was a kind of euphoria surrounding the work, a very positive attitude. The second version was worked on a year later and already

Audience at the Belcher Building enjoying *The Akron Color Line Project Performance* Version 1

we found ourselves more critical in our approach to racial conflict—the second version was more edgy.

India: ...and the cast in the second version included people who were more vocal—they each had something to say and were comfortable saying it. The second cast included people who had undergone some sort of injustice or had been through a situation where they had to think more concretely about race.

I remember you had us bring in recent news articles that dealt with racial issues from the local papers and I started to realize how much race was a huge factor in how and what gets reported. And especially in any violence issues....

Jim: There was a rash of violence around that time for you personally, wasn't there?

India: Yes, my little cousin was murdered during the second week of rehearsals. And there were other cases—lots of violent events, unsolved murders, cold cases. And the other black performers working on the piece could all empathize...

Jim: One of the news stories that was current at the time concerned a group of African American teens attacking a family outside their house on the Fourth of July. We all understood the reporting to have been unfairly one-sided and we became very sensitive to the way in which the media reported events such as this one. In fact, the media's representation of race became a theme throughout the second version of the performance.

AVERY: Akron is a high place.◆

INDIA: Akron is a low place.

> ♦**Pat:** The media is a powerful presence in people's lives—impacting how people are socialized to think about others as well as themselves.
>
> **Jim:** We started the play with a walkaround. The title, the "walkaround," comes from the nineteenth-century minstrel shows. Back then, it was usually used as a finale, a kind of competition, where each performer would move to the edge of the stage, one by one, and perform a short, virtuosic dance. But we used the walkaround as a way to introduce the cast and the city of Akron to the audience. Different "characters," historical facts, and impressions of the city were highlighted in our version of the walkaround.
>
> **India:** I remember it all came from a song. I started out singing. For some reason, I was doing Sojourner Truth everywhere that year. I already knew the "Ain't I a Woman" speech by heart so you had me break it into little bits and pieces. Someone would do something, perform an action, and you had me respond to them with a little bit of Sojourner Truth's speech.
>
> **Jim:** Our walkaround ended as everyone lined up—upstage—with Treviel doing the rap he composed from Martin Luther King's "Letter from the Birmingham Jail."
>
> **India:** And we all added our voices to it.

YULIA: Akron is no place.

TREVIEL: Akron is my home.

INDIA: Akron is a high place.

AVERY: Akron is a low place.

YULIA: Akron is some place.

TREVIEL: Akron is my home.

T. J.: Akron is where Sojourner Truth delivered her "Ain't I a Woman" speech in 1851.

CHRIS: Akron is John Brown.♦

> ♦**Donna:** Samuel Lane, the first sheriff of Akron and author of *Fifty Years and Over of Akron & Summit County*, devotes a chapter to John Brown and calls him "Our own John Brown." When John Brown asked the citizens of Summit county to canvass the village of Akron on behalf of his cause to help keep the state of Kansas from becoming a slave state we read: "At a small but enthusiastic meeting, to whom he gave a graphic account of the bloody struggle, a committee was appointed to canvass the village in behalf of the good cause of which committee, it was the privilege, and the pleasure of the writer to be a member" (584–92). Samuel Lane, retired sheriff of Akron, wrote this about 1856. Less than fifty years later, Akron experienced The Akron Riot and only twenty years after that the largest Ku Klux Klan membership in the country. What happened to create this change of heart?

SARAH: The Underground Railroad.

T. J. & YULIA: Freedom.

TREVIEL: Akron is my home.

CHRIS: Akron is—

AVERY: Akron was—•

> •Jim: Most of the things we said about the city came from lists that the actors made. In rehearsals we would sit and make lists about different aspects and impressions of our life in Akron and how we viewed and experienced the city.
>
> India: And there were lots of things that arose at other times during the rehearsals that were brought in as material for us to work on.
>
> Bill: What does this mean, specifically? It seems to partly mean you drew from personal experience, and perhaps from whatever everyone says about Akron. This seems smart, but I would like to hear... what are the types of impressions that came up, what aspects were highlighted, was there any disagreement and how was that reconciled?
>
> Jim: Bill, India, and I are talking here about the walkaround specifically. Each line that is spoken by the actors came from the lists that we generated as a group. Answers to questions about the city and life in the city. I don't recall any disagreements. Certainly, my role as instructor/director came into play here in making the final selection of what worked or what didn't work and sometimes I had to assert some "authority" in giving tasks to the various cast members to research things like John Brown's relationship to Akron or the context of Sojourner Truth's speech. But this was all part of the learning process, the creative process. The impressions that came up are those included in the script. Nothing was really eliminated unless it was redundant or clearly took the tone of the play in another direction.
>
> Carolyn: In the field of social science research known as cognitive domain analysis, lists are a vital source of data. The theory is that when people share a social position or a cultural context—a domain, they have a largely shared understanding of the components of that domain. By asking people to list items or elements of particular experiences related to the domain, we can begin to understand not only how the domain is constructed (components' interrelationships and relative importance) but also the degree to which each is shared by the various members of the group. Knowing that particular attributes of membership will increase or decrease the likelihood that a person includes an element on a list can tell us about dimensions of difference and give us greater understanding of the workings of access, power, privilege, and counter-narrative.
>
> Jim: Carolyn, I think my early training with anthropologist James Spradley and his approach to ethnographic research has influenced my creative process more than I realized. I see this script very much as an ethnography of Akron told from our little culture's point of view.

SARAH: Rubber Capital of the World.

TREVIEL: Akron is my home.

SARAH: Akron is the factories—

YULIA: The soot—

AVERY: The filth

T. J.: It's an opportunity .

AVERY: It's a trap.

TREVIEL: Akron is my home.♦

> ♦**Amy:** John Brown, a hero of the abolition movement, might today be characterized as a terrorist.
> **Bill:** "Home community" is nearly always a complex and contested concept, because it involves including "virtuous citizens" as insiders and excluding "disruptive subjects" as outsiders in the very process of constructing the community itself. So a statement like "Akron is my home" can be very mundane even as it is also multilayered and ripe with power and subordination implications.

A stop moment while T. J. speaks next.

T. J.: Akron is built on the blood of hundreds of thousands of Africans, South Americans, and Asians, tortured, mutilated, and killed collecting rubber.

ERIKA: Akron is the place I want to leave.

ROSILYN: Akron is the place I want to stay.

AVERY: Akron is improving.

YULIA: Akron is decaying—

T. J.: Coming together—

CHRIS: Falling apart.

A stop moment while Sarah speaks next.

SARAH: Akron is where Bill Clinton held his first Town Hall Meeting on race in 1996.♦

> ♦**Amy:** Clinton's reason for visiting Akron was to launch a national conversation about race. Sadly, that conversation was derailed by the Monica Lewinsky scandal that broke shortly after his visit. I've often wondered if racial tensions might have been ameliorated

had this conversation taken place. I also thought it was pretty darn brave of Clinton to
address the proverbial elephant in the room—race! He could have done what so many
others have—ignored the problem, thereby exacerbating it.

Bill: True. And he chose Akron because of the Coming Together Project, which had done
great things to bring black and white into one conversation…but later fizzled and is
now gone. Sometimes the stories that need to be told do not have happy endings.

ERIKA: Akron is a battleground—•

•**Pat:** That is why the renewal of conversations on race through avenues like Story Circles
is imperative.

ROSILYN: And a promise.

SARAH: It's what we got.

ERIKA: Akron is our home.

The walkaround ends with everyone singing Treviel's rap.

ALL: "We are caught in an inescapable network of mutuality, tied in a
single garment of destiny. Whatever affects one directly affects all
indirectly."

Everyone ends upstage in a line facing upstage.

India comes out and says:

INDIA: Those are the words of the great Martin Luther King written
from the Birmingham Jail in 1963 in the heat of the Civil Rights
Movement. Throughout its history, Akron, our home, has often
found itself at the center of racial conflict. *(India sings "Hang on to
the World.")*•

•**Jim:** I never asked you where that song, "Hang on to the World," came from. It was a
Donny Hathaway song?
India: Yes, at the time I was listening to a lot of Donny Hathaway. I thought it brought
hope to the situation. It became relevant to the performance because it rang hopeful in
relation to the material on the Civil Rights Movement. Later on in the play, we sing
one of Sam Cooke's songs—the song he wrote that became an anthem for the Civil
Rights Movement—"A Change is Gonna Come." You had put me in charge of the
music and I felt the two songs mirrored each other.
Jim: The story of "That Akron Riot" was a new scene for the second version of the play.
I found it in a newsletter from Akron-Summit County Public Library. I remember when

Jim Slowiak and India Burton in *The Akron Color Line Project Performance* Version I

I first brought the story into rehearsal everyone was freaked out by it. First, we performed the story as a contemporary newscast and then it sort of morphed into a television game show. I think that by using familiar frames to view this material, it allowed all of us to engage the material as more than ancient history. It became something alive and still possible. We all felt that certain members of the cast (specifically Avery and Treviel) might easily find themselves in a similar situation even today.

India: The thing I remember is that rehearsing this scene is when it got really real for the cast. It was at this point that the white actors didn't know if it was okay to say "nigger." Rosilyn sang that counting rhyme with "catch a nigger by the toe" and she wasn't saying it all the way.

There were several of these awkward moments when the white actors wanted to be respectful to us, but for the sake of the show it was necessary to tackle the ugly realities.

I remember, Jim, that you said you used to say that rhyme when you were little, but that you didn't really think about what it meant.

Jim: Yes, growing up in the fifties and early sixties in a small town in north-central Wisconsin, this version of "Eeny Meeny Miny, Moe" was our usual way of counting out on the playground. I don't think any of us realized what we were saying. No one had ever seen a black person (unless you count Sidney Poitier in *Lilies of the Field* or Nat King Cole on TV). In fact, thinking about it now, I was always the kid who was last to be chosen for any team sports or anything, so deep down I think I empathized with the subjects of these kinds of rhymes, "Eeny, Meeny, Miny, Moe" or "Ten Little Indians." They were the ones being marginalized, stepped on, laughed at. "My mother says to pick the very best one. Out goes you!" It's so cruel. When I was selected in second or third grade to perform a solo version of *Little Black Sambo* for the PTA, I remember the

strangeness, the uncomfortableness, of the experience. I think I started my personal journey of "integration" long before I realized what any of it meant.
Carolyn: I grew up saying "catch a tiger by the toe."
Jim: That's what the difference of about ten years can make.
India: I didn't know that rhyme until I heard it in rehearsal.

Everyone moves as if soaking up the rays of the sun. Sarah, India, Avery, T. J., Yulia, Chris, and Treviel form a "horse-drawn carriage."

THAT AKRON RIOT

REPORTER (ERIKA):[1] One hundred and ten years ago, on August 22, 1900, one of the most violent and racially motivated events in history occurred right here on the streets of Akron. The riot made headlines around the country and became known as "That Akron Riot." The story begins with a six-year-old girl named Christina Maar. Monday night, August 20, little Christina was found "wandering aimlessly," crying and all alone on Merriman Road. Earlier that night, around five p.m., she had been playing in her yard (on East Avenue) when a witness saw a man riding a horse attached to a road cart come by and "entice" her to take a ride. She was then later found at seven p.m. that night on Merriman Road, "so badly frightened and her sufferings were of such an intense nature that she was not able to give a very good description of the fiend…" (*Akron Beacon Journal*, August 22, 1900). Akron Police were led to believe that someone attempted to rape and assault little Christina, and they were determined to find the perpetrator.✝

✝**Pat:** Jim—thank you for sharing that profound memory. Ballads like "Ten Little Niggers" appeared relatively "harmless" but actually shaped social and cultural race consciousness, and the ultimate legacy that this and other such "rhymes" leaves behind is the belief of black inferiority.
Bill: Jim, you note the value of connecting the riot to familiar frames. I can see the value (and have seen the magic you do), but I wonder: to what degree was there also a cost? By making the disruptive familiar, what did we lose? Why did this juxtaposition of the disruptive and familiar result in (as India put it) a major move toward making it real? There seems to be more to this story…can you unpack it a bit for me?
Jim: Exactly, Pat. That's why I felt it was necessary to include the rhyme in this story of "That Akron Riot." We researched the period when this rhyme became prevalent and

it fit in with the time frame of the story so we went with it as a way of showing the kind of atmosphere that shaped those events in 1900 Akron. Bill, you're asking a lot in your question/comment: an analysis of the power of parody and satire as well as a comparison of the effects of realistic drama to other more expressionistic or agitprop forms. Film can do "realism" much better than theatre. There is no way that a theatre production could depict the horrors of slavery in the same way as *12 Years a Slave*, for example. However, theatre does something else. Theatre can make us believe that a simple chair is a king's throne and a toilet brush is his sceptre. By framing "That Akron Riot" in a contemporary manner, I believe that we actually brought the material more to life than if we had merely illustrated the events as they had happened. The actors engaged personally with the material and the audience was able to see and hear the story in a less emotional, more active way. The great twentieth-century theatre director and playwright Bertolt Brecht believed that empathy meant acceptance. If the audience empathizes emotionally they somehow feel excused from taking any action against what they are seeing and if the actor performs within the given circumstances of the story without questioning those circumstances (as an actor must do in a realistic rendering of a story), the actor is accepting implicitly the circumstances as unchangeable. Our way of handling the story in this production forced each of us to have a social/political point of view about the material. We could not stay neutral in the face of what we were doing. Nor could the audience. It was pure agitprop, I admit it. But it was also pure theatre.

Rosilyn sings "Eeny, Meeny, Miny, Moe." The carriage stops to "entice" her. Rosilyn gets on the carriage. The carriage proceeds upstage and to center. Rosilyn sings "Eeny, Meeny, Miny, Moe." The carriage stops center with the line "catch a nigger by the toe." Everyone runs off, leaving Peck (Treviel) and (Reporter) Erika center.

REPORTER: It was discovered that night that Louis Peck, an African American, had secured a horse and carriage from Pringle's livery stable located on North Main Street. The horse and carriage had been returned around eight p.m. by a different man. The police told Mr. Pringle that they were looking for a man who was riding a horse attached to a road cart. Mr. Pringle did not suspect Louis Peck at first, but then changed his story and told the police that it must be Louis Peck they were looking for. Beacon Journal reporters interviewed witnesses in Christina Maar's neighborhood and they all seemed to believe that it was an African American that abducted the little girl.

T. J.: I saw a man in a cart. He was a nigger.

ROSILYN: It was a nigger. Definitely a man of color.•

India: Another thing that was interesting about this scene was when we all as a group became the horses and carriage—and later there was a scene when we became a bus.

Jim: Yes, it was a different kind of performance style for all of you. We had no set and few props and you all worked out how to transform into what was needed with only your bodies. It's very basic storytelling and physical theatre technique, but extremely effective and often theatrically more interesting than if we had an actual carriage, bus, or real working water fountains.

ERIKA: Police showed a photograph of Peck to one of the witnesses, and Peck was identified as the assailant of the little girl.

CHRIS: This is a photograph of Louis Peck. Is he the one who kidnapped the little girl?◆

Jim: The Louis Peck story was the first material we worked with that didn't come from a story circle and I think it allowed us more freedom as performers. With the story circle stories we were careful and concerned not to lose the integrity of the story—not to lose the person's actual words—so we were cautious in how we staged the stories at first. The Louis Peck story was historical and we were stimulated to explore all the aspects of the story and look for different ways of presenting it.

This story gave us, as a company, permission to turn the stories into theatre in a variety of ways. We found the freedom we needed to approach the other stories.

I remember John O'Neal advising us to narrate less and open up the stories—to be more theatrical. This began to happen as we worked on the Louis Peck episode.

India: And this story also brought the content firmly back to Akron and made us focus on the familiar in a different way. Akron is just Akron for us but it took on an historical, almost mythical, dimension in this story. The cast became more interested in doing research into the history of Akron and we began to realize the connection between Akron, racial violence, and even the rubber atrocities in the Congo and South America.

Bill: The freedom provided "made us focus on the familiar in a different way. Akron is just Akron." This is like a Zen koan. Brilliant. Simple. Powerful.

YULIA: He's the man. He's a colored man.

REPORTER: Peck was arrested after he returned from Youngstown on a passenger train Tuesday night after midnight.

Police siren, then movement.

REPORTER: He was taken directly to the Summit County courthouse, and a confession was quickly obtained. Peck pled guilty to the crime as charged and was arraigned within twenty minutes.

Peck is taken upstage and beaten.

REPORTER: Sheriff Frank G. Kelly and other authorities believed it was
  prudent to get the prisoner out of the city as a cautionary measure in
  case public outrage started something unpredictable in light of the
  Maar incident. Around four on Wednesday afternoon, Peck was
  taken to Cleveland, to the Cuyahoga County jail, for temporary
  custody.

Peck is taken across to stage left.

REPORTER: As it would turn out, Sheriff Kelly was right in his
  thinking because something very unpredictable and terrible did
  occur on that August night.

The ensemble (except Treviel and Erika) begins the riot.

INDIA: Lynch Louis Peck!

ALL (EXCEPT TREVIEL AND ERIKA): Lynch Louis Peck!

T. J.: Any nigger will do!

ALL: Any nigger will do!

ROSILYN: The police shot and killed two children!

ALL: The police shot and killed two children!

CHRIS: Take the city building down by force!

ALL: Take the city building down by force!

AVERY: Bricks, stones and dynamite!

ALL: Bricks, stones and dynamite!

YULIA: It's blood we want! Blood! Blood! Blood!

ALL: It's blood we want! Blood! Blood! Blood!

SARAH: Set the City Building ablaze!✝

✝**Donna:** This series of brief violent statements is in keeping with the contemporary
description of what happened that night. Ordinary citizens became enraged and violent.
When it was over they went home and except for two children who were accidently
killed by the police, everyone went back to being ordinary citizens.

Ensemble makes "fire" with bodies.

PECK (TREVIEL): Damn, Damn, Damn....

ERIKA: Firemen fought to keep the fires under control all Wednesday
   night and into early Thursday morning.

*The rioters form a single file, holding "rifles," and march upstage. Then they face
downstage, pointing the "rifles." Then they face upstage.*

ERIKA: Ohio Governor George K. Nash ordered the Ohio National
   Guard to take the city under martial law but was not able to get
   assistance as quickly as he requested. Companies from the Ohio
   National Guard entered the city by special train at eight thirty on
   Thursday morning. They proceeded to march down to the corner of
   Mill Street and Main Street, where they were headquartered at the
   Hotel Buchtel. There were also several National Guardsmen
   brought in to protect designated spots downtown, including the
   County Courthouse. Mayor Young made a declaration that in the
   meantime, all city saloons were to be closed so that the influence of
   alcohol would not be allowed to further cause any other crimes or
   up risings.

CHRIS: I need a drink!

T. J.: All the saloons are closed.

CHRIS: It's that nigger's fault!

ERIKA: I was able to interview Louis Peck at the Cleveland Jail. *(Goes to
   him.)* What do you recall about the crime you are accused of?

PECK: Oh I was drunk and didn't know what I did. Even after I had
   sobered up and was arrested I couldn't imagine what it was for.
   After I reached the jail and they told me what I was charged with, it
   began to dawn upon me what I had done, and the enormity of the
   crime almost set me crazy...

ERIKA: What do you plead?

PECK: I will only plead guilty to the charge if they do not sentence me to
   life in prison. And get me the heck out of Cleveland because it's
   entirely too close to Akron.

Kyle (T. J.) Josza, Treviel Cody, Sarah Taylor, and Christopher Laney in rehearsal for Version II

ERIKA: On Thursday, a special grand jury was empaneled and Louis
    Peck was brought back to Akron to receive his final sentence.
    Welcome to Akron's very own version of Jeopardy with special
    contestant Louis Peck!

*Cast sings the Jeopardy theme. They form a V-shape. The "Contestants" make one
step forward when it's their turn, and then step back in line.*

SARAH: My name is Louis Peck.

ERIKA: Ding!

ROSILYN: My name is Louis Peck.

ERIKA: Ding!

INDIA: My name is Louis Peck…I mean, I got all the
    qualifications…I'm black!

ERIKA: Ding!

PECK: My name is Louis Peck—1900.

ERIKA: Ding!

CHRIS: Contestant Number One! If we went out to a fancy dinner what would you order?

SARAH: Assuming you're buying. . . .

CHRIS: Wrong!

SARAH: I just want a handful of candy.

ERIKA: Ding!

AVERY: Contestant Number Two! If we were going out on a date, what mode of transportation would you use?

ROSILYN: Something classy. Like a horse. A horse-drawn carriage. Final answer.

ERIKA: Ding!

YULIA: Contestant Number Three! Tell me, how much wood would a woodchuck chuck, if a woodchuck could chuck wood?

INDIA: If I was a woodchuck, I'd know what a woodchuck would chuck. But I'm not. I'm Louis Peck.

ERIKA: Ding!

T. J.: Contestant Number Four! Why did you assault and rape an innocent little white girl?

PECK: Say again?

ALL (EXCEPT TREVIEL AND ERIKA): Guilty. Guilty. Guilty. Guilty.

They form a tight circle around Peck.

PECK: No-o-o-o-o-o-o-o!!!!

ERIKA: With only one witness, Peck was indicted on the charge of rape. Peck pled guilty and was sentenced to a life in prison all within an hour and a half. On Friday afternoon, he was taken to the Ohio Penitentiary.

INDIA: This is an awful story.

ROSILYN: (*To Erika.*) Yeah. Why are you telling us this story?

T. J.: Is this how race relations in Akron began?

CHRIS: Whatever happened to Louis Peck anyway?

PECK: Louis Peck was eventually pardoned on May 6, 1913 by the Ohio
State Board of Administration, former warden of the Ohio
Penitentiary E. T. Jones, and Governor James M. Cox. The
members of the State Board of Administration were of the opinion
that there were grave doubts as to Peck's guilt, and he was given no
opportunity to establish his innocence. Peck's lawyers also believed
that he had been railroaded into pleading guilty.•

•Donna: This would also be a good story. Who fought for Peck's pardon?
Jim: I found in the Journal of the Senate of the State of Ohio that Louis Peck was pardoned on the recommendation of the warden and the Ohio Board of Administration
based on an affidavit from "the family physician of the injured girl that while attempt
had been made no rape had actually taken place. Peck's prison conduct had been good
and the warden found employment for him at once in the state of West Virginia" (56).

ROSILYN: So what happened next?

AVERY: In 1917 the NAACP formed a chapter here in Akron. The
African American population grew rapidly due to the many job
openings in the rubber factories.

CHRIS: In 1921, the Ku Klux Klan started a chapter in Summit County.

T. J.: During the twenties, the Summit County chapter of the KKK grew
to be the largest chapter in the United States with over 52,000
members, many of whom were prominent figures in the Akron
community and city government.

SARAH: In 1929, the Summit County chapter of the KKK officially
disbanded.•

•Carolyn: I found this glimpse into the terrifying jeopardy of being black when a white
child went missing really chilling when it was performed. Since then, I have walked
past those sites in downtown Akron mentioned in the story and felt a shiver. It is not
surprising to me that the NAACP sought to set up a chapter here when they did and
also not a surprise that the KKK arrived. What does surprise me is the disbanding of
the KKK in 1929. Can any of you shed light on why this element in the pressured landscape of race relations in an industrialized town disbanded?
Donna: John Lee Maples' 1974 master's thesis, "The Akron, Ohio Ku Klux Klan, 1921–
1928" was written as a result of interviews with contemporaries of the Klan members.

Though elderly when interviewed they recounted stories of Klan control of the Akron School Board, the Sheriff's office, and the Mayor's office. In a dramatic scene, the head of the Akron Klan was asked by the National Grand Dragon to step down from his leadership position just as the Akron contingent was about to march in Washington, DC. Upon return to Akron most Akron Klansmen quit the national Klan and formed a new organization. A dispute over Klan funds between those loyal to and those who were leaving the national organization signaled the end of the Klan's power in Akron.

To go back to Carolyn's question, I find it equally puzzling to understand why the Klan became so powerful in Akron. Many local leaders seem to have been members of the secret organization. They were particularly powerful in the Akron School Board where they were in the majority for most of the 1920s. Though they did not favor integration with blacks, their target was primarily Catholics.

Pat: I was just reading an article on the growth of hate and extremism in our country since the 2008 Election of President Obama. Currently the numbers of KKK groups is holding steady at 163 chapters nationwide with a strong presence in Ohio.

INDIA: During the 1930s and 1940s, African Americans flocked to Akron for the new jobs. They settled between Euclid Ave and the Ohio Canal near the B. F. Goodrich factory complex and in the little Cuyahoga Valley along North Street. Howard Street became the center of their activities. (*Pause.*) Howard Street—a place for jazz music and black entrepreneurs.

A NIGHT OUT

India sings "At Last."

Sarah and Chris come on stage and start dancing to "At Last."

SARAH: As a teenager, I always wanted to go down to Howard Street to see Bobby "Blue" Bland, B. B. King, and Benny Rivers. But by the time I got old enough to go, I had two boys and a husband.* *(Chris and Sarah sit in chairs facing the audience.)* So me and my husband would pack up the boys in their pajamas and make sure we brought blankets and something to eat. *(Two actors, Rosilyn and Yulia, playing the boys, run up behind Chris and Sarah.)* Oh, and, of course, something for them to tee-tee in. *(Sarah gives the boys a "can" and they turn away and "tee-tee," then give it back to Sarah.)* And we headed on down to Howard Street. Now, we made sure we got there early. Sometimes they got stars on both sides of the street. Oh, it was like a fashion show. *(Two actors, "the fashion models," each on*

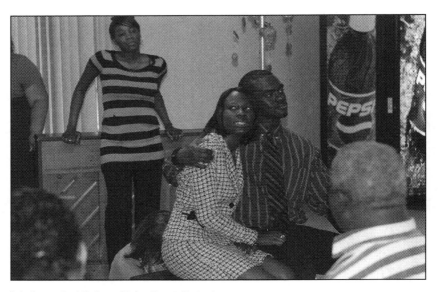

India Burton, Sarah Taylor, and Robert Grant in Version I

either side of the stage walk from upstage to downstage and back.) Me
and my husband, we enjoyed watching the stars. Now, eventually,
the boys would fall asleep. (*The boys fall asleep.*) And me and my
husband would just sit there and listen.

⁺Carolyn: This quiet comment on women's lives slipped by me in the play. I wonder now
what Sarah thought about it and whose story the line wells from.
Pat: You are right, Carolyn. There is an even greater narrative on women's lives behind the
shadow of this brief comment.

India sings "At Last."

Sarah puts her head on Chris's shoulder.

SARAH: It was our night out.•

•Donna: I loved this story in the play. It also shows us what can be lost in the rush to
Urban Renewal.

INDIA: Howard Street was the place to be.... (*T. J., Avery, Erika and Treviel do their "In the Ghetto" dance routine.*) Bars and clubs, that's all we had in Akron.

SARAH: You can say that again.

Chris blows a whistle and becomes a white cop. The whistle "wakes up" Rosilyn and Yulia who become streetwalkers. Other actors create a street scene.

CHRIS: "When you see a white man and a black man together, the black man is in bad company." According to my grandfather, this statement summed up the feelings of the Akron police in the thirties and forties. At that time, there was only one black policeman on the force. There was no easy assignment for this guy anywhere in Akron. There was great racial hostility on the force, and in the community. There were only two predominantly black neighborhoods—the first was Howard Street, and later out Wooster Avenue. My grandfather spoke to my father only once about taking black people into the station. He said they never went to court. Differences were settled in the alley.♦

♦**Donna:** None of the stories about the "blight" on Howard Street are as compelling as the stories about the creativity there and this is true even in the later version of the play.

Actors engage in their "Howard Street" actions, creating the atmosphere of life in the neighborhood in the 1950s.

MIKE'S STORY

MIKE (T. J.): My dad was also a policeman on Howard Street from about 1946 till about 1955. His beat was nothing but Howard Street. In 1953 my brother Dick, who went under the name of Ron Harrison at WAKR, was the youngest disc jockey in Akron. He started at the age of fifteen. By the time Dick got to be eighteen or nineteen years of age he used to go down to the Top Hat and the Green Turtle, which were two nightclubs on Howard Street. All these celebrities would come in and perform at Tangiers, Bill Palombo's, The Mayflower—places of that sort.

Audience at Belcher Building responding to seeing their stories on stage

*Song: "It Don't Mean A Thing If It Ain't Got That Swing," with the actors also vocalizing the "musical instruments."**

*Jim: Our first prompt for collecting stories in the field was about Howard Street. The whole project really began with Donna Webb's efforts to create artwork about the history of Howard Street in a senior citizen's residence on North Hill in Akron. Our initial task was to do a performance about Howard Street. And, especially in the first version, Howard Street became the center of the piece.

It was a Howard Street that was very rose-colored, however, and that always bothered me. A kind of Norman Rockwell vision of life in the black neighborhoods. So wonderful—just jazz and good times on Howard Street. The task in the second version became how to reconcile that whitewashed memory with one more connected to the reality of segregation, job insecurity, discrimination, and eventual urban decline.

India: We got some great lines from those first stories. Like "In them days we was walking all the time." And the story about the $300 dress and the observation from the one lady about there being more prejudice up north than in the south.

Jim: I remember we had a white actor tell the story of the $300 dress in the first version. But that wasn't working. We decided in the second version to have white actors play white and black actors to play black. Color became more important in the second version.

India: That's right. I think that was an important change. In a piece about race the visual aspect can't be ignored. I remember in one rehearsal Treviel was really upset during the

> \$300 dress scene. It really pissed him off that there was a time—and still is—when you could walk into a store and run into this wall of prejudice. A white actor performing that story wouldn't have the same reactions.
>
> **Carolyn:** India's point about the need for white to play white and black, black in the second version of the play is interesting to me. In theater and in life, I wonder about when we decided to stay with imposed categories and when we decided to deny or defy them. It sounds like in the very raw story of the dress, it felt necessary and right to let the experience stay where it belonged. I was lucky enough to be involved at the margins of another production of India's. At the time of this writing, middle school students are touring their performance of a play called *The Diversity Play*. India and the middle school drama director worked with more than forty children to create the play which, like the one here, used a compelling combination of history, personal narrative, and creative writing to explore experiences with discrimination. In that play, the children sometimes represented the dimensions of difference being focused on (black girls versus white girls on a playground were roughly divided by actual skin color) and sometimes physical or phenotypic categories were deliberately defied as in the case of a very thin girl who portrayed a child living with the social stigma assigned to people who are over-weight.

MIKE: After hours they were not allowed to stay at the hotels downtown—they had to go to the hotels in the black area.

Song: Same as above but slower and somewhat distorted.

MIKE: But before they went to the hotels, they would go to the nightclubs on Howard Street and perform with the local musicians. And my brother would be down there with his equipment and interview all the stars that came in. And I was with him. I was an artist and I would sit there and sketch all these musicians that were performing. I met people like Lena Horne, Eartha Kitt, Ella Fitzgerald, Dinah Washington....Dear God, just so many...Cab Calloway, Billy Eckstein. (*Each time he mentions a jazz performer one of the cast members physically takes on that persona and sings a fragment from one of their hits or does a very short solo.*) All these people came in and performed. My brother would interview them and a lot of times we'd become friends. They would come to my mom and dad's house and have dinner with us.

Dinner action. All, except T. J., sit at a "table" downstage.

INDIA: I remember when we were young; all we did was fight at the dinner table.

ERIKA: My mother's lemonade was so sweet; I swear she used all the sugar.

TREVIEL: Oh, and Mama's sweet potato pie!

AVERY: Oh, and the fried chicken was to die for.

YULIA: One time we had nothing but Saltines.... (*Pause.*) For Thanksgiving.

ROSILYN: One time my mom was chasing my dad around the table, and the dog bit my dad on the butt!

TREVIEL: Is the dog still in the family?

SARAH: Speaking of teeth, you know my Grandma's got false teeth. She took a bite of an apple and her teeth just popped right out of her mouth!

CHRIS: I have no good memories of family dinners.

Actors return to their places.

MIKE: We did that kind of thing for many, many years. I also used to go down to Howard Street for a lot of other things. I got my hair cut at a black barbershop. I wore my hair in a flattop and he did a beautiful job on my hair. I would go down there to get my shoes polished. I wore braces because I have cerebral palsy.• Other places that I went to get my shoes shined, whenever they would polish my shoes, my foot would move back and forth. But Mr. Washington at Mr. Brown's Barbershop built me a little vise to set my foot in so he could polish my shoes. I was only allowed one pair of shoes a year because of the price of the braces. Howard Street had dress shops and millinery shops. They had a poultry place that you could go and get live chickens. They would slaughter them for you; they would pluck them for you. (If you wanted them plucked. Otherwise you could take them home and do them yourself.) They had a fish market down there where you had live fish, live lobster, live crabs—all that kind of thing. You couldn't get any fresher than that! People ask me now: "Weren't you afraid to go down on Howard Street as a kid, because it was all black and you were white?" And I tell them: "No. I had no problem whatsoever. My dad was a policeman and

every one that had businesses down there knew that. They watched
out after me. In a way, everybody was my mother and father. I
couldn't get away with anything down there."* Howard Street was a
wonderful place. It was like the Fairlawn for the blacks. Everything
that black people needed was down there. And it was absolutely
wonderful. And I met so many nice people. And, uh, I just enjoyed
myself. That's all. That's it.

*Jim: This storyteller from a story circle—Mike—was the one who really gave us the
sense of nostalgia about Howard Street. His stories were so detailed and sincere. But
clearly from the perspective of a youngster. And a privileged white youngster.
India: Yes, but he really had this affection for black people. He was handicapped (cerebral
palsy) and he told a story about being supported and defended by black women in the
Howard Street neighborhood where his dad was a cop. He never saw black people as
the enemy or as someone to fear.
Jim: For Mike, Howard Street was a kind of paradise. Much like the visions we often have
of Harlem during the 1920s, the Harlem Renaissance. Other people told us stories of
the long-gone black districts in their cities and towns and the stories were often infused
with this same kind of nostalgia. However, there is something for me in these stories
that doesn't sit right. Why are we romanticizing a past that didn't really exist? How can
we forget the discrimination, prejudice, and racism that created these neighborhoods
and then allowed them to decay and often (as in Akron) get razed?

*Jim: I liked how in the second version we created a more balanced picture of Howard
Street. Yes, it was a wonderful place, peopled with a rich, vibrant community of entrepreneurs, entertainers, and businessmen, but it was also a ghetto, where this community
of people remained restricted and separated from the rest of the city.
India: And we showed the disintegration of Howard Street with the entry of drugs and
prostitution.
Bill: First, both performances were transformative. Second, I did not see nearly enough
of showing the disintegration, since most of that was due to external forces.
Carolyn: I would like to know more about the decline of Howard Street. I know Donna's
work with the residents of Cascade Village has yielded many stories about Howard
Street across time including the heyday of that amazing sounding deli/grocery store
and the dangerous nature of the space once it was deserted by entrepreneurs and par-
tially torn down. Perhaps there is material here for a new production?

BARBARA BURTON (INDIA): I remember there was prostitutes and
bars up and down Howard Street when I was a kid. You could buy
anything on Howard Street from clothes to food to (*sung*) sexual
healing!*

Donna: I understand the desire to offer a more balanced picture of Howard Street. I remember that we were all surprised at the positive nature of the stories that we heard at the Belcher Building. I too wonder why we didn't hear more about prejudice and violence and heart break. HOWEVER, I think that we should respect the storytellers. These were the stories they chose to tell. It would be interesting to do some story circles where we design a prompt that specifically gives permission to tell less positive aspects of their life experience. Clearly asking them to tell a story about their experience with race was not the prompt to bring forward their most difficult experiences. Does anyone have a thought about why this might be?

All women turn into streetwalkers and position themselves stage left.

HISTORY OF PIMPING IN AKRON—PART I

TREVIEL: Howard Street, was, I guess, it was maybe a black Utopia for a street hustler, meaning prostitution and pimps. A big reason for that is because back in the days when the rubber companies and stuff were in Akron, you had a lot of money coming through and with a lot of money that comes through, a lot of people came through, you know, whether it be for jobs, or for some of the rubber companies—the rubber capital of the world! Now, me, truthfully, I don't know what makes some women do that, you know, it's not a big secret, but there is something…it can be done, as far as looking at it from the male point of view. As for the woman's point of view, ah…I don't know what would make a woman do that, you know.

INDIA: I'll tell you what can make a woman do it! Not being able to feed her kids by any other means, that's what!

SARAH: Maybe. I've heard that some people can't think of any other job they can do, but I don't necessarily think it's true.

YULIA: Low self-esteem. They have no respect for their bodies!

ERIKA: It's being desperate. You'll do anything to put food on the table to feed your children!

ROSILYN: A lot of women who become prostitutes have really bad childhoods. Probably were molested by someone close to them, like a father or an uncle. And they feel they're good for nothing but sex.•

Jim: I remember that the first prompt at the Belcher Building was to tell stories about Howard Street. I don't think we mentioned race at all. The first version of the performance stuck to stories from story circles, but the second version utilized found information, our own stories, interviews, and we went back to the original storytellers for clarifications and more stories. This made the piece much more complete. We still respected the stories and the storytellers, but we also put things into more of a context.

India: For the material about prostitution, I interviewed a woman named Tina who had AIDS. She just died last year—was murdered, actually. I saw her one day and I just went up to her and she began to tell me about her life and prostitution being like a drug—once you get into it you are hooked....It goes along with all the rest of the violence we've been talking about. You know I have lost five or six cousins to gang-related violence, murder, in the past couple of years. Just a lot of murders happening all the time.

Jim: That reminds me of a story: I was babysitting in West Akron, off Copley Road, for some of the New World Performance Lab actors while they were rehearsing. I was in the living room on the sofa, reading, and I heard a gunshot and then a bullet came through the front wall and hit the wall on the other side of the room. I hit the floor and then crawled up the stairs to check on the baby. I stayed huddled on the floor of the kitchen until everybody came home. It was terrifying.

India: That is a lot of people's daily reality. It's sad, but that's the ghetto.

Bill: Amazing. I had no idea about Tina, India. Thanks for doing that.

Carolyn: Whew, both Jim and India, you have both sacrificed for your art, I know, but in very different ways these comments show what it means to engage with the community.

Pat: This is very powerful. This performance (and this volume) serves as a legacy for Tina's story.

INDIA: Sometimes women have to make that sacrifice for their families. In one night they can make what they would make in two weeks working nine-to-five. It's an easy way of making money, if you're in a tough situation.

The men move to stage left for the next scene. Chris, Rosilyn, and Yulia are upstage right quietly creating the atmosphere of 1960s street life, very "hippie"-like.

AT THE SHOE SHINE SHOP
TREVIEL: But in the 1960s Howard Street, the jewel of Akron, was beginning to lose its brightness.

India, Sarah and Erika sing "Baby Love." An apprentice is shining a shoe. Avery (the shoeshine shop proprietor) steps out of the group and turns off "the radio." The sound of the singing fades. The girl group reacts silently to being turned off.

PROPRIETOR (AVERY): Those girls sure can sing! (To the apprentice.) How are you doing there, boy!

APPRENTICE (T. J.): Alright, Sir!

PROPRIETOR: (*Looking at the shoe.*) You missed a spot right there. (*Takes the rag and shines the spot. Then returns the shoe to the apprentice.*) There you go. Very good, young man, very good.

APPRENTICE: Thank you, Sir.

The door to the store opens offstage and the bells are heard ringing. The pimp enters and greets the proprietor with a special handshake.

PIMP (TREVIEL): Give me some skin on the black hand side.

The proprietor motions to the chair.

PROPRIETOR: OK, Sir, put your foot right there.

The pimp gets into the chair. The apprentice begins to shine his shoes.

PIMP: Alright now! Alright now! (*To the apprentice.*) How are you doing, young brother, man?

APPRENTICE: Fine, Sir. And you?

PIMP: I'm alright, I'm alright.

PROPRIETOR: This is my new assistant. He'll shine up your shoes like a brand new Cadillac.

PIMP: Now, that's what I'm talking about.

PROPRIETOR: What you been up to Mr. Sundance? You still with that fine foxy chick I saw you with last week?

PIMP: Now you know, if she ain't with me, she ain't working for me!

PROPRIETOR: Mm-hm!

PIMP: (*Looking at his shoes.*) Look at this! This boy's doing a real good job! Oooeee! Let me give you something there, young man. You did such a good job! (*Gives apprentice a coin.*)

APPRENTICE: Thank you, Sir!

PIMP: (*Raises his fist.*) Power to the people!

The ensemble in *The Akron Color Line Project Performance* Version II

PROPRIETOR: Now, you've got to be careful with all that "Power to the people" and "Black power." Some of these men got just enough power to shoot you, you know.

PIMP: Now, that's the old school stuff. Now, you know, we ain't Negroes, or none of that sort. We're black. And me—I am Black Power! Say it loud....

ALL: I'm black and I'm proud!

Everyone raises their fists and the "Hippies" join by making peace signs.

The pimp gets up and leaves with the special handshake saying:

PIMP: Give me some skin on the black hand side.

PROPRIETOR: *(Quoting Martin Luther King.)* "Free at last! Free at last! Thank God Almighty, we are free at last!"

The Proprietor turns on the "radio": "We who believe...." The procession moves to stage right, the "hippies" have joined. Erika becomes the last person in line. She remains center stage.◆

*India: This scene, "In the Shoe Shine Parlor," was fun. Treviel took on the persona of the seventies pimp. The black girls were the radio singers (The Supremes) and it was great when Avery turned the radio down and we got attitude because he turned us down.

Jim: And then we showed the passage of time and raising of consciousness because when he turned the radio back up you were singing "Ella's Song." We all learned about Ella Baker (1903–1986) when Professor Zack Williams from the University of Akron History Department came and talked to the cast and presented a brief history of the Civil Rights Movement. I remember how important his talk was for many of you in the class because some of you had never met a black professor in your college career. Ella Baker cofounded the Southern Christian Leadership Conference with Martin Luther King and helped form the Student Non-Violent Coordinating Committee. Martin Luther King was the public face of The Movement, but Ella Baker was the one behind the scenes, organizing, and administrating. A real unsung hero.

India: Who had her own song composed for her! "We who believe in freedom cannot rest until it comes!"

Bill: Reading your margin notes I am learning more about the stories. I did not see all these dimensions.

Jim: I am very interested in this idea of how humans do not differentiate between skin color until it's pointed out in some social framework. I am using this idea in staging *As You Like It* right now. I was rereading Jan Kott's book, *Shakespeare Our Contemporary*, and he says something like if everyone in the culture is black then the real black person is a white man playing a black person and the real white person is a black man playing a white person—you only see difference when you don't see it through yourself (270). The same point seems to hold about gender. There are two *As You Like It* casts: one all men and one all women. So the question becomes how do we determine what is femaleness or maleness then? How do we determine what is black and what is white?

Carolyn: Yes, I think I experienced both my Americanness and my whiteness when I was living in Swaziland in southern Africa.

Jim: Therefore, it seems very accurate, as several of our storytellers pointed out, that racism in the south, under segregation, was a very different kind of racism than African Americans experienced in the north—where racism, and even segregation, was less apparent.

THE DEPARTMENT STORE

Erika is humming a country song. The group begins to tease her from stage right.

ERIKA: I didn't know I was black till I came to Akron in 1958. I realized I was black because my cousins were teasing me hilariously.✝ (*Laughter from the group. Pause. Erika is talking over them.*)• Because if you are black, you're not supposed to know country songs. (*More teasing from the group. Erika pauses and waits until they settle down.*) This woman at Yeager's department store got fired for taking me to the new floor where the restrooms were located. The blacks were only allowed to shop for returned goods. They weren't allowed on the new floor. In

Robert Grant in Version I

the South there were signs to tell you what to do: "Whites Only." Here in Akron you had to figure it out for yourself.♦

♦Bill: This is a thread worth expanding. Tell me more.

Carolyn: Speaking to this what we recognize as difference and how we value it, Kinzler et al. (2009) did some interesting work on children's parsing of difference. They asked children to identify which of two choices of faces they preferred to become friends with. In a series of experiments, they drew out English-speaking childrens' relative comfort with/preference for pictures of potential friends with different skin tones and with different languages and accented English. They found that children most preferred to make friends with others who looked AND sounded like themselves but barring that, they preferred native accent over same skin tone.

Donna: According to the proceedings of the British Philological society, the root words for color and skin are the same in Greek and Latin. If this is so it points to a very early recognition of differences in skin color. It may be that people with different skin colors or language were viewed as strangers, outsiders and potentially dangerous. This may have been a survival mechanism for early man. If so, recognizing that we might be acting on instinct when we recoil from others unlike us would be an important first step in overcoming a response that is no longer linked to survival and in fact is counterproductive in that regard.

◆**Pat:** This also reminds me of the Clark (African American psychologists) 1940s experiments using dolls to study children's attitudes about race. You probably have heard of how African American children (as young as three years old) were shown "a black doll and a white doll," following which, children were asked "which doll is nicer?" and "which doll is prettier?" The children were then asked to identify the doll that looked most like herself (himself). Just like the white children, the African American children showed a preference for the white dolls. Their findings suggest that racial stereotypes learned so early in life are linked to dominant culture preferences and tied to issues of self-esteem and self-concept.

◆**India:** The rules were clear in the south.

Jim: But here, in the north, you had to figure it out for yourself. In the north, the same rules actually applied, but they were hidden. For me, that was an important discovery about Akron in the pre-Civil Rights years. Just the idea that people were not allowed to use the same restrooms in the big department stores or even shop on the same floors shocked me. In the late 1950s, I just didn't imagine that kind of thing happening in a northern city.

India: It really didn't surprise me. In the south, it was just more external. In the north, it wasn't that it didn't happen but—it wasn't really more tolerant—it was more covered. It just doesn't surprise me. It still happens and it is 2013.

Donna: I think that in Ohio, the racism was generally more, well, subtle (and sometimes not so subtle). Cities had "sundown laws" stating that no blacks could be within city limits after sundown. It was also quite common for deeds to have restrictive covenants prohibiting the sale of the home to black or, in the case of a home I formerly lived in that was built in 1924, blacks or Jews. Subtle, yes, but also effective in terms of accomplishing the same impacts as blatant Jim Crow laws in the south.

THE MERRY-GO-ROUND◆

◆**Pat:** The film *Race—The Power of an Illusion* demonstrates that today communities are still "separate and unequal" and the gap continues to grow, long after the Civil Rights era and the outlawing of discriminatory policies. The film notes that America has "inherited a legacy of inequality" that continues to shape segregation practices because they are so deeply entrenched in the institutions that structure our society.

Erika is on a merry-go-round, riding and singing, "All around the mulberry bush the monkey chased the weasel. . . ." Rosilyn, T. J., and Yulia (Chris's relatives) have formed a carousel upstage right. Sarah is a ticket seller. There are popcorn and cotton candy vendors, etc.

CHRIS: When I was a little boy my parents, aunt, uncle and I all went up to the Summit Beach Amusement Park. It was nickel day and there were all kinds of crowds because, you know, the tickets only cost a nickel. (*Chris buys a ticket from Sarah upstage right*). And each horse on this racing merry-go-round had two seats. There was just one seat left beside a little girl. I thought for a second, and thought oh the heck with it so I jumped up on the seat beside her. (*Chris "rides" next to Erika.*) And we had a good time! (*Chris gets off the "merry-go-round" and waves to Erika. Rosilyn, T. J. and Yulia become Chris's relatives.*) I got off the merry -go-round, and my parents and my aunt and uncle were all mad at me because the little girl that I climbed on the seat beside was black. I wasn't supposed to do that. They were mad all day.

Rosilyn, T. J. and Yulia turn away from Chris. Actors form two lines that pass each other upstage, the African American and the white. All actors stay upstage, except Sarah and Rosilyn, who come downstage.

CROSSING THE MASON-DIXON LINE

Shirley Ann, a polite and serious person, a "military brat," is with a carefree and fun-loving person, a "bobby soxer."

SHIRLEY ANN (SARAH): I grew up in Norfolk in Portsmouth, Virginia.

BOBBY SOXER (ROSILYN): I'm from Ravenna!

SHIRLEY ANN: I really didn't know there was a racial difference because it was a navy town.

BOBBY SOXER: I'm a small-town girl. Akron was the hot spot!

SHIRLEY ANN: And the diverse people that are on navy ships and in the service and much of the marines were from all kinds of countries, so I thought that was what the world was like. People from India, people from Africa, people from Puerto Rico, people from southern Ohio and southern United States just all came together and I didn't know there was a racial difference.

BOBBY SOXER: So, me and my girlfriends always made it a point to go to Akron every chance we got.

SHIRLEY ANN: But once when I was a child, my mother and I went to the southern part of the country, down to Alabama on a Greyhound bus.

BOBBY SOXER: So we hopped on the bus and headed towards Akron. But after a long bus ride I had to use the bathroom.

SHIRLEY ANN: My mother had packed a bag, packed a shoebox with fried chicken, potato salad, potato chips, hot rolls. I fell asleep and was sleeping comfortably.• But when we got to a certain point on the highway, the bus driver pulled over and the entire bus had to shift their seats.

•Donna: The great thing about stories is that they include things like this; lists of foods lovingly packed for a child. It makes the loss and unfairness of racism so much clearer and unbearable.

Slowly they change places on the "bus."

BOBBY SOXER: *(Notices Sarah and walks up to her.)* At the Akron bus station, in the bathroom, I noticed a woman, and she was giving me a towel. And I thought, why is she giving me a towel?

SHIRLEY ANN: At that time we were called "colored."

BOBBY SOXER: *(In a whisper to the audience.)* Then I realized she was the only black person I had seen since I had gotten to Akron.

SHIRLEY ANN: All of the colored people had to move to the back and all of the white people sitting in the back had to move up to the front, because we were crossing the Mason-Dixon line.

BOBBY SOXER: So I went up to her and asked, "Excuse me, but I was just wondering why are you the only black person in the bathroom? And why are you giving me a towel?"

SHIRLEY ANN: And I couldn't understand it. My mother had to drag me back because I was happy with the seat I had. And I just couldn't understand it, because at that time I was only about ten or eleven years old.

Sarah goes behind Rosilyn and both face stage right.

BOBBY SOXER: So, she just said....

SHIRLEY ANN: "That's how it is."

SHIRLEY ANN AND BOBBY SOXER: (*Looking towards the audience.*)
That's just how it is.

THE BUS

All begin to sing the lines "Ah ha, hush that fuss / Everybody move to the back of the bus" from OutKast's song "Rosa Parks" and get into the "bus" formation, with Chris as the "bus driver." The bus makes a counterclockwise circle from downstage right to more upstage right.

AVERY: I'm not gonna move to the back of the bus! (*Avery goes from the back to the front and gets some looks from the white people on the "bus." Sarah and Erika step out of the "bus."*)◆

> ◆**India:** One rehearsal, Jim told us to just become a bus. Chris Laney was the driver and we had to move together rhythmically and in coordination. Sarah and I just simultaneously and spontaneously began to sing the "Rosa Parks" song by OutKast.
> **Jim:** You know a lawsuit was filed on behalf of Rosa Parks against OutKast claiming that it misrepresented her and her accomplishments. I think it was eventually settled out of court and OutKast agreed to develop educational programs for Rosa Parks' foundation. So it's interesting that the song actually served us at this key moment in the play when we showed the crossing of the Mason-Dixon line and the move to the back of the bus. It was just at this point that we realized that we needed to separate—create and live with a color line in our cast. We couldn't represent going to the back of the bus if we didn't separate the cast into black and white. It wouldn't make sense.
> **Donna:** It is so powerful to me when Jim's actors move, dance and sing. The physicality of the work really brings it home.

WHITE WATER, COLORED WATER

SHIRLEY ANN (SARAH): When I got to Alabama, I found out that I can't just go to any water fountain to drink because some water was white and other water was colored and nobody had described for me or explained to me what those white and colored differences were.✦

> ✦**Jim:** My mother came to see the performance at E. J. Thomas. It was the first show she had seen that I directed in many, many years. In a later conversation, she quoted the story about the water fountains, not remembering that it was from the performance. She thought she'd seen it on television or something. And she started to tell me the story as if I didn't know it. I had to tell her, "Mom, that was in my play!"

Carolyn: It's interesting to me that the story is so iconic/familiar and yet powerful that your mom could transfer it from stage to her wider world so easily.

Jim: Exactly. It's like a story that we've all heard before.

India: This was one of the funniest scenes to perform because the water fountains came alive and chased the actors. It was like a cartoon.

Jim: When I envisioned this scene I always saw it as a kind of cartoon or illustrated children's book from the 1960s. The child's point of view is so present in the story. And that's what I wanted to amplify by having the water fountains actually come alive. I think this story would make a wonderful children's book with illustrations.

Bill: "It is like a story we have all heard before." But our experience with story circles makes it clear that we each hear familiar stories differently. That "familiar" story is told a bit differently here, with a North-South personal dimension. At the same time, when I was watching this scene I had this deep sense of missed opportunity, as if the familiar suffocated the difference.

Jim: Bill, I'm not sure what you're commenting on here. Are you talking about the story itself or the stylistic choice of how it was performed? I sense sometimes that you prefer a more "realistic," graphic depiction of the stories. Certainly, a version of this story with real water fountains, the hot, humid atmosphere of the South, and real children would have a different effect on the audience. Is one way better than the other? No, they have a different effect. I also believe that the "familiarness" of the story came from the audience having to engage more fully in the storytelling. They had to fill in the blanks, so to speak. And this allowed them to hear the story "differently" and made it seem "familiar" at the same time. It's one of those wonderful paradoxes that we in the theatre deal with constantly.

Donna: Again the physical portrayal of the horses and carriage and carrousel and water fountains…create a visceral understanding of the story.

Pat: I remember how watching this scene took me back to my first drink from the colored water fountain.

ASHLEY (ERIKA): My mamma never let me go anywhere by myself; it just wasn't safe for a girl to be walking around by herself. I was so excited when she asked me to go to the store to pick up some groceries. So I went down to the local grocery store, got what my mamma told me to get, and hurried on back. *(Pause.)* It was real hot out that day, and as I made my way back, I got thirsty! Just ahead of me I saw two water fountains!

Two sets of water fountains appear, one "Colored Only" and the other "Whites Only," stage left (Treviel and T. J.) and stage right (India and Yulia.)

SHIRLEY ANN: I always knew water was white and clear so I went to the white water and of course it was a big issue in the heart of

The Version II ensemble performing "White Water, Colored Water"

Mobile, Alabama, with the white people in the park and this little colored girl drinking out of the white fountain.

Both Sarah and Erika approach the water fountains.

ASHLEY: As I went to drink from the coloreds only, a notion comes up on me. I wonder what the white folks' water tastes like. Did it taste better? Did it taste the same? And if it did taste the same, how come we got different fountains to drink from?

SHIRLEY ANN: I didn't understand the difference between the water. My mother had to explain to me that white water was for white folks, but the water that came out of the colored fountain was not colored.

Ashley looks at the whites only fountain, then the colored only. She does this a couple of times.

ASHLEY: So I looked around to make sure no white people saw what I was about to do. Lord knows what might happen to me if one of them saw!

SHIRLEY ANN: I had to try to understand the difference between white water and colored water and it was just a terrible, terrible time. It was my eye-opener that there are differences in how people are treated based on their skin color, who they are and what their background is. (*Ashley creeps over to the whites only fountain.*) And that began to shape me to try my very best to treat everybody equally and fairly and I do. I think I go out of my way to try and embrace people into understanding because I still have that taste in my mouth. I still remember to this day the fact that I was told....

Ashley takes a sip from the whites only fountain. The whites only water fountain tries to grabs her.

WATER FOUNTAINS (ROSILYN, CHRIS, T. J. & YULIA):
(*Loudly.*) Colored people can't drink this water!

Sarah runs, being followed by Yulia counterclockwise. Erika runs, being followed by T. J., clockwise. When they make full circle, Sarah and Erika duck and Yulia and T. J. get back in their places. Everyone turns upstage and sees that Avery has been lynched, his body presenting the image of a man hanging from a tree. India solemnly sings "Strange Fruit."•

> •Jim: In the lynching scene we have an example of the power of physical theatre. Film can show all the blood and gore. But without any rope or any tree, Avery was able to create a physical image of a man hanging from a branch. It was so real that the image is still imprinted on my mind.
>
> Carolyn: Oh, Jim, comment further about this!
>
> Jim: What does an actor need to do in order to "make the invisible visible" (as Peter Brook says), to take an event from the past and make it live again in the present? This is what Avery did. In order to do it, he had to call upon his own personal associations, images, and fears. In some way he had to imagine with full detail a "possible future" for himself. But in doing so, his own identity and ego dissolved and he was able to "not pretend." He became a living sign, an icon, what the great theatre visionary Antonin Artaud (1958) describes as "a martyr signaling through the flames" (13). It was simple. It was true. And Avery probably had no idea of the power of his performance. He just did it.

THE THREE-HUNDRED-DOLLAR DRESS
WIFE (INDIA): I'm from the South, and you'd be surprised—the people in the South are not as prejudiced as they are in the North.

HUSBAND (TREVIEL): They are more prejudiced up here than they are in the South, and where we used to live in the South—white here, black there, and we all played together.

Two groups of "schoolchildren" form, African American, upstage left, and white, upstage right. At first they only play within their separate groups. Then they notice each other, tease each other, and finally attempt to play "throwing" a "ball" across the stage.

WIFE: We all didn't go to school together—we had our different schools....

HUSBAND: That's right, we had our different schools. *(Pause.)* Yes, we did.

WIFE: Yes, we did, dear. But we all played together.

HUSBAND: Oh, we played together alright, but, of course, when we went to visit them, we had to go through the back door.

WIFE: That's right. We couldn't go through the front.... *(Pause.)* But we all...played together...We played together.

HUSBAND: When did we come to live up here? Was it '54?

WIFE: Yes, it was 1954. And when we first got here I said "Oh, my gosh, they are more prejudiced in the North than the South.

HUSBAND: Those people in the South, if they like you, they like you.

WIFE: And they are very nice. Very nice.

HUSBAND: Yes, dear.

WIFE: Remember that store we went to when we first came to live up here after we got married?

HUSBAND: The one in Fairlawn?

WIFE: The one in Fairlawn.

HUSBAND: How can I ever forget!

Husband and Wife are in a department store. Wife is admiring a dress. Chris, Rosilyn and Yulia become the store mannequins.

WIFE: That's a beautiful dress! And it's in my size, too! *(She takes it off the rack and holds it in front of her figure.)* What do you think?

HUSBAND: I think it would look very good on you.

WIFE: You really think so?

HUSBAND: Of course, I do. You are so beautiful—everything looks good on you!

WIFE: Oh!.. You're just saying it because you love me!

Suddenly a store clerk rushes towards them shouting.

CLERK (T. J.): *(From a distance.)* Excuse me! *(Rapidly approaching.)* Excuse me! Excuse me, but this dress costs over three hundred dollars! *(Pause.)*

HUSBAND: *(With utter indignation.)* Well, I don't give a damn what it costs! If she wants it, I can pay for it!"

WIFE: Oh, my goodness! *(Clerk goes away to tend to the store's mannequins—Rosilyn, Chris and Yulia. Husband and Wife are back in the present. Wife speaks to the audience.)* So, he paid for the dress.

HUSBAND: *(Stubbornly. To the audience.)* Yes, I did.

WIFE: I took the dress home. *(Back to the past. Wife is now taking the dress out of its covering, taking it off the hanger, examining and admiring it. Then she speaks sternly.)* I'm taking the dress back tomorrow.

HUSBAND: I just wanted to let the clerk know that I could pay for that dress!

WIFE: But I did take it back, so we could get the money back.

She returns the dress to the clerk. T. J. gives money and he and the mannequins very quietly emit contemptuous laughter.

HUSBAND: That's when we realized: um-um, what a difference!

All mannequins laugh louder and transition to a white "Tire-Making Machine" downstage right. Another type of machine is formed by the African American actors upstage right.

MACHINES: Goodyear, Firestone, General Tire, Seiberling. Goodyear, Firestone, General Tire, Seiberling. Goodyear, Firestone, General Tire, Seiberling. (Etc., etc., etc.)

Benjamin Reread (performer and assistant director) interacting with a storyteller at the Belcher Building

THE RUBBER CITY

RITA DOVE (SARAH): My name is Rita Dove and I grew up here in Akron. There are times in life when, instead of complaining, you do something about your complaints. During World Wars I and II, African Americans came to Akron in search of better jobs and a better life. What they found were the worst jobs in the rubber factories.◆

◆Jim: The stories about the rubber factories all came from the book, *Wheels of Fortune: The Story of Rubber in Akron* by Steve Love and David Giffels. We didn't have time to gather more stories and here was a resource that included fantastic stories that had already been collected. I contacted David Giffels, who is now on faculty in the English Department at the University of Akron, and he said he didn't own the rights and I was welcome to use any of the stories as far as he was concerned. *The Akron Beacon Journal* owned the rights and they gave us permission to use the stories as long as we credited them. Ben Rexroad, who served as assistant director in the second version, also contacted Rita Dove who gave us permission to use her poems in the performance. In the end, the poems didn't really work, but we did choose to use Rita Dove as an actual character. She told the story of her father and the other rubber workers.

In order to create the rubber factory experience and the intense segregation that existed in the workplace, we created a white tire-making machine and a black tire-making machine. The black machine was working harder. It was hotter and dirtier. And the white machine got more water breaks.

India: It was important for us in the cast not to tell these stories or play these scenes giving the impression that blacks should be thought of as victims. The idea was to have the stories told and understood but not for people to feel sorry for us.

Jim: A friend of mine told me recently that he walked out of *12 Years a Slave* because he felt the film was presenting the material in too polarized a fashion. I don't know. I think we have to show these events without any compromise, no cloaking. Otherwise, the facts are too easy to dismiss. Dismissal is the status quo. It's what has always been done and continues to be done. But it's hard to dismiss the inhumanity that takes place in *12 Years a Slave*. And it's hard to dismiss the kind of discrimination that took place in Akron and in the rubber factories. It was wrong and people suffered. A lot. And we continue to deal with the reverberations of these years of denial and inhumanity on our streets and in our neighborhoods. People need to see that and understand it.

I was very moved by reading the comments in Amy Shriver Dreussi's chapter about the play. I had not seen those comments before. There were students that said the performance had changed their lives. For all of the performances, we had talkback sessions in which the actors were able to respond to questions and comments from the audience and the audience often engaged in more storytelling or affirmations provoked by what they had just witnessed. For me, these talkbacks are one of the most exciting aspects of live performance.

India: I remember in the talkback session after the play, a biracial girl said that she wished there could be a play like this about the biracial experience.

Jim: New World Performance Lab is working on a new piece about Akron and rubber called *The Devil's Milk*. I started exploring the material with UA students in the Creating Performance class in Fall 2013. *The Devil's Milk* will carry some of this material forward and explore more deeply how rubber and racism are intertwined in the story of Akron and how we must fight to get out from under this heavy history.

Carolyn: India, I also heard a student in one of the talkbacks say something similar. He added that he wished his own stories and his family's could be in such a play. Someone near him commented that he should just gather the stories and do it. His comeback was that he might. It would be interesting to explore outlets for an endeavor like that so we could supportively encourage it.

Jim: Carolyn, let's teach a class in Psychological Anthropology where each student has to dramatize his/her "autobiography!"

TREVIEL: We mostly swept floors.

INDIA: Cleaned spittoons.

ERIKA: Scrubbed toilets.

Talkback at The Belcher Building

TREVIEL: Some of us worked in the mill room. Here raw rubber was mixed with carbon black.

AVERY: Others of us worked in the pit—

INDIA: It was hellishly hot.

AVERY:—where we cooked the tires into the finished product.

Chris gives a "factory" whistle. Both machines stop working.

OTIS SPURLING I

OTIS SPURLING (TREVIEL): We was paying union dues but were not allowed to go further than the mill room, the pit and janitorial service.

RITA DOVE (SARAH): Across Akron, the line was drawn.

BOSS (CHRIS): (*In a bad mood.*) Spurling, I've got bad news. You are being laid off.

OTIS SPURLING: Laid off?!

BOSS: It's not your fault. They've got too many workers in the mill room. You were one of the highest paid ones, so they had to let you go.

OTIS SPURLING: What about training me as a tire builder? There's job openings for tire builders. Did you put in a word for me?

Awkward silence. The Boss lowers his head.

BOSS: Colored people don't work as tire builders. It's a white man's job.

Treviel goes upstage and sits on the bench next to India. Chris rejoins the white actors and they form a "cafeteria" table where they "eat" and quietly interact.

CLARK SMITH

RITA DOVE (SARAH): Clark Smith began working at Firestone in 1941, and at that time the African American workers were not allowed to eat with the white workers. Segregated cafeterias did exist, but the mechanical building had only one cafeteria—for the whites. The black workers ate lunch in the locker room, in the basement.

AFRICAN AMERICAN WORKER (ERIKA): *(Downstage left. He is holding his food in his lap.)* It's like we're having a picnic, right, Smith?

CLARK SMITH (AVERY): *(Smiles.)* Maybe... But I think it's more like a park. Because when you eat on a park bench, there's no place to put your food, except in your lap.

AFRICAN AMERICAN WORKER: You're right. This is exactly like the park. Except that instead of pigeons, we've got rats down here.

CLARK SMITH: You know, I've been thinking....

AFRICAN AMERICAN WORKER: What?

CLARK SMITH: I've been thinking—this is no way for any human being to eat his lunch.

He gets up, takes his food and starts for the white people's cafeteria. The other African American worker tries to stop him.

AFRICAN AMERICAN WORKER: Are you crazy? We are just lucky

Avery McCullough and Erika Kinney rehearsing Clark Smith's story

to have jobs. We've got a place here—this is our place. Why ask for trouble? Hey, Clark, wait a minute! You're not serious?*

> *Amy: I remember this section of the play so vividly. People sitting around me were shocked to learn about the segregated lunchrooms. It's such a simple thing and so emblematic of the racism that was sometimes not so subtle up north. Sometimes the big picture of racism is hard for folks to grasp, but these "little" things? They go right to the heart.
> Bill: The everyday, micro aggressions....
> Pat: Yes, unfortunately these microinsults and microinvalidiations incidents have become a commonplace experience for many people of color.

The white workers begin an audible discussion of a Cleveland Indians' game. Clark Smith walks over to the whites only "cafeteria." He stops just before he enters the "cafeteria" and takes a deep breath. The white workers stop talking and look at him. Clark Smith sits down at a separate but nearby "table" in the whites only "cafeteria." Clark Smith exhales.

RITA DOVE: Before the Civil Rights Movement I was always holding my breath. When the Civil Rights Movement began I was finally able to exhale.

Avery, Sarah and Erika sing, "We shall not be moved."

OTIS SPURLING II
Chris gets up, goes to downstage left and "dials" the "phone." The phone rings (Yulia). Otis Spurling picks it up.

OTIS SPURLING (TREVIEL): Hello.

BOSS (CHRIS): Spurling, is that you?

OTIS SPURLING: Yes, this is Otis Spurling....

BOSS: Do you still need a job?

OTIS SPURLING: Yes.

BOSS: Then I've got some good news. There are two job openings in the tire room. We are considering hiring you and another colored man to be trained as tire builders. Are you interested?

OTIS SPURLING: Yes, Boss, I'm very interested. I haven't worked for a year. I need the money.

BOSS: Can you start tomorrow?

OTIS SPURLING: I'll be there.

BOSS: Oh, and...Spurling? Spurling, are you still there?

OTIS SPURLING: Yes, I'm here.

BOSS: Expect trouble, Spurling. *(Silence.)* You know, there's going to be trouble.

Otis Spurling and two other African Americans come to work as tire builders. This is their first day. They form another Machine. The white workers are very unfriendly. They are protesting and won't work with the African Americans.

WHITE WORKER I (ROSILYN): I won't work next to Niggers!

WHITE WORKER II (YULIA): Me neither! Hey, you, go back to Africa!

WHITE WORKER III (T. J.): Them or us!

ALL WHITE WORKERS: *(Chanting.)* Them or us! Them or us! Them or us! Them or us! Etc.

The ensemble rehearsing for Version II

Chris gives a "factory" whistle.

AFRICAN AMERICAN WORKER (AVERY): My hands are
  bleeding. I can't take it any more.

OTIS SPURLING: My hands are bleeding, too. Keep going. Don't let
  them see it's getting to you. This job is where the money is.

AFRICAN AMERICAN WORKER (ERIKA): To hell with the
  money. I quit.

AFRICAN AMERICAN WORKER (AVERY): I quit.

*Two African American workers walk away. Chris whistles again. Otis Spurling
goes upstage to India.*

OTIS SPURLING: Minnie, honey, I can't do this job.

MINNIE (INDIA): Isn't there other men who are doing this job?

OTIS SPURLING: Yes.

MINNIE: Then you can do this job.

Otis Spurling goes back to work. He is alone working. The Boss goes to the white workers and tells them:

BOSS: Either go back to work or hit the road!

India sings, "It's been a long, a long time coming, but I know change's gonna come. Oh, yes, it will."

Fearing the Boss, the white workers join Otis Spurling, and one by one, all the actors join and form a single machine, singing India's song.

RAY DOVE
RITA DOVE (SARAH): You have to imagine it possible before you can see something.• You can have the evidence right in front of you, but if you can't imagine something that has never existed before, it's impossible. For my father, even a master's degree did not translate into a better job at Akron's rubber factories.

•Pat: Such a profound statement.

VICE PRESIDENT (T. J.): *(To his Secretary.)* Ray Dove... Ray Dove... that name sounds familiar... Any way, he has an excellent academic record. He earned a bachelor's degree in chemistry in 1947. Graduated second in his undergraduate class. Earned a master's degree in chemistry in 1953. Sounds like he's exactly the kind of analytic chemist we are looking for. Have him come in.

SECRETARY (ROSILYN): Yes, Sir.

The Secretary leads an African American man into the Vice President's office. They shake hands.

RAY DOVE (SARAH): Ray Dove. Good to meet you, Sir.

VICE PRESIDENT: *(There is a look of recognition.)* It's good to meet you, too, Mr. Dove. I remember you now. You're the elevator operator here. *(Pause. Another handshake.)* Keep up the good work. Goodbye, Mr. Dove.

The Secretary sees him out.

RITA DOVE: One after another my father's classmates got jobs in their
   field and he was still punching elevator buttons. Everyone was
   afraid. Someone had to make the decision to incorporate a black
   within their organization for the first time. Someone had to
   imagine it.

OTIS SPURLING (TREVIEL): I returned to work the second day. I
   studied the specification manual backward and forward.
   Determined to succeed, I stayed on that job at Goodyear for
   twenty-one years.

ERIKA: Clark Smith was Akron's Rosa Parks—the first African
   American to sit down in Firestone's whites-only cafeteria. From
   then on, black workers and white workers ate together. We ate at
   separate tables, though. Not because of any rule. It just happened
   that way. It still happens that way today.

RITA DOVE: In 1953, my father, Ray Dove, put on a tie and began the
   work he was meant to do. He became an analytic chemist in
   Goodyear's research department. Goodyear wasn't sorry. My dad
   retired in 1986, having advanced to senior research chemist, and
   then to section head, overseeing people with whom, thirty-four
   years before, he wasn't allowed to work. And I grew up to win a
   Pulitzer Prize and to become Poet Laureate of the United States—
   twice!

CLARK SMITH (AVERY): But how much had things really changed?
   Long after the day I sat down in that cafeteria, I found this card on
   the company bulletin board: "Racial Purity is America's Security.
   Invisible Empire Knights of the Ku Klux Klan." Across Akron, the
   line is still drawn.

*The African American and the white students form two separate parallel lines
facing each other.*

AKRON RIOTS OF 1968*

◆Jim: When we first started collecting stories, no one wanted to talk about the riots of
1968. I remember we would bring up the prompt and people would say things like, "Yes,

there were riots." Then silence. There was still a kind of fear of talking about what had happened and a lot of anger. It was too near, too present. I mean, when you think about it, the scars of the riots are still visible along Copley Road and elsewhere. The geography of the city is a direct result of the riots, including the razing of Howard Street. So it's no surprise that people were reluctant to talk. Yulia interviewed several people and I asked each cast member to get stories from their family members. That material allowed us to approach the scenes for the Akron 1968 riots.

INDIA: I remember coming out of high school in Akron in 1967 and our class went to Perkins Pancake House one evening and we sat there forever, it was like our homecoming night. We went there and there was approximately thirty to forty students, and they wouldn't serve us. And we were all sitting in there, and they wouldn't serve us, you know. And they would not give us service! Those are some of the things I remember from back then. Where you could go to Woolworth in downtown Akron and you wouldn't get served, and if you were served, you didn't get glass, you got paper cups.✝

✝**Jim:** The stories of Perkins Pancake House and the downtown Woolworth's with the paper cups were the catalyst for staging this scene. We all became so angry when we heard those stories. And I think this scene galvanized the work of the black actors in the performance. We created compositions inspired by photos of the riots from the *Akron Beacon Journal* archives, too. The photos and resulting compositions were very compelling and helped us to enter into the chaotic world of that time. I remember that you all (with Ben Rexroad's help) found the *Soul Train* action as a performative metaphor for approaching the violence of the riot and there was a kind of ownership of the material that took place after that point. A fierce and exhilarating quality entered the work that all of you were doing. And I felt truly humbled in the face of these scenes and how each of you were bringing them to life. I think all of the white members of the performance team felt that way. And it was also scary. When some people saw this scene in rehearsal they thought that perhaps it was too much—too polarizing. We all spoke about it as a cast and I think we actually toned down some of the venom for performance.

Donna: I had a student once who grew up in Akron in the 1950s and 1960s. She was biracial and she told a story in class about how her mother used to take her to eat at the lunch counter at Woolworth's downtown. Her mother would urge her to eat quickly because she was afraid that they would ask them to leave.

All African Americans say "paper cups."

AVERY: I remember people were just tired and fed up with the way we were being treated back then.

The ensemble, Version II

SARAH: We got tired with being called "Nigger" and having to take it.

YULIA: Tired of you taking our jobs.

ERIKA: Tired of substandard housing.

CHRIS: Tired of you spoiling our neighborhoods.

TREVIEL: Tired of discrimination.

T. J.: Tired of you.

INDIA: We were just fed up, so these were the triggers that just set everybody off.

ROSILYN: OK, then, what do you remember about the Wooster Avenue riots in 1968?

"Snapshots" begin. The actors form a series of compositions based on Akron Beacon Journal photos of the 1968 riots.

AVERY: I remember a police officer killed somebody young, a young person, and that started one riot.

SARAH: I remember Martin Luther King was killed on April 4, 1968.

TREVIEL: I remember there was another riot after that—it was July 1968.

ERIKA: I remember buildings being looted.

T. J.: I remember buildings burning.

INDIA: I remember they built us a grocery store on Wooster Avenue after the first riot.

YULIA: I remember during the second riot, they looted that grocery store.

CHRIS: I remember the warehouses were looted.

AVERY: I remember thousands of people, thousands of people just everywhere. It was hot—ninety degrees!

ROSILYN: I remember buildings smoking and burning.

SARAH: I remember people running with packages.

INDIA: I remember—one thing I particularly remember—I remember an old lady coming out of a grocery store, and she looked at me. She was an elderly lady, she had to be good in her eighties. She had a six-pack of Pepsi, a cane, and a brick in one hand. She had a brick in one hand!

Performers form a gauntlet, dancing in place, clapping their hands together, as on the seventies television show "Soul Train."

AVERY: I remember on Edgewood it was like a gauntlet. Because somebody would be down on the far end of Edgewood and when a car would come down, they would say, "Brother! Sister!" you know, and the car would go through. But another car would come through, they would say, "Whitey!" and by the time the car would get down there, they were pelted with bricks on both sides, so by the time they got through, say , a couple of hundred people, their car was really in bad shape.

The white people end up lying on the ground "in really bad shape" after going through the "gauntlet." The African Americans begin to chant, "The roof, the roof, the roof is on fire. / We don't need no water, let the motherfucker burn," from the 1984 song by Rock Master Scott & the Dynamic Three.

A "snapshot" moment from "The Riots of 1968"

TREVIEL: I remember they blocked off Copley Road. They blocked this whole area off very quickly with the National Guard and the police department. You could go as far as, towards about Mull Avenue, about as far as you could go.

ERIKA: I remember you couldn't get out of the neighborhood.

SARAH: It was all blocked off. And there was a curfew.

AVERY: Right. Nothing could come in here; nothing could go out of here! And at that time maybe 70 percent of Akron's African Americans lived right here.

SARAH: Right here.

INDIA: In this West Akron area. They had it blocked off, so nobody could get in or out.

SARAH: I remember one thing they did to calm down the riot—they brought in Pepsi trucks and potato chips.

The white people get up and one after another give the African Americans "Pepsi" and "potato chips."

AVERY: After the riots were over, they built us…they gave us…a swimming pool and a grocery store, I guess, to calm us down.

INDIA: And nobody could get in or out.

TREVIEL: Shit, it's still damn hard to get out.

AKRON NOW AND THE CIVIL RIGHTS

DRUG DEALER (AVERY): Man, fuck the white people! They ain't the ones we have to worry about these days, it's the niggas that's killing each other. But as far as the Civil Rights, I don't think there's such a thing. Especially in the hood, man. When you gotta mama that's on crack and no good, and dad in jail, tell me, what you gonna think about the Civil Rights? Sometimes I say to myself, "this shit ain't fair," but what the fuck fair got to do with reality? The reality is I'm a fucking nigga. And I'm a mean muthafucka too! *(Laughs.)*

TREVIEL: White people always gonna be holding they purses and reaching for they mace. Then people say that black people oppressing themselves. But who started all this oppression? The white folks! I mean, I don't hate white people, but I don't trust them muthafuckas as far as I can throw 'em. 'Cause truth be told, white people will do anything to bring blacks down.

SARAH: Yeah, what're they calling it now? Reverse discrimination? Don't they realize that affirmative action is just trying to create some equal opportunity? The social structure gives whites a lot of artificial advantages. And sets up artificial blocks for people of color. I don't want to take someone's job if they're more qualified than I am. But if we're both equally qualified I want the same opportunity to fight for the job as anyone else.

ERIKA: If we're gonna create a just society, where everyone can prove themselves on their own merits, we gotta understand what race means and what it's meant for this country, for this city.

AT A PARTY
Everyone is dancing.

A YOUNG WHITE WOMAN (ROSILYN): Last summer I took a class called "Black Experience." I took this class to see what has been left out of my history lessons. All my life I've been taught the Eurocentric way. So, I took this class and it was very interesting. And I went to a party over the summer, and I saw a girl there who was Korean, who was a friend of one of my friends there. She asked me what I've been doing all summer and I told her I took this class, I told her why I took this class and I told her that it was very interesting. And she laughed and I wondered why she laughed and I asked her, what's so funny? And she said, "Well, I guess I'm just a little bit racist, because I grew up in Akron." And this was very confusing for me, because I grew up in Akron also, but the exact opposite happened to me. And also, she was Korean, and doesn't everyone experience racism? I've even experienced racism, and especially someone of a minority.

AKRON NOW AND THE CIVIL RIGHTS (CONTINUED)
DRUG DEALER (AVERY): I believe drugs is the reason why the civil rights movement really stopped. And I believe the whites was behind it. When crack came into the picture in the eighties, niggas ain't have no chance, man. Our parents was the ones on that shit, so now we feeling it. My mama told me that she used to buy from some crackers that live in Bath.... That's the shit that piss me off.... These white people living in Bath, selling to the poor niggas of Akron!

T. J.: You know, whites abuse alcohol and drugs more often than blacks and Latinos. Statistics show it!

WOMAN (INDIA): *(Talking to the other woman.)* The Civil Rights movement was all that Martin Luther King stuff and Rosa Parks.... I mean, does it really matter? 'Cause what happened then was what happened then. Me or anyone in the ghetto can't really think about the Civil Rights when we got mouths to feed. It's hard enough thinking about these no good baby daddies. But yeah, I do wish people would pay more attention to what happened during the Civil Rights movement, 'cause niggas these days will settle for anything white people tell 'em. Back then they was proud to be black. *(Pause.)* Anyway, it ain't about the black people believing in the Civil Rights. Do the white people believe in it?

OTHER WOMAN (ERIKA): Are you for real?

WOMAN: Girl, I'm serious!

T. J.: It all starts with education.

ROSILYN: Teachers do make a difference.

INDIA: Yeah, growing up, back in school, the way teachers talked to the little white girls was different from the way they talked to little black girls. I remember this one friend of mine, Martinette, she didn't go to school with the kids back home, because she was sent to a school for talented kids. I remember she was eight years old and in third grade....

THE AWARD

TEACHER (YULIA): I almost forgot, but our very own Martinette has won an Academic Achievement Award. Congratulations, Martinette! Let's all give her a hand! *(Everybody claps with the nails of their thumbs.)* This is a very prestigious award, and you should be very proud of your accomplishment.

MARTINETTE (INDIA): *(Excited.)* I worked very hard, Mrs. Jones, but still, this is very unexpected. Is there going to be a special ceremony, you know, when I get up on stage to get the award? I hope my grandmother can come, if she's feeling well. She'll be so proud of me!

TEACHER: *(Hesitant and evasive.)* Well...yes, there will be.... But, you see, Martinette, we've decided, I know you will understand...You see, Judy will accept the award on your behalf.

MARTINETTE: Judy, Mrs. Jones? But why Judy? It's my award, isn't it? Isn't it, Mrs. Jones?

TEACHER: Oh, yes, yes, yes! Of course, it's your award. It will have your name on it! Now you're all worried, but there's nothing to worry about! Judy's just going to go up on stage, shake hands with the mayor and have her...I mean your...I mean her picture taken, with the mayor, you know, for the newspaper.

Judy goes up on stage and accepts the award, shakes hands with the mayor and has her picture taken.

INDIA: Sure enough, there was a picture of Judy, who was white, with the mayor, and under the picture, there was Martinette's name. The mayor knew Martinette's grandmother, and was probably wondering why a white girl was picking up that award. Poor Martinette! She wasn't good enough to go to school with the kids back home or good enough to accept her own award! And that's the way things still are.

SARAH: I've seen some bad times, but these are the worst times.

CHRIS: Crime is definitely worse in Akron in the last couple of years.

TREVIEL: No jobs! Foreclosures!

T. J.: Every one's hurting right now.

TREVIEL: But African Americans in Akron have been hit harder. Much harder.

ALL WHITES: Stop whining!

AVERY: Incomes are dropping.

SARAH: And less income means less ability to take care of a house.

ERIKA: We was doing good in the nineties. With good ole Bill Clinton.

INDIA: Now everyone's running off to the suburbs.

ERIKA: Better schools.

ROSILYN: Safer neighborhoods.

INDIA: And then there's those of us left behind.

TREVIEL: A lot of black men with prison records!

AVERY: If a white man with a prison record can get a job easier than a black man with no record, where does that leave a black man with a record?

ALL BLACKS: Shit! No one will hire him!

CHRIS: So what do you do? Just walk around getting into trouble?

YULIA: Robbing and stealing because you can't make it?

ALL BLACKS: I can't provide for my family!

T. J.: Some people would say blacks gotta take more personal responsibility.

CHRIS: Shooting each other is not taking personal responsibility. There's some areas of Akron we should be issuing helmets and flak jackets.

AVERY: And when one black man commits a crime, all of us are suspected, because the police can't tell us apart!

Everyone laughs. Everyone, but Avery and Treviel, goes upstage.

WE ALL LOOK ALIKE

KEVIN (AVERY): *(Reacts to the police cars.)* Please allow me to illustrate. My buddy calls me at, like, nine a.m. *(On the phone.)* What's up man?

FRIEND (TREVIEL): Hey, Kev, you wanna ride with me to Akron to pick up my mom?

KEVIN: Yeah, man, no problem. So, we in Cuyahoga Falls, comin' down State Road. We see police cars everywhere. If you ever been on State Road it veers off Howard or Main Street. So we took the Howard way. We goin' down Howard, we see Akron police out, too.

FRIEND: Apparently somebody shot somebody with a shotgun and it's like a three-hundred-pound black dude, maybe four-hundred-pound...

KEVIN: So we get down by Howard, goin' down the hill, and all the cop cars all the way up the hill. They was following us the whole way....

FRIEND: We didn't know somebody got shot til afterwards.

KEVIN: So they pulled us over in the middle of the hill.

FRIEND: They said the guy was in a rusty Chevy Capri, mind you, a blue one! But I have a Chevy Capri four-door, but I've got a very clean one. So there is no way you can get it mixed up with this clean-ass whip.

KEVIN: So they pulled us over. A lieutenant, he pulled right in front the car trying to ram us.

Chris Laney, Avery McCullough, and Treviel Cody performing "We All Look Alike"

FRIEND: He cut us off so I had to throw my car in park, so I wouldn't hit the cops...

KEVIN: So, he hopped out, they all hopped out, surround us, like, six cars with their guns. I was scared, like, "what's going on?"

FRIEND: "Get your hands up! Get your hands up!" His hands were already up... he yanked him outta the passenger side, you know, to get down on the ground.

KEVIN: The dude just, I dunno, if he just didn't like black people.

FRIEND: You could tell the Sergeant wanted to shoot him. He had the Taser in his face and he had the regular gun in his face.

KEVIN: I was really scared.

FRIEND: And he yanked us out of the car and he threw his arm behind his back, like all in one motion.

KEVIN: I was already on my knees and he like just kinda like throw me to the dirt. And I remember his partner just comin' over and just stomped me in the face. Like my tooth gone till this day right here. Just stomp me in the face, kicked at least three times....

FRIEND: The suspect they was lookin' for was in a rusty car, a three-hundred-pound dude.

KEVIN: So this is a big dude. You know, I'm a little dude. I just think it's sad how they just 'cause one black person did something we all suspects.... I guess I heard the sayin', you know, I guess we all look alike, but, you know, you can't get me mixed up with some three-hundred-pound guy.•

•**Carolyn:** The traffic stop story here and several others I heard as part of story circles with Bill in the summer of 2009 at the Akron Urban League strike me as especially important. Listening to the young men tell their stories which flowed one to the next in my circle, the traffic stops worked as a trope for them, invoking by the mere reference not only stinging personal experience but also enraging frustration with the seemingly unassailable structural injustice being perpetrated by law enforcement. Finding a way to tell these stories so that people who do not experience law enforcement as unjust can hear them is an enterprise that requires patience, humor, and tolerance from the storytellers…something I think listeners don't always appreciate that they are asking for.

AKRON NOW AND THE CIVIL RIGHTS (CONTINUED)•

•**Jim:** This whole last part of the play wrote itself—more or less. We had the stories "They All Look Alike" and "The Award," but the rest of the material came from the cast's personal experiences and thoughts about the way things are now in Akron. We questioned very much how to handle the anger and bitterness of this last section. I asked each of the research team members (the authors of this book) to come to a rehearsal and to react specifically to this part of the play because I was unsure as to how it would be received by the spectators. After that, the cast was able to focus what they wanted to say in this section. When Avery began his rant after the Civil Rights section, the immediacy of the topic of racism became strikingly clear. There was no escaping what each actor on stage was feeling and expressing. Character and history became less and less important as the play went on and we found ourselves at a point where the line between character and actor, between story and storyteller, was extremely transparent. Who was telling the story? And the play suddenly and strikingly became the personal story of each member of the cast. And each member of the cast, black or white, had to confront his or her feelings about race and racism in our community. I think, looking back on this experience, that the whole play was a revelation, a confession or a plea, that each cast member enacted during the performance. And it was stunning to see each actor vulnerable and open at the end, asking the spectators to question themselves in the same way—and to take action.

Bill: "The whole play was a revelation, a confession or plea." This is exactly how I experienced it as an audience member. If you can be less than humble for just one moment Jim, because we can learn from this, how did you direct them to this place?

Donna: Yes, Bill this is the question I most want to hear Jim answer as well. I guess that this crafting of an authentic experience is what theatre has to teach us.

Jim: I approached the directing of this project much like the story circles themselves. For me, it was important to acknowledge what each person was bringing into the rehearsal studio each day and make sure that they were heard. Unfortunately, many people believe that theatre is about ego and that attitude of kill or be killed, climb to the top. I try to create an atmosphere of working for the other in my rehearsals so that the actor is free to reveal his or her vulnerability. I can't say that there is any particular method to this process. Each play, each cast, is different and demands different tactics and solutions. I think it's very similar to what each of us experiences at the end of the semester when a class has gone really well or has failed miserably. It's a subtle dance. There are so many variables. But the only thing we can do is be present and listen and the class will tell us where it needs to go, what it needs to spend more time on, or can skip over. Rehearsals are the same. It's not about method. It's about the underlying principles that guide each of us as teachers or directors or even human beings. The way we put those principles into practice is going to transform with each new situation, but the principles remain the same.

WOMAN (INDIA): I mean, I love being black, but being black is like a scar. Like a scar you get when you're little and it never goes away. Like when you walk into a room and the white people automatically assume that you are a certain way. You're with all those white people now and you know how to talk to them. But I ain't gonna lie, white people piss me off.

OTHER WOMAN (ERIKA): *(Smiling.)* Sometimes, they piss me off, too!

WOMAN: Yeah, but I've seen some shit happen in the hood, you don't even know about. You got out of this shit, and sometimes I wish I followed you. I'm tired of not knowing who gonna be next. Who gonna die.

DRUG DEALER (AVERY): Man, I ain't no educated nigga, but there's two things I paid attention to in school. Math, 'cause I have to know how to count my dough. You know, niggas be tryna play you

"What are we waiting for?"

and shit! And slavery. I mean, that shit'll fuck a muthafucka up. . . . That's all I'm saying. . . . Man, I just don't got nothing else to say 'cause I'm getting pissed. . . . (*His cell phone rings. He looks at it.*) Plus, my baby mom calling me . . . (*Laughs.*)

Shots are heard offstage. Everyone stops.

OTHER WOMAN: (*On cell phone.*) Someone's been shot! We need an ambulance here quick! Arlington Street in Akron.

WOMAN: This is messed up. What a waste!

T. J.: We have all this waste out here in Akron. Wasted labor. We've got all these people who aren't working. All this wasted property. Wasted talent. We need a fundamental change in our system, in our community.

CHRIS: We do not need a fundamental change in our system. People simply need to behave, follow the rules, and copy the behavior which succeeds.

SARAH: The problem is that kind of lack of vision.

YULIA: And lack of commitment.

ERIKA: You know, it's just about choice.

TREVIEL: What are you saying? We have to choose to change old behaviors and habits.

AVERY: It's not just about choice. Guys, wake up! Racism is institutionalized.

T. J.: That's right. Enough already with that old "just pull yourself up by the bootstraps" myth. It doesn't work for everyone.

INDIA: That's why the stories have to be told.

ROSILYN: So that we can rethink and reframe how we talk about race and racial conflict.

TREVIEL: The stories are important.

ERIKA: We need things rebuilt and newly built in this country.

CHRIS: OK, I get it. So, let's start with this city.

YULIA: With our own community.

SARAH: I guess there's a lot of work to be done.

INDIA: What are we waiting for?*

---

*Donna: The language of the original stories was used in the text of the play. I was there for some of the original story circles and recognized them as I was watching the play. I feel it is very important to analyze the stories and to use them as data, but they also stand on their own and will tell us something about ourselves and the storyteller. I believe they can do this sometimes BECAUSE they are so understated and not over-explained.

Donna: I feel privileged to be in on this discussion. It resembles one of the most important aspects of the story circle; that is; being listened to. In story circles the storyteller truly has an audience. In this book we each also have an attentive audience, one that is listening and providing cross talk here in the margins.

Jim's play, *The Akron Colorline Project Performance* is a shining example of the transformative power of stories. It changed my life and I believe it had a positive impact on everyone associated with it. I don't think we have seen the end of its "cascading effect" on our community. Kudos to Jim and all of us and The University of Akron Color Line Performance Team including India Burton, Treviel Cody, Yulia Gray, Rosilyn Jentner, T. J. Josza, Erika Kinney, Christopher Laney, Avery McCullough, Benjamin Rexroad, Sarah Taylor, and everyone else who contributed their creativity and energy to writing and performing it.

NOTES

1. Much of the language of the reporter comes from Mary Plazo's account of this event for the Akron Public Library's newsletter. Our thanks to her for granting permission to do this. Also note that several of the stories in the script come from the book *Wheels of Fortune* and are used with the permission of the *Akron Beacon Journal.*

REFERENCES

12 Years a Slave. 2014. Directed by Steve McQueen (France: Video France Télévisions Distribution, 2014). DVD.

Adelman, Larry, executive producer. 2003. *Race: The Power of an Illusion.* Narrated by C. C. H. Pounder (San Francisco, California: California Newsreel). DVD.

Artaud, Antonin. 1958. *The Theater and Its Double.* New York: Grove Press.

Brook, Peter. 1996. *The Empty Space.* New York: Touchstone.

Clark, Kenneth, and Mamie K. Clark. 1940. "Skin Color as a Factor in Racial Identification of Negro Preschool Children," *Journal of Social Psychology* 11: 159–69.

Kinzler, Katherine D., Kristin Shutts, Jasmine DeJesus, and Elizabeth S. Spelke. 2009. "Accent Trumps Race in Guiding Children's Social Preferences." *Social Cognition* 27, no. 4:623–34.

Key, T. Hewitt. 1854. "On the Etymology of Certain Latin Words." *Proceedings of the Philological Society* 5 , no. 114: 103–9. https://books.google.com/books?id=aHkhAQAAMAAJ.

King, Martin Luther. Letter from Birmingham City Jail, April 16, 1963. *Online King Records Access (OKRA) Database.* Martin Luther King, Jr., Research and Education Institute. http://okra.stanford.edu/transcription/document_images/undecided/630416-019.pdf.

Kott, Jan. 1974. *Shakespeare Our Contemporary.* New York: W. W. Norton.

Lane, Samuel. 1892. *Fifty Years and Over of Akron & Summit County.* Akron, Ohio: Beacon Job Department.

Love, Steve, David Giffels, and Debbie Van Tassel. 1999. *Wheels of Fortune: The Story of Rubber in Akron.* Akron, Ohio: University of Akron Press.

Plazo, Mary. 2010. "That Akron Riot." *Past Pursuits: A Newsletter of the Special Collections Division of the Akron-Summit County Public Library* 9, no. 2: 7–9.

Ransby, Barbara. 2003. *Ella Baker and the Black Freedom Movement A Radical Democratic Vision.* Chapel Hill: University of North Carolina Press.

"Report of Reprieves, Commutations and Pardons Granted by Governor James M. Cox, from January 13, 1913 to January 11, 1915." 1915. *Journal of the Senate of the State of Ohio 106.* https://books.google.com/books?id=pE9Bw4puLBsC.

Spradley, James. 1979. *The Ethnographic Interview.* Belmont, CA: Wadsworth.

———. 1980. *Participant Observation.* New York: Holt, Rinehart and Winston.

Concluding Thoughts

Storytelling and Democracy*

*Bill: Initially we considered a different title for this chapter: Deliberative Storytelling and Democracy. Conversation ensured…

Donna: The emphasis on respect for each person's story and the restraint required to listen without comment is at the core of what separates story circles from other methods of inquiry. For me the concept of deliberative storytelling gets in the way and seems less important. If it is important to this chapter, it might be helpful to discuss how it is similar to and different from other story circles.

Bill: Good question. I agree on titling the chapter. My point was to emphasize the structural preconditions that transform mere discussion into deliberation, which (often, but not always) seems to happen in story circles.

Carolyn: What you two raise here draws two thoughts from me. First, for those of us using story circles in the classroom to help build toward engagement with difficult dialogues, to build empathy, and to help students link academic content to the lived experiences of themselves but also others in the classroom, I am right with Bill. But I, and I suspect all of the other authors, have also employed the story circle method primarily as a way to establish respect and restraint (listening) which invites intimacy and self-exploration in order primarily to build community within the participant group. Identifying shared understandings and points of divergence on "hot" topics may be an outcome but—as with the middle schoolers working on *The Diversity Play*—there was no grade or performance-need riding on the story circles' outcome. Content that might feed the development of the play was secondary to camaraderie that would feed to souls of the players.

My second comment is that I like Donna's question because it forces us to take apart the story circle one more time and consider more carefully what these exchanges actually do when we undertake them. Is it possible that the deliberative process is separate from the storytelling? The notion of deliberation or a conscious, shared process of exchange with a goal of achieving a shared or balanced understanding among the parties is explicitly present in the phase of the story circle after the stories have been told. When the participants share "snapshots" and then discuss the themes that emerged in the stories, and also when participants create a means to report out from their circle to the assembled group, at all these points deliberative process arises and dialogic moments are possible (Buber 1958; Cissna and Anderson 1998, 2004). What these moments may do is alter understanding of key issues for participants and possibly then alter relations among participants (see McNamee and Gergen 1999).

Is it possible to leave the stories unconstrained and only enter into the deliberative and dialogic process once the stories are in the air or is there a risk here that we are constraining the expression of the stories if we are steering participants toward dialogic moments? Is this an argument for not articulating a clear prompt? Or is this an opportunity for another study in which we compare content of and experience in story circles to see how they differ for participants in the same broader gathering if half the circles learn in advance there will be a discussion of emerging themes after the stories are told and half do not?

Story circles are a structured format to encourage and enable us all to reincarnate our deeper selves, in communion with others, on the basis of listening in the present moment, a skill which has been less and less nurtured in the academic environment.• We have observed, as Donna Webb put it once, that "listeners are often moved to empathy rather than distance," as we have all been so moved through this sometimes awkward opportunity to be in a safe place where we can put our faith in each other.

•Pat: Bill you are right here and I think Donna's point and Carolyn's metacommunication of the story circle process brings clarity to a crucial aspect—listening. Recall that the rules indicate:

"Story circles are primarily about listening. Listening is more important than talking. Do not spend time thinking of your story. Instead, listen actively to all of the stories and trust that the circle process will bring you a story when the time is right...."

In my communication classes, we discuss that many of us are guilty of critically evaluating what is being said before fully listening to understand the message that is being communicated. In his book *The Lost Art of Listening*, Michael Nichols maintains that our lives are coauthored in dialogue and learning to be an effective listener is essential to improving relationships and perception of others. Story circles lead to mindful and intentional listening.

Jim: I have to agree with Pat here. For me, the key to the story circle process is listening. It is only in listening to another's story that we will find the voice to tell our own story. In listening to the other, we begin to learn to listen to ourselves, the deep voice within, the voice of our heart or even soul, if you like. As an artist, learning to listen is the key to finding one's own voice. So, for me, all the deliberation, dialogue, and analysis is secondary and can actually block an authentic experience from occurring. Jerzy Grotowski often told us to hold any questions until the end of the work and only then, if the question had not been answered in the course of the work, was it a valid question. I think of this when I see students interrupting a learning process with constant trivial questions and not allowing the experience to give the answer. The obstacle is an inability to listen.

Bill: *Allow the experience to give the answer* is beautiful and reminds me of a phrase in Mark Juergensmeyer's *Gandhi's Way* (2002): "conflict is the crucible" (16).

Donna: The comments from Bill, Carolyn, Pat, and Jim have brought me full circle in my thinking about the deliberative nature of our story circle process. I considered the stories that we all gathered at Cascade Village to be just a part of my larger project, Cascade Village Public Art. As I lived with the stories during the following year and as I wrote my chapter for this volume I came to understand the stories in a much deeper way. They have become a resource for me in my search for the importance of art in the community. The stories continue to have a life. Three of the stories have been retold four times. They are included in this volume, have been told to more than fifty children as well as to an audience of nearly one hundred people at the Akron Art Museum. We may never know how many people will deliberate on the stories we have called forward as they are told and retold.

Story circles changed our lives and created the Akron Story Circle Project community that is the source of this book. Using story circles in our classrooms we have learned to better transform "hot moments" where conflict, disorder, and discomfort might reinforce stereotypical divisions, into learning moments.✦ With our students, in a community of learners, we are then able to move from statistics to narrative and back, shifting from platitudes to revelation. We transform classroom community and skill building into an accessible and illuminating microcosm for practicing the skills required to meaningfully participate in the ongoing struggles to make democratic deliberation both possible and desirable.

✦**Carolyn:** I would add to this that I have "learned to better transform those 'hot moments'" in my classrooms through the use of this method but also through the pedagogical dialogue (and storytelling) surrounding its use. This happened because a group of faculty chose to engage with story circles together. This society of teachers and our ongoing exchange of ideas has been key to my own pedagogical development.

Together, we share stories to integrate self and culture without pretending as we, in Jim's words, assume "the responsibility of incarnating those stories for others to experience," so we might—experientially—as Pat noted "break down our provincial ways of looking at the rest of the world." We share stories Face2Face as Carolyn and Sandra put it, in order to "explore human experience" in all its richness, using traditional tools and our own creativity as educator-learners to connect communities with individual identities to "convey the essence of what it is to be successfully human" as Donna so eloquently described.

STORY CIRCLES, CIVILITY, AND COMMUNITY

The classes described in this volume were, or included, structured public deliberations about race, racial conflict, crime and punishment, and more. Our larger enterprise has been to engage in deliberative discourse with each other, our students, and communities on these subjects. Well-structured public deliberations can bring people with *opposing* views together. The use of storytelling within our courses is open-ended and inviting; through them we can all participate and transform hot moments in the classroom into deep learning.

> *I learned a lot through the stories, not only about other students, but myself. I never really thought about racism that I have experienced in my workplace and ways to prevent it in the future.... The first story circle I participated in Monday was one of the biggest rushes I've ever had in a classroom. I was really nervous and when the story came to me it just spilled out. I don't know how to explain it.*

For those of us who describe using them in class, our story circles structured conflict directly into the syllabus from day one. We wanted to avoid fear of conflict resulting in withdrawal from participation or half-hearted listening.* We also built a serious analysis of the best available data into the conversations to avoid a retreat to familiar, but empirically suspect, platitudes about race and power. And we structured classroom interactions to be critical and collaborative, dialectical and detailed, designed to constantly revisit and re-think and reconsider earlier data and stories, in concert.

---

*Amy: Fear of conflict is central to most tenants of classroom management. Student storytelling is a different form of "flipping" the classroom—surrendering the power of narrative, of delivering the compelling content, to students.

One way that story circles help me better understand the data we have previously discussed is by allowing specific and unique personal experiences to be shared with our classmates. In the second story circle my group discussed a situation where I had been pulled over for several violations, making a U-turn, blinding a cop with my bright lights, and not having my seat belt on when he came up to my window.

I was doing practically everything wrong and the cop just let me go. But a black student in my group was telling a story of when he was pulled over and searched for no apparent reason. The cop made him get out of the car and onto the ground. This specifically reflects the argument made in the article where the farther African Americans traveled from their neighborhood the more likely they were to get stopped.

Hearing this story in which the speaker connected a peer's experience with the scholarly data brought conversation to a full stop. Everyone in the room was compelled to think and re-think about what divides us and also about what unites us.• White students struggled with new stories, describing experiences in an America very different from their own.• Story circles highlighted experiences that connected both to the aggregate data in our scholarly readings and to a deeper understanding of the ways that our concrete lived experiences are linked to our perspectives on race and crime, police discretion, and the incarceration explosion. Stories were heard; interpretations were challenged.

•**Pat:** Yes, this reinforces that stories told in story circles function as a vehicle for sharing meaningful events of our lived experiences.

♦**Carolyn:** New stories, or rather stories new to them, make me think about the importance of even minor opportunities to engender empathy in these exchanges. Barth said "everyone is necessarily the hero in their own story" but is that true for children who identify with parents who are backgrounded or resemble the anti-heros/antagonists in the collective cultural narrative? Certainly Toni Morrison didn't think it was so and fought to raise awareness and to change this externally-shaped, internally-imposed deprecation in her storytelling. I'd like to think that the processes we engage in our classrooms and at community events described in this volume are adding to a shift in the old collective cultural narrative.

Jim: I think it's true that the old collective cultural narrative no longer functions as it did in the past and has to undergo some kind of shift or transformation. There was a time (in ancient Greece, for example) where everyone who attended the theatre shared a common belief system and mythology. This common narrative no longer holds true. At one play at The University of Akron the audience will consist of Christians,

Muslims, and Jews, blacks, whites, immigrants, rural and urban dwellers. Our culture is not becoming more homogenized as many fear. As we careen into the twenty-first century and try to refashion our mythologies to make sense of this post-human world, we are in danger of becoming more fragmented and segmented—a culture of niches, each of us in his or her personal bubble of likes and dislikes with no regard for the common good. I have pointed out to my students how often one of them will begin to tell a story ("I had the most incredible dream last night" or "Do you know what happened to me at the store just now?") and the response of the others has nothing to do with the story just told. The response is totally egotistical. It's usually something like: "Oh, let me tell you about the dream *I* had. It was even more incredible," or "Something even worse happened to me at the store." They totally negate the first teller's experience and their story doesn't really have anything to do with the first teller's story, except on a superficial level. This behavior doesn't occur in story circles, but outside story circles, in daily social interactions. For me, it's a good example of how story circles actually serve to engage us in a deeper level of listening and human connection.

Donna: Jim, I agree that one-upmanship is common in daily conversation but does not happen in story circles. I wonder why this is? It is very refreshing. It is as though there really is respect for each person's story.

University of Wisconsin political scientist Katherine Cramer Walsh noted in summarizing research on similar dialogues that the type of work we are doing here deepens learning about how politics works (and sometimes does not work) and, with particular relevance to our struggle with civility today, suggests that story circles can serve as a "potential antidote to political polarization . . . [where we learn] to address divisions within [our] communities in a productive fashion." She goes on:

> studies of students demonstrated that participating in interracial dialogues improves views of intergroup conflict, increases intercultural communication skills, and results in motivations to learn about other social groups, which in turn seems to spur perceptions of greater importance and confidence in reducing prejudice and promoting diversity. (Walsh 2007, 244)

Walsh calls the type of communicative action we are structuring into class here "public talk" and explains that it places more of an "emphasis on listening to and understanding others" than on "reaching a decision" (Walsh 2007, 3).✦ Since our story circles were connected to larger scholarly conversations about race, our storytelling was both the less formal public talk Walsh refers to and also an explicit building block for more formal public deliberations about policy decisions and community building.●

✦Amy: Our students are awash in information—live newsfeeds, tweets, posts, pins, and snapchats. Storytelling, whether in Face2Face conversations or story circles, delivers information in a genuine, personal manner. These conversations are so much more compelling than the less personal world of social media. That they take place in an academic environment is all the more surprising and moving.

●Pat: In addressing the notion of community, Gudykunst (2004, 346) observed that "a community is not a group of like-minded people; rather, it is a group of individuals with complementary natures who have differing minds." Thus, building community with people from different group memberships is an essential process for positive inter-group relations.

Bill: Yes...complementary, like players on a team, Pat. This is part of Walsh's point too, in storytelling like in community, we reject the either/or approach to diversity versus unity and see the interconnected value of both, of civility and contestation.

Jim: Yes, Pat, and we must create these communities by creating the stories. It's real hands on work.

Story circles enable discussion and application of theory to the real world experiences of my classmates. It is one thing to read about police stopping someone because they are black, but it is entirely different when you can put a name to the face. Story circles make the data more real. Sometimes when reading data it is difficult to get the picture that racism happens to people, living, breathing, talking people that have families and friends—not just numbers.

I think the data helped me understand the differences between implicit and explicit racism and the problems that we face in bringing the implicit to the explicit [the phrase we used in class was 'making the implicit explicit']. I learned more about myself and my classmates.... After doing the story circles I really wanted to talk about race to everyone, and when I did I realized how blind most people are to the implicit racism that still permeates society. It was an entirely different way to learn, which I loved.✦

✦Carolyn: I am repeatedly struck by how positive the experience of participation can be. In my own classes and events, there certainly have been less good circles and less enthusiastic people. Earlier in the volume we noted that there have been some very raw moments in which personal hurt has been shared. But the dominant experience I have seen is one of warmth and sometimes euphoria. Students, participants in general, find this way of connecting intellectual work to human experience powerfully moving. They also often find real bonds develop, as we, the Akron Story Circle Project did.

Pat: Yes, our group has had discussions of the one student in my class who had an unpleasant reminder of an unfortunate situation during the story circles, but I am also inspired by the overwhelming positive experiences that come out of each story circle session. In reflection on the reason why, I am taken back to our early story circles. I will never forget Donna's story about her mother "driving" her to school in a wheel barrel, Bill's raw and honest disclosure of his family's reaction to his first wife, and Carolyn's beautiful song—sung as a (what seemed to me at the time very unusual but wonderful) means of "reporting back." Jim's script clearly reveals that a story sinks in, and we remember it. The stories told in story circles often involve a change of heart. They give the best examples of how to change and why to change.

Amy: My story is not about storytelling, but it is related. One of my earliest memories of teaching was when I was a grad assistant leading a discussion group. I asked a particularly quiet member of the group his opinion on a topic I no longer remember. He looked up at me with real fear in his face. He said, in a trembling voice, "No one ever asked me my opinion before." I vowed then to ensure that my students have ample opportunities to form and express their opinions.

Storytelling is one source of knowledge produced through this vigorous contestation, *balancing civility and contestation* in the listening and telling required to overcome blindness this student observed around her.[1]

LISTENING TO REJECT DUALISTIC THINKING

What Walsh concluded on the basis of her multi-method, empirical analysis of storytelling is that the conversations she observed demonstrated a pragmatic rejection of "either/or" thinking. Dualistic thinking is expressed, for instance, in conventional banalities about the need to focus either on unity and shared values or on difference and diversity. Instead of either/or thinking, she observed citizens and elected officials of all races and economic situations embracing "both/and" thinking. The type of both/and thinking that is highlighted in conflict management literature and essential to both learning how to navigate difficult dialogues and mastering the skills of democratic citizenship, can be encouraged through good humor.[2] *

*Amy: Rene Hicks appeared at one of our early years of Rethinking Race. Reading my students' papers about her message taught me how incredibly effective humor can be in defusing tense situations. Humor seems to allow people to let their barriers down and allow them to receive information in a more open fashion. We've seen this year after year in Rethinking Race data.

Hicks used laughter to address serious issues, that otherwise are too taboo to talk about in public so freely. She coined the tactic, "comedy activism." The logic was different from the way I had looked at talking about race related issues, but Hicks made sense to me. The issues she would talk about usually I would cringe down into my seat if in a private setting these issues were talked about openly with blacks and whites present.

Diogenes, a famous, ancient Greek cynic who farted openly to disrupt public lectures, used improvisational humor and incivility to challenge hierarchy by enlivening the audiences' imagination. Jon Stewart, Dave Chappelle, and Steven Colbert among others play similar roles today (see, for example, Drew, Lyons, and Svehla 2010, 154–61). All of these social thinkers, along with Rene Hicks and our students, are rejecting dualistic, either/or, "sucker's choice" thinking to reframe our conversations as both more interesting and more illuminating.• Our student-peers are transformed into both student and peer with specific stories and experiences unlike ours. We can see both difference and unity, and we have taken a concrete step toward realizing ways to bring an appreciation of difference into our lives to strengthen a sustainable (if more contingent and indeterminate) conceptualization of unity, community, and democracy.

•**Carolyn:** It would be interesting to compare the central themes of stories gathered in story circles after speakers like Michelle Alexander vs. comedians like Mark Cryer at Rethinking Race.

CONFLICT AS OPPORTUNITY AND CRUCIBLE

Is this easy? No. In fact, if it feels easy, we are likely wasting time with platitudes and posturing. As Jay-Smooth put it in describing how elites dodge accountability for racist words or actions, we want to avoid framing racist actions or remarks as a "who you are conversation" because this is a "rhetorical Bermuda triangle where everything drowns in a sea of empty posturing until someone just blames it all on hip hop and we forget the whole thing ever happened." Instead, we need to be uncomfortable about our current racial arrangements.◆

Sharing my story made me uncomfortable. It was a rush that I've never felt before. Feeling uncomfortable like I did made me more conscious that racism really is a problem in my workplace and after talking about it I realize that a change needs to be made.

◆**Jim:** I think that someone who is a better social commentator than I am needs to reflect a bit on the current controversies surrounding Donald Sterling and Cliven Bundy. How do these two stories intersect with what we are doing with story circles and Rethinking Race?

Donna: Good question, Jim. When we engage in Rethinking Race or in telling stories about race we rarely are shocked in the same way that we have been by the comments of Sterling and Bundy. I think that we continue to do work to defeat racism because we know that those terribly devastating experiences are out there. What we wonder is why we don't often hear personal stories of racism during story circles? Is it because there is a shame associated with the experience that people don't want to share? Or maybe we are not using effective prompts? It may be that issues around race are not automatically negative and therefore when we use the word race we are not activating memories of unfair treatment. Maybe we need to ask specifically about exclusion, powerlessness, shame, or pain that might be a part of their racial experience but not the whole of it.

Walsh rejects dualistic platitudes in well-structured "public talk" in favor of treating conflict, and even very uncomfortable conversations about racial conflict, as potentially productive rather than inherently divisive.

> At the heart of their strategy is an emphasis on listening rooted in the practical need to learn to communicate across lines of difference....I conclude that people implementing and participating in civic dialogues around the country are pursuing a practical politics that balances unity and diversity, listening and scrutiny, and dialogue and debate. The results suggest a rethinking of the place of conflict in deliberative democracy and an acknowledgement that it is the ongoing struggle with difference that provides unity in contemporary civic life. (Walsh 2007, 14)

This puts our recent focus on civility in context. Successful deliberative storytelling is *civil contestation* and connected to *achieving* unity. Our story circles publicize conversations that might have previously been kitchen table only, reminding us that notions of "civility" are themselves agreements, always open to renegotiation, and making this explicit is particularly important in a university classroom.

> *It helped me to see both sides of the situation. The data was reinforced by actual events that people just like me have faced such as being pulled over because an African American was in the car with you and being harassed. It was easier for me to understand the data and believe it when there were real people describing it to me. The data gave me a starting point to trying to see what was really going on in the world and allowed me to question certain aspects of society and how the world we live in works. The stories gave me*

real examples that I was able to understand a lot more and create data in my head that showed a clear picture of what was going on throughout society.

We found that our story circles encouraged both a deeper learning and more grounded (in both concrete relationships and in the scholarly litera-ture) self-reflection for our students, particularly for the white students and a similarly deepened understanding of the both different and similar expe-riences, perspectives, and values of their differently situated peers. And as Walsh found, we experienced that the listening, supported and enabled within structures like story circles, was a key element that compelled par-ticipants to "face the reality of different realities" (Walsh 2007, 8).*

*Pat: Sharing stories through story circles is an effective way to connect, find common ground and acquire a frame of reference for how to relate to one another and the world at large.

Jim: I would say that this is an argument, not just for story circles, but for art in general and for the need of arts education in our schools and universities.

BLACK & WHITE CLASSROOMS

Our classrooms are overwhelmingly white. Most of our faculty team on this project are white including our political scientist... and every other faculty colleague in his department is white. Most of political science is white.•

Although there is serious, fractious, ongoing debate within this research, there is also nearly unanimous consent among these scholars that, to borrow from Cornel West, race matters. Social scientists may disagree about how or why it matters, but there is a broad agreement that racial considerations continue to influence the ways that White citizens think about politics and policy in America. There is another, far more insidi-ous agreement among scholars of race politics. It is usually unstated and implicit, but the consensus exists nonetheless that black people don't matter." (Harris-Lacewell 2003, 222; emphasis in original)

•Donna: It might be helpful to talk about the difference between stories told by white people and those told by black people. We see different themes in the white and black stories included in this volume.

Bill: This certainly appeared to be the case in the story circles in my classes. Maybe ten percent of the white students would tell stories that either asserted they have no expe-rience with racial conflict or a story where they or their family turn out to be the white racial heroes of the story because "they do not even consider their neighbor to be black."

> At the same time there were a small number of stories from black students who grew up in white super-affluent suburbs who (similarly?) asserted that they have never experienced racism. I agree that this would be a very interesting dimension to study.
>
> **Carolyn:** I find that most young people who have recently arrived at university and who are in the middle of the pack—not standing out for their socioeconomic, age, gender/sexuality, disability, racial, or ethnic qualities—in my introductory classes are anxious to talk. They want to be known, to share personal information in order to make a connection. It seems to me that we need to recognize these dimensions of difference because these students may need to come to the practice of listening and also of sharing in ways that are different from those who are not in the center of the pack. Okay. I just read that over and it seems fairly obvious. Does it need to be said?
>
> **Amy:** Absolutely, it needs to be said. Our traditional students have had so little experience with persons different than themselves that I feel like this point is crucial to the entire endeavor.
>
> **Bill:** Your insight, Carolyn, was not obvious to me. I now wonder if I spend too much time encouraging everyone to speak and participate, without devoting similar energy and attention to ensuring that those who are most eager to speak learn to listen and create additional space for those eager to listen to learn to speak.

Despite new research techniques, the study of racial attitudes still omits black voices and black agency (Harris-Lacewell 2003, 223). As a result, we are asking the wrong questions when scholars assume that "disagreements over racial policies are about political rather than racial attitudes ... [and that] prejudice is not a meaningful explanatory variable in White policy attitudes" (Harris-Lacewell 2003, 226).

African Americans are political agents with interesting and illuminating stories to tell. Stories white Americans need to hear; stories that reflect racial conflict, power, and subordination, not just routine policy disagreements. Story circles are one tool for bringing in black voices, with precisely the issue-frame disruptive qualities that Harris-Perry suggests we should expect, invite, and demand. Suddenly our conversations no longer simply assume a black culture of violence, suspect work ethic, or that citing the racial composition of prisons demonstrates, once and for all, black criminality.◆

> ◆**Carolyn:** At the incredibly simple level of proxemics, story circles put all the listeners in the same position in, as O'Neal so appealingly insists be a "proper circle" where each participant can clearly see the participant on the far side of the person next to them. This is functional of course but symbolically resonates with Harris-Perry's message. "Invisibility exclusion" of others' experiences is less possible in the story circle.

Jim: I am reminded here of the controversy surrounding *Saturday Night Live's* perceived exclusion of the black female voice. They rectified the situation by hiring several African American women as performers and writers. But one of them, Leslie Jones, made some very hard-hitting "slavery jokes," creating even more controversy and exposing the double-standard in both the black and white communities concerning the voice of an African American woman as opposed to an African American man. She defended herself by saying that Chris Rock or Dave Chappelle or any number of rap artists could say things that she said, make "slavery jokes," and no one would bat an eye. We can argue whether or not the sketch was funny or mature or subtle enough, but the fact remains that she's breaking the mold and making us hear the stories of racism in a very different way—from the contemporary black female perspective.

Melissa Harris-Perry argues that failing to hear black voices means that researchers fail to account for the fact that blacks think about race often, while whites do not. This changes the meaning of the stories they tell (Harris-Lacewell 2003, 235) and makes us, as a community of citizen-scholars, more likely to overlook alternative explanations.

Dr. Martin Luther King observed in *Where Do We Go From Here: Chaos or Community?* that "power without love is reckless and abusive and that love without power is sentimental and anemic" (2010, 38). He similarly noted in his sermon "A Tough Mind and a Tender Heart" that we are called to "combine the toughness of a serpent and the tenderness of a dove. To have serpent-like qualities devoid of dovelike qualities is to be passionless, mean, and selfish. To have dovelike qualities without serpentlike qualities is to be sentimental, anemic and aimless. We must combine strongly marked antitheses" (1977, 18).✦

✦**Jim:** Once again we are reminded of the power of paradox, the necessity of including opposites in one's work methodology. This way of thinking is essential to the creative process: structure and spontaneity, playful and sacred.

Dr. King is rejecting dualistic thinking. We tried, similarly, to structure the ongoing, collective, thoughtful, and productive rejection of dualistic thinking about race into the course work described here. We need to both engage with power (with serious tough-mindedness) and engage with love (with an open mind and shared goal of achieving agreements) if we want our classrooms and public spheres to be places where the vigorous contestation of ideas links individual freedom with collective prosperity.●

> •**Pat:** Bill, I am so glad that you reminded us of Dr. King's ethic here. His words power-fully remind us that there would be no genuine progress for African Americans or other socially marginalized groups unless our contemporary American society turned toward greater justice and "love is the foundation of justice."
>
> **Jim:** In Don G. Campbell's book, *The Roar of Silence*, he tells the story of a young monk who asked the Buddha why he was the Buddha. "Is it because you have mastered all your desires?" "No," was the reply. "Are you the Buddha because you can levitate?" Again, no was the answer. "Because you can know all things?" Once again, the simple answer was "no." "Then, why are you called the Buddha, the Enlightened One?" The Buddha's response was, "I am only awake" (22). It is to this state of "only awake" that story circles have the possibility to bring us—a state that does not get caught in judgment, criticism, or egotistical self-consciousness. It's a difficult state for the educated Western mind to comprehend. But it is the state of creativity and harmony. In other words, democracy and community.
>
> **Amy:** I'm reminded of Cornell West's comment at Rethinking Race 2012, "Justice is what love looks like in public." Phew.

The work described in this volume has used story circles to bring schol-arly data to life through storytelling, it has used storytelling to build com-munity and open pathways for both unity and direct, difficult dialogue about diversity. It has shown the reader some of the ways that this process leads to creative new channels to share the results of the exploration, deepen the connections forged in the process, and shift the cultural narrative that it is our enterprise to engage with. The use of this method requires us all to be both fully present and humble, skilled at balancing both civility and scrutiny, dialogue and debate, love and power, because it is out of these conversations that we achieve agreements, create communities around unity and diversity, and make democracy both possible and desirable.

NOTES

1. Dr. Martin Luther King, Jr. uses the image of blindness to describe racism and other evils in more than one place in his writings. In *Strength to Love* (1981, 51) he says that there are three steps to answering Jesus' call to love our neighbors and love our enemies. First, develop a capacity to forgive. Second, separate the sinner from the sin. Third, never seek to humiliate our opponents, but instead make "every word and deed con-tribute to an understanding with the enemy." In explaining the second step Dr. King says "we see within our enemy-neighbors a measure of goodness...." Dr. King notes that Jesus' prayer on the cross "is an expression of Jesus' awareness of man's intellec-tual and spiritual blindness. 'They know not what they do,' said Jesus. Blindness was their trouble; enlightenment was their need" (43).

2. For example, see Juergensmeyer 2005 and Fisher, Ury, and Patton 1991.

REFERENCES

Barth, John. 2002. "The Remobilization of Jacob Horner." In *Esquire's Big Book of Fiction*, edited by Adrienne Miller. New York City: Context Books.

Buber, Martin. 1958. "The I-Thou Theme, Contemporary Psychotherapy, and Psychodrama." *Pastoral Psychology* 9, no. 5: 53–57.

Campbell, Don G. 1989. *The Roar of Silence: Healing Powers of Breath, Tone and Music*. Wheaton: Quest Books.

Cissna, Kenneth N., and Rob Anderson. 2004. "Public Dialogue and Intellectual History: Hearing Multiple Voices." In *Dialogue: Theorizing Difference in Communication Studies*, edited by Rob Anderson, Leslie Baxter, and Kenneth N. Cissna, 193–208. Thousand Oaks: SAGE Publications.

———. 1998. "Theorizing about Dialogic Moments: The Buber-Rogers Position and Postmodern Themes." *Communication Theory* 8, no. 11: 63–104.

Drew, Julie, William Lyons, and Lance Svehla. 2010. *Sound-Bite Saboteurs: Public Discourse, Education, and the State of Democratic Deliberation*. Albany: SUNY Press.

Fisher, Roger, William Ury, and Bruce Patton. 1991. *Getting to Yes: Negotiating Without Giving In*. London: Penguin.

Gudykunst, William B. 2004. *Theorizing About Intercultural Communication*. Thousand Oaks: SAGE Publications, 2004.

Harris-Lacewell, Melissa. 2003. "The Heart of the Politics of Race: Centering Black People in the Study of White Racial Attitudes." *Journal of Black Studies* 34, no. 2: 222–49.

Juergensmeyer, Mark. 2005. *Gandhi's Way: A Handbook of Conflict Resolution*. Oakland: University of California Press.

King, Martin Luther. 1997. *Strength to Love*. Minneapolis: Fortress Press, 1977.

———. 2010. *Where Do We Go From Here: Chaos or Community?* Boston: Beacon Press.

McNamee, Sheila, and Kenneth J. Gergen. 1999. *Relational Responsibility: Resources for Sustainable Dialogue*. Thousand Oaks: SAGE Publications.

Nichols, Michael P. 2009. *The Lost Art of Listening: How Learning to Listen Can Improve Relationships*. New York City: Guilford Press.

Smooth, Jay. 2008. "How To Tell People They Sound Racist." YouTube video, 3:00. July 21. https://www.youtube.com/watch?v=boTi-gkJiXc.

Walsh, Katherine Cramer. 2007. *Talking About Race: Community Dialogues and the Politics of Difference*. Chicago: University of Chicago Press.